SAUDI ARABIA LABOR LAW AND PRACTICE 2025

MICHAEL O'KANE

ANDALUS
PUBLISHING

Saudi Arabia Labor Law and Practice 2025

Publisher's Cataloging-In-Publication Data}
(Provided by Cassidy Cataloguing Services, Inc.)
Names: O'Kane, Michael, 1955- author.}
Title: Saudi Arabia Labor Law and Practice 2025 / Michael O'Kane.
Description: Los Angeles : Andalus Publishing, [2026] | Includes index.
Identifiers: ISBN: 9781945979347 (print) | 9781945979354 (ePub)}
Subjects: LCSH: Labor laws and legislation--Saudi Arabia. | Foreign workers--Legal status, laws, etc.--Saudi Arabia. | Personnel management--Law and legislation--Saudi Arabia.
Classification: LCC: KMT1270 .O532 2025 | DDC: 344.53801 --dc23

CHAPTER 1

INTRODUCTION TO THE 2025 EDITION

IN 2001 I started keeping an outline of Saudi employment law developments. Over time, the outline grew as laws tend to do. One obstacle to the Saudi Labor Law was the fact that the law's articles, though numbered, were neither indexed nor named. I added unofficial, descriptive names as a finding tool to facilitate access to the law's contents. At the time, naming articles in Saudi laws was not a convention and I am happy to see that other agencies tend to identify articles in the laws they promulgate. This is still not the case with the newly named Ministry of Human Relations and Social Development so I have kept the unofficial identifiers and created new ones for new articles still lacking names.

The result of this naming is a detailed table of contents which permits quick identification of relevant sections of the law. Additionally, an index makes finding answers to every questions a simple exercise.

Much of what happens in Saudi Arabia happens online and labor law is no exception. The detailed model employment contract was replaced by a less-detailed, online version, a copy of which is included here for guidance. Calculation of the Saudi End-of-Service benefit was always somewhat tricky, but now the Ministry provides a helpful online EOSB calculator on its website.

The Saudi government continues to move aggressively to find jobs for Saudi citizens. The program, called "Saudization," "Saudiization" or—perhaps easier to pronounce "localization" requires certain businesses to maintain specified levels of Saudi employees.

Women have moved into the labor force en masse. Gone are the days when Saudi businesses were forced to create "Ladies" sections and their abolition created more opportunities for the employment of women.

The Ministry announced the overhaul of the country's work permit rules. Access to the Saudi work permit, called the *iqama* will now be classified based on skills needed in the Kingdom and focusing on insuring that non-Saudi workers possess the necessary qualifications for the country. We can expect that over time, categories of employees will be adjusted based on national need and not necessarily the need of a particular employer. The availability of qualified Saudi employees makes this initiative possible. Nevertheless, with foreign workers constituting 80% of the Saudi workforce, mass reduction of foreign workers will be a gradual process.

Questions, complaints or comments about this guide can be directed to me at mok@mu7ami.com.

Michael O'Kane
August, 2025
Riyadh

CHAPTER 2

CHAPTER 2 SUMMARY AND PRACTICE UNDER THE SAUDI LABOR LAW

INTRODUCTION

SAUDI LABOR LAW is a moving target. The labor law of Saudi Arabia was amended in 2006 to reflect the Kingdom's rapid modernization. Royal Decree No. M/51 dated 23/8/1426 (27 Sep.2005); Council of Ministers Decision No. 219 dated 22/8/1426 H. The previous law dates from 1969. In April, 2015, Royal Decree No. M/51 dated 23/8/1436 was published in issue 4563 of the Official Gazette. The Royal Decree contains thirty-eight articles and makes substantial changes to the Labor Law. These changes are incorporated in the full text of the Labor Law set out in the Appendix. One year later, the Implementing Regulations were amended again in accordance with Ministerial Decision No.1982 dated 28/6/1437H (06 April 2016). The full text of each article of the implementing regulation follows the affected article of the law. While a considerable body of custom and practice had developed to aid in the interpretation of the old law, the new law has been seen as a break from previous practice. Nevertheless, many provisions in the old law are carried forward to the new legislation, so it is helpful to refer to the older legislation as an aid in explaining and understanding the new.

Still further changes were made in August 2024. The Council of Ministers recommended changes to forty-seven articles and the changes were effected by Royal Decree that month to take effect on February 25, 2025. Cabinet Decision No. 117 dated 2 Safar 1446 H (6 August 2024); Royal Decree No. 44 dated 8 Safar 1446H (12 August 2024).

The Labor Law is a tool to assist in the implementation of social policies; namely, the creation of employment opportunities for Saudis, the protection of foreign workmen and to discourage labor unions. The treatment of labor affairs differs considerably from practices seen in Western jurisdictions.

There have been a few new developments. In 2019, the Ministries of Labor and Civil Service were merged and the new agency named the Ministry of Human Resources and Social Development.

In 2021, the first steps were taken to abolish the "Kafalah" system of restricting free labor. The practice, tying employees to their sponsors, is common in the Middle East but is a target of a great deal of criticism. The system ties an employee's immigration status to his employer sponsor. Unfortunately, efforts to abolish this sponsorship move at a glacial pace. In practice, employee mobility only obtains where an employer has failed to meet Saudiization requirements. Clearly, one should have nothing to do with the other. It will be some time, if ever, before immigration status is disentangled from immigration status: in case of an employee who dies on the job, the Passport Office has a role to play.

Saudiization numbers for the *nitaqat*have again and then again been revised to the point where *nitaqat* tables have been removed from this book. Eventually, the Ministry will require that a company's workforce consist of at least 90% Saudi national employees. In some industries this percentage is attainable, in others perhaps not. Already there are reports of employees not being able to renew their work permits (*iqamas*) because the Ministry determined that the company lacked a sufficient number of Saudi national employees.

In another case, a company decided to abandon a Capital Markets license as they could not be assured of transferring employees currently working in London. As a consequence, the Saudi employees they planned on hiring lost their job offers.

Employment disputes are decided in Saudi labor courts which are not known for their speed. Employers routinely delay cases in the hope that the employee will abandon the case and all too often win in this fashion. It is still the rare company that funds the required End of Service Benefit.

This revised edition corrects certain errors of translation and is set in a format that is easier to read. The article titles are for the sake of convenience and do not form part of the law. The Arabic language version is the only authentic, official version of the law.

Historical View

Saudi Arabia is at the same time the most visited country on the planet and the most difficult country to visit. Those who do not come to the country for religious purposes otherwise have no right to visit. You cannot simply decide to visit Saudi Arabia. A visitor first needs an invitation from a Saudi national. If the visitor meets certain requirements, the Saudi consulate will issue the appropriate visa. The country's ruler, King Salman bin Abdulazziz Al-Saud's official title is "Custodian of the Two Holy Mosques"and both the King and the government take this responsibility seriously. Making the pilgrimage to Mecca, or *hajj*, is one of the five fundamental elements of Muslim faith, often called the "five pillars" of Islam.

In recognition of that fact, any Muslim, from any part of the world, regardless of nationality, has a right to make the pilgrimage, subject only to reasonable numerical restrictions. There are over one billion Muslims in the world, and it would be chaos if all were to descend upon the city of Mecca at the same time.

In the 1970's, following the nationalization of the Aramco, the American oil company and the spike in oil prices during the 1974

October war, Saudi Arabia rapidly modernized. The boom that followed those events and which continues to this day, has made Saudi Arabia into a technologically advanced and economically sophisticated nation.

The country's manpower resources were insufficient to manage such rapid and comprehensive growth. A decision was made to seek needed manpower from other countries. Millions poured into the country to meet the needs of Saudi employers. Saudi Arabia had both jobs and money to pay employees. In countries where unemployment rates are high, a job in the Gulf promised a better life. Millions came.

Historical antecedents influenced the development of the country's labor laws. Slavery was only abolished in the 1960's. Even today, critics of the Saudi labor system complain that too much of it recalls indentured servitude. The employer issues the visa invitation letter under which the employee must work only for the original employer, who is also called the employee's sponsor. Normally, the sponsor is responsible not only for payment of wages, but for provision of housing and transportation. Until 2001, a laborer was not permitted to travel from one province to another without the written permission of his employer.

It wasn't that long ago that at the end of the employment contract, employees were given a final exit visa and their pictures published in the newspaper to warn anyone who had done business with them that they no longer represented the employer. Worse still is the language used to describe some of these relationships such as language suggesting that an employee has "escaped" or "absconded." Some might say that traces of indentured servitude persist today, especially regarding domestic servants. As roughly 80% of Saudi households employ domestic servants, this is no small matter. Newspapers routinely refer to housemaids who "escape" their employers. That a housemaid would resign her position is hardly news, but the use of the word "escape" underlines the fact that there is a complex web of responsibilities and duties enveloping the employer/employee relationship that are simply not seen in other countries.

The first iteration of the Implementing Regulations of the Labor Law, published in 2007, provided procedures for common tasks in the human resources sector such as placing Saudi or foreign job candidates, transfer of employees and licensing of employment agencies. While perhaps excessively bureaucratic, the employer reporting requirements are extensive and enforced by labor inspectors. Forms are provided for the collection and reporting of data required by the Ministry of Labor. Record keeping requirements are similarly extensive and records and registries required to be maintained must be made available to labor ministry inspectors. In addition to day to day record keeping, annual reports must be filed with the Ministry.

Employees on "free" visas are not permitted. Council of Ministers Resolution No. 1235 of 12/10/1397 H(11 Nov. 1977) abolished so-called "free"visas, that is, those visas issued to workers who come to the Kingdom seeking employment without having been hired for a specific position. The Regulations make clear that there is no free labor market in the Kingdom. Whether this is due to artifacts of indentured servitude or merely an aftereffect of a protectionist economy is a question best left to historians. What is clear is that workers may not enter the Kingdom except while under the sponsorship of a Saudi national. In most cases, a worker must complete one year of service with that sponsor before becoming eligible to switch to another sponsor. In some cases, such as where the original sponsor merges or is acquire by another company the employee is automatically transferred if he consents. There are service requirements even for intracompany transfers.

An employee must complete three months of service before requesting an amendment to his job title or obtaining a new position within the same company An intracompany transfer requires all of the formalities of a new foreign recruitment and approval of the Ministry of Labor is required.

Saudi citizens are granted preference with respect to any job vacancies in the Kingdom. A prospective employer seeking to hire foreigners must not only show that there are no Saudi nationals available, but be in good standing with respect to required Saudization percentages. In the case of a specific government contract, the relevant ministry's decision that foreign labor is required is given deference.

For foreigners, employment, housing and immigration are all linked. A change in one affects the others and requires amendment of contracts or official documents. Because an employee is admitted to sponsorship in regards to an undertaking to perform specific work, the employee's functional job duties cannot be changed without reviewing his eligibility to work in the Kingdom under the new position.

The new law also obligates workers to remain in their employer's service until the expiration of the contract. While the Implementing Regulations potentially ameliorate this requirement, an employee must nevertheless complete a certain minimum employment period before becoming eligible to change employers in addition to obtaining the consent of both employers as well as approval by the Ministry of Labor. Royal Decree No. 35 dated 28/7/1422 (16/10/2001 H) provides for an administrative fee of SAR 1000 when an employee seeks to change his profession or change employers, assuming that the requirements for such a change are met.

Employers who fail to comply with the regulations or instructions promulgated by the Ministry will lose the right to hire foreign workers.

The Implementing Regulations set the standard for the operation and licensing of both employment agencies and recruitment offices. Employment agencies must have a minimum capital of SAR 100,000. There are two kinds of employment offices: one is for Saudis seeking employment and the second is for foreign workers recruited to work in the Kingdom. There are separate regulations for each. Recruitment offices may recruit employees under their own sponsorship and then provide manpower to contractors. To insure performance of all financial commitments, recruitment offices must obtain and post a bank bond of SAR 300,000 from which the

Ministry will make deductions where employees are not paid or in case of financial awards in labor disputes. There is a serious question as to whether the amount of the bond is sufficient, especially given the relatively large amounts of End of Service Benefits. Employment agencies or recruitment offices that violate Ministry of Labor rules are subject to progressive discipline and face license cancellation for repeated violations.

Businesses that employ fifty or more employees must organize or obtain training programs and train at least 6% of their Saudi workforce annually. Businesses with 500 or more employees are permitted to determine qualifications for a given position outside of published Ministry guidelines. A training database must be maintained and is subject to inspection by labor inspectors.

The regulations also flesh out procedures for managing dispute resolution and identify the number of paid holidays (nine). Employees who come to the Kingdom with a recognized special or professional skill are not subject to the mandatory retirement age of 60. The requirement of maintaining first aid kits and their contents is specified in the Regulations as well.

Recent Developments

Saudization principles became even more important with the Minister of Labor being granted powers to deny business licenses to firms that fail to meet the requirements and setting up a reward system to compensate those who report violations.

In 2016 new implementing regulations were issued. The government frequently tweaks its targets for increasing the presence of Saudi nationals in the workplace. Positions restricted to Saudi nationals are opened up if insufficient local labor can be found; where local labor is not in short supply positions may be closed.

In the summer of 2013, the government announced the strict enforcement of immigration and sponsorship provisions. Free workers, that is, workers who entered the country under the sponsorship of one Saudi employer were to be deported unless they regularized their sponsorship situation. It had been commonplace for Saudis charge a fee to sponsor workers even though they had no jobs for them. The free workers were on their own once they were in the country and had to find jobs. Though technically none of these workers existed, in fact they did, and in large numbers. For a variety of reasons, their actual employers did not change the sponsorship of the workers from the figurehead sponsor to the actual employer. Sometimes the actual sponsors disappeared. Sometimes the actual sponsors even had real jobs for the new workers, but could no longer afford them because of losing contracts or a downturn in business.

No matter the reason, the government insisted on regularization and thousands of workers were unable to meet the new government requirements. The government extended the enforcement deadline several times as pictures of workers and their families passing out in the heat while waiting in long lines were publicized around the world. Eventually the deadlines passed and the government started arresting workers. The result was that major construction projects were halted and businesses shut down because workers failed to report to work.

Enforcement activities have been aggressive. Professional secondments have heretofore been common, but without approval of the Ministry of Labor are now prohibited. Workers have stayed home fearing arrest. Embassies have been swamped with requests for assistance from workers who cannot find their long-gone original sponsors and so cannot obtain exit visas to leave the country. The government has even announced the creation of camps to intern these so-called "illegal workers." It will be a question of time to see if the government remains steadfast and deports thousands of people or whether there will be some kind of economic accommodation or amnesty.

Domestic Servants Regulations

The treatment of domestic servants in the Kingdom has been the subject of great criticism over the years. The past several years have seen arrests of Saudis who traveled with their domestic servants who brought charges against them upon arriving in another country. Saudis are now advised to contact their Embassy in case of any problems overseas and to educate their servants as to their responsibilities. Practices common in the Kingdom, such as the retention of the worker's passport by the employer, are severely criticized outside the Kingdom.

2013 saw the publication of the long-awaited Domestic Servants regulations. Among other features, the rules provide for a paid vacation after two years of service and require the payment of End of Service Benefits after four years of service. A six day work week is established by the law and sick leave is provided for as well. The employer also must provide health insurance.

Unfortunately, the law contains provisions which have been harshly criticized outside Saudi Arabia, such as a prohibition on leaving employment without the consent of the employer during the contract term. Transfers are now permitted. It is now much easier for domestic workers to switch employers. Facilitation of the transfer is through the government's Musaned platform.

In any event, while the lot of domestic servants in the Kingdom is far from ideal, the new law is at least a step in the right direction. An employer who fails to heed the requirements of the law can be fined and prevented from hiring new domestic servants. A committee was created within the Labor Ministry to hear claims filed by domestic workers and to mediate disputes between workers and their employers. The government has recognized that domestic workers have rights and has pledged to enforce them. Whether the new law will be a success remains to be seen.

Update 2025

Amendments continue to be made to regulations governing domestic servants or to use the politically correct term, "helpers." As of January 1, 2026 wages must be made via an electronic salary transfer through the Musaned [1] platform. This applies to all domestic workers in the Kingdom.

> [is a]comprehensive system to integrate and organize the Labor Recruitment process from the providing countries, digitally authenticating the contract between the Employer and the Laborer...Guided by the Ministry of Human Resources and Social Development, [Musaned] aims to facilitate the Labor Recruitment Process and protect the legal rights of the contracting parties...

Aside from domestic workers, the Skills Classification guidelines promise a major revamp of work and resident permits in Saudi Arabia. As a statistical measure, the new system allows the HRSD to fine-tune labor force numbers by increasing or decreasing the number of visas open to particular specialties. By requiring proof of possession of claimed skills, the Ministry seeks to insure that work permits are not granted to the unskilled and an inevitable testing regime will confirm that an individual who claims to possess a skill in fact does so.

As the Ministerial Resolution only became effective in July, 2025, it will be some time before the full effects are seen. Have no doubt, however, that these guidelines will affect every foreign worker in Saudi Arabia.

On August 1, 2025 new rules went into effect regarding official

1. musaned.com.sa

recognition of the end of the employer/employee relationship. At the end of the worker's contract, an employer may submit an absence report only if there is both no work contract and the employee's *iqama* is valid for at least sixty days.

At the end of the employee's contract, the employee has sixty days to sign a new contract with his employer or a new contract with a different employer. In the case where no employment contract is signed, the employee must leave the Kingdom within that sixty day period.

If the employee has signed no new work contract but has remained in the Kingdom, the (now former) employee has overstayed his visa dn is subject to immigration sanctions.

The implementation of this new policy gives a worker two months to find a new job without the necessity of having to leave the Kingdom and return.

These matters are discussed in the Ministry's *Procedural Guide for Ending the Contractual Relationship*, available on the Ministry's website at: https://www.hrsd.gov.sa/en/knowledge-centre/decisions-and-regulations/regulation-and-procedures/1170532.

I. The Employment Contract

The Labor Law is applicable to every contract according to which any person is bound to work for the interest of the employer and under his administration and supervision in return for salary. However, the Law does not apply to all workers, such as domestic workers, as the amended versions of Articles 5 and 7 make clear. Additionally, the law does not apply to non-Saudi workers who come to the Kingdom for a specific task of less than two month's duration.

1. Right to Work

The Saudi citizen's right to employment is found at found in Article 3 of the Labor Law. The right is, unfortunately, aspirational, as there is a great deal of unemployment in the country, suffered especially by young Saudis. Still, the provision of a right to work clause tends to establish, at least on a theoretical and adjudicative level, a balance between employer and employee. In other words, an employer is not performing a favor for an employee by hiring him; instead, an employer is merely implementing a right recognized by the country's laws in respect of employment.

2. Government Employees

In a change from prior practice, all employees of the government are subject to the Labor Law, as is the government itself. This corrects a previous practice in which government workmen were subject to the Labor Regulations, but government civil servants were exempted.

3. Contents of the Employment Contract

A copy of the model employment contract is found at Annex 6 of the Implementing Regulations herein. The employment contract should be written, though an oral contract will nevertheless be binding. Two copies of the employment contract should be made and each of the parties should retain a copy. The contract must contain, at a minimum:

- Name of the employer and name of company, if any;
- Name and nationality of the worker;
- Identification of the worker (Saudi identity card or foreign passport);
- Wages to be paid;
- A description of the employee's duties;
- Identification of the duty station, or place where the work will be performed;
- Date of appointment;
- Length of the contract.

Saudis may have contracts for an indefinite term; contracts employing non-Saudis must be for a limited term. If such a contract does not specify a term, it will be deemed to be limited to the term of the employee's work permit. Note that the repeated renewal of a definite term contract may cause it to be converted to an indefinite term contract.

Council of Ministers Resolution No.1235 makes it clear that employees of employers with government or specific project contracts are to be provided housing. This applies to all labor contracts and so need not be specifically mentioned in individual contracts, though in case an employer or labor commissioner is unfamiliar with the resolution it is not a bad idea to specifically mention this requirement.

A contract executed in a language other than Arabic is valid but the Arabic language version is always controlling. It is common practice in the Kingdom to create a bilingual contract, with the Arabic and English texts written side by side for easy reference. In case of a labor dispute, all proceedings will be conducted in Arabic and all documents, including the Labor Contract, must be submitted to the court in Arabic. One way to avoid potential problems is to include a provision that the English text is to be used as a tool to interpret the Arabic version in case of any ambiguity.

Many prospective employees are told that their contracts are provisional or can easily be modified upon arrival in Saudi Arabia. *This is almost never the case.* Once a contract is signed, an employee is bound. Despite what some agents may say, Saudi employers rarely modify signed contract terms. After the expiration of a contract, however, employer and employee are free to negotiate different terms. An employee is expected to perform services under the employment contract and will owe damages to the employer for failure to do so. These damages include the cost of foreign recruitment, if applicable.

4. Probation, Contract Duration

An employment contract may specify a probationary period of up to 180 days, not including holidays or sick leave, for a new employee. Previously the probation period could not be greater than 90 (ninety) days. During this period, the employee may be terminated for any reason at the convenience of the employer and the employee has no right to complain or to require the employee to reinstate him. The requirement of a probationary period and its term must be included in the contract otherwise no probationary period will be deemed to exist. An employee may be made to serve only one probationary period, unless the by agreement of the parties where the second probationary period is for a new position. The employee's right to leave employment during the probationary period must be specifically spelled out, otherwise the right to leave during the period is held solely by the employer. An employer may be compensated for his damages where an employee has failed to complete his contract.

One of the changes of the Labor Law is to provide that contracts of limited duration that are either renewed three times or extend for a period greater than four years are converted into indefinite term employment contracts by operation of law. This rule in practice only applies to Saudi national employees because other regulations tie the term of the employment contract to the expiration of the employment's residence permit. These permits are issued on an annual basis only.

An employee who is terminated during the probationary period is entitled to whatever leave was earned during that period.

5. Relocation of Employees; Change in Duties

One of the consequences of requiring the inclusion of a job description and identification of an employee's duty station is the fact that these cannot subsequently be changed without the consent of the employee. Article 58 of the Labor Law prevents an employer from transferring an employee where such a transfer would require the employee to change his residence. Article 21 of the new Implementing Regulations answers the question of dual or even multiple workplaces: an employment contract may even specify the whole of Saudi Arabia and the employee's consent to transfer or rotation is presumed by his signing the work contract. Employers who want maximum flexibility should include broad geographical assignments in the original work contract while employees who need to remain in a specific location should make sure that only that location is specified. If there is a legal reason for the transfer which is required by the "nature of the work," such transfer will be permitted. The Labor Law permits occasional transfers of up to thirty days without the employee's consent.

An employee cannot waive his rights under the Labor Law. It is questionable whether an employee may waive his right to object to a transfer or agree in advance to a transfer. A waiver may be agreed in the employment contract. In addition to the prohibition on depriving employees of minimal rights protected by the Labor Law, such consent would seem to fall afoul of the Islamic contract prohibition on uncertainty ("*gharar*") in contracts.

Except in emergencies or for special periods not exceeding thirty days per year (such as during an audit or taking inventory) an employee's duties may not be varied from those specified in the contract of employment. An employee cannot be made to waive this right in advance. For this reason, the job description should be written in very general language and include the phrase, "and other duties as required" so as to give the employer maximum flexibility.

6. Termination of the Employment Contract

In a major change, employment contracts can now be cancelled without just cause. Nevertheless, employees who are dismissed without cause are entitled to severance pay. An employee who resigns without cause is entitled to compensate his employer for real and moral losses.

In the case of an employee who has been recruited from overseas, the damages could be substantial. The death of an employer does not terminate the employment contract unless it is a personal services contract.

Many employers have long complained about the difficulties in terminating an employee. The provision for providing for reinstatement of illegally dismissed employees has been rescinded. It is not clear how this will operate in practice because the practice has been so ingrained for so many years. The Labor Law provides for the calculation of a severance payment, establishes reasonable leave during the notice period for the purpose of job-seeking, but reinstatement of a dismissed employee is no longer the law.

7. Employee Discipline

The following conduct by an employee constitutes legal grounds for dismissal:

- Assaulting the employer, a manager or supervisor;
- Failing to perform his principal duties; or ignoring posted safety-related instructions after having been first warned in writing;
- Engaging in dishonorable or dishonest behavior;
- Theft or negligence which permitted theft, where the crime has been reported to the authorities within 24 hours after the employee's confession;
- Submitting false documents in order to obtain employment;
- Failure to satisfactorily complete the probationary period;
- Absence without excuse as follows:
- More than 20 days during one year where there has been a warning after ten days; or
- More than 10 successive days at any time, where there has been a warning after 5 days;

- Using professional status (i.e., his position with his employer) for personal gain;
- Unauthorized disclosure of trade secrets.

The following conduct by an employer entitles the employee to terminate the employment contract and to damages:

- Failure to meet contract obligations;
- Cheating the employee concerning conditions of employment;
- Changing the employee's job duties without agreement;
- Assaulting the employee;
- Failing to remedy an acknowledged dangerous condition at the workplace;
- Paying the employee's final salary and End of Service Benefit with a bogus explanation in order to trick the employee into thinking he had violated the contract.

Conduct outside the workplace is normally not grounds for dismissal. An employee may not be disciplined for behavior outside the workplace unless it is work-related or relates to his relationship with his employer or manager.

This is an important innovation since employees are under the general sponsorship of the employer, and, more likely than not, live in housing that is either owned by or subsidized by the employer. These relationships outside the workplace tend to involve employers in the lives of their employees in ways that are not common in Western jurisdictions, so a clarification that employee misconduct outside the workplace unrelated to job performance will not impact the employee is a welcome clarification. The references to misconduct relating to the employer or manager in charge refers most likely to paragraph 1 of Article 80, which provides that an employee can be terminated for assaulting his employer.

The Labor Law specifies how collected employee fines may be used.

8. Discrimination in Employment

Generally, there is no discrimination in terms of conditions of employment. Some of the terms of the Labor Law are specific to expatriates, such as Article 3 of the law, entitled, "Employing non-Saudis." Provisions concerning foreign recruitment, repatriation and related matters obviously do not apply to Saudi nationals. Article 58's restriction on changing an employee's residence does not apply to non-Saudis, since they are not domiciled within the Kingdom. The provisions requiring training for 12% of the Saudi workforce is not applicable to non-Saudis. Apart from the general rule that Saudis are entitled to preference in employment, employers are to make a 2% of salary contribution to GOSI on behalf of all employees. An additional 9% pension contribution is required only on behalf of Saudi employees. The End of Service Benefit is to be made to all employees regardless of nationality.

Muslim employees are permitted breaks for the purposes of prayer. During Ramadan a distinction is drawn between Muslim and non-Muslim employees with with respect to working hours. Muslim family law rules are also recognized in some cases, such as in the case of a death of a spouse.

9. Immigration

The employer is the employee's sponsor for immigration purposes. A copy of the employment contract is required for issuance of the visa. A medical examination is required to obtain a residency permit, and this examination is repeated upon arrival in the Kingdom. According to new labor regulations, the costs of the residence permit, as well as the costs of renewal of same and entry-re-entry visas or permits for annual leave must be borne by the employer. However, an employer is not responsible for the costs of visas or resident permits for an employee's family. The Kingdom has recently announced a substantial increase in fees for such visas, causing the return of accompanying family members to their home countries. It is unclear whether these high fees will be retained in the future.

II. Conditions of Employment

1. Workday/Workweek

The workday cannot exceed eight hours per day and the work week cannot exceed 48 hours per week. For Muslims, the workday during Ramadan cannot exceed six hours per day and the work week cannot exceed 36 hours (Article 98). An employee's pay period cannot be changed without his written consent (Article 59). For government employees as well as many in the private sector, the weekend in Saudi Arabia now consists of Friday and Saturday, but the observance is not universal. Proposed, but not enacted, provisions of Royal Decree No. M/51 would lessen the work week to 45 hours and formally establish a two day weekend for all.

2. Payment

In a major change from past practice, employees may no longer be paid in cash but their wages must be deposited in a bank account in a bank approved by the Saudi Arabian Monetary Agency. The purpose of this provision is to crack down on illegal or occasional workers. Bank accounts for foreign workers are tied to their labor permits. If a labor permit expires or is cancelled, even if due to a clerical error, funds in the employee's bank account will be automatically frozen.

3. Overtime

Overtime is to be paid at the rate of 150% of the employee's regular wage. (Article 107) Overtime is owed for work performed on national holidays.

3. Breaks

An employee may not be forced to work five hours without being given a one-half hour break. Lunch, rest and prayer breaks are not included in the calculation of working hours. Friday is a day of rest. Breaks are chargeable to the employee and time taken during a break does not count towards an employee's eight hour daily work obligation. However, an employer cannot require the employee to remain at the worksite for more than twelve hours.

For workers at remote sites, the weekly breaks can be accumulated for no more than eight weeks upon agreement with the employees and approval by the Ministry of Labor. Overtime is required to be paid at the rate of time and a half, or, 1.5 times the employee's hourly rate.

Employees must be given time for daily prayers. The determination of prayer time is not left to the discretion of the employer but is instead in accordance with accepted, Kingdom-wide Islamic religious principles. A minimum of one-half hour per prayer time is the norm. Travel time to the nearest mosque or prayer room is required. Many businesses have prayer rooms for the convenience of their employees, and every neighborhood has a mosque which is reachable in a few minutes. Time necessary for prayer does not constitute a break chargeable to the employee.

4. Treatment of Professional and Managerial Employees

Professional and managerial employees are not bound by the hourly provisions of Articles 98 and 101 above. The Implementing Regulations exempt these employees from the mandatory retirement age of 60 for men and 55 for women. *See*, Article 15(9).

5. Leave

Employees are entitled to 21 days of vacation per year. Salary must be paid prior to the employee taking his vacation. After five years, the employee is entitled to 30 days per year. An employee must be paid prior to taking leave. Untaken leave is to be compensated. Untaken leave does not expire with time.

Employees are entitled to one day leave for childbirth, three days for marriage and three days in the event of the death of a spouse, parents or children. A female employee is given fifteen days leave in the case of the death of a spouse. An employee who is enrolled in school must be given leave to take exams. An employee who has at least two year's tenure must be given ten to fifteen days leave to make the Hajj, or pilgrimage to Mecca.

An employee with a proven illness shall be given paid sick leave for the first thirty days, then 75% of wages for the next sixty days, and no pay after ninety days.

An employee is now entitled to maternity leave during her first year of service.

An employee may take leave without pay by agreement with the employer. During such leave, the employment contract is suspended.

For the purposes of annual leave, weekends are included in the calculation. The law does not provide that leave days are business days only. An employee is not entitled to additional leave because of an intervening weekend during leave.

Because leave is to be taken in the year in which it is earned, an employee may take annual leave without first completing twelve months of service.

6. Holidays

The Kingdom grants its workers nine paid holidays per year. In accordance with the Kingdom's Basic Law, No. A/90, dated 2/10/1412 H (21 Aug 1991), these are: Eid Al-Fitr (four days) and Eid Al-Adha (four days). Later, the Government added the national day, September 23rd. Government offices usually close for a week or more during the Eid holidays, which are moveable feasts. Private sector offices usually are closed for a shorter period. Ministerial Order No. 812 dated 16/11/1394 H (28 Oct. 1974) provides that an employer may increase the number of holidays and if he does, these days may be used to extend any of the holidays established by law.

Saudi Arabia now has a two day weekend beginning on Friday and ending on Saturday. The first day of the business week is Sunday; banks are open on Sundays. Many employment contracts still specify a six-day work week, in those cases, Friday is the day of rest.

Saudi Arabia now shares five business days with its Gulf neighbors and four with the West.

7. Part-Time Employees

Except for working hours, the part-time labor contract is treated as any other employment contract under the Labor Law and the provisions of the Labor Law control. The Labor Law requires the Ministry of Labor to issue comprehensive rules and regulations concerning part-time employees. If the term of employment exceeds ninety (90) days the temporary contract will be converted to a full-time contract governed by and subject to all of the provisions of the Labor Law.

According to Clause 4 of Ministerial Decree 1/2837 (6/9/1427 H), part-time employees are subject to the provisions of the Labor Law with respect to leave, the definition of weekend, holidays and overtime. Part-time employees are not entitled to the End of Service Benefit.

The hiring of seasonal staff on successive discrete contracts would preclude payments of many benefits available to full-time, regular employees. Where an individual is hired seasonally for a limited term, at the expiration of the term, there is no employer/employee relationship. Note however, that even part-time employees, assuming that they have completed their probationary period, are entitled to the End of Service Benefit. This issue may be addressed in the promised regulations.

If a contract is for a specific job (such as construction of a specific project) the employment contract shall terminate at the end of the job agreed (Article 57). This article is a new development as well and permits the use of "project" or "temporary" employees without requiring an employer to provide permanent employment for an individual.

There is some tension between Article 6's ninety-day limit and the project project limit for projects which take more than ninety days to complete. Resolution of this conflict will have to be decided on a case by case basis pending issuance of a clarifying regulation.

8. Workman's Compensation

An employee injured at work is entitled to employer-paid medical care. An employee who is temporarily disabled shall receive the full amount of his salary for thirty days, then 75% thereafter during the treatment period. If the disability lasts for one year, the employee is considered permanently disabled and entitled to the end of service benefit.

Employees who suffer permanent injury are entitled to compensation based on regulations issued by the Ministry of Labor. Employees who are permanently disabled shall receive an award of three times their annual salary, but in no event less than SAR 54,000. The heirs of an employee who loses his life on the job are also entitled to three year's salary or SAR 54,000, whichever is greater (Article 138).

9. Health Insurance

Employer-provided health insurance is mandatory. Premiums roughly are as follows: for a premium of SAR 2,500, coverage up to SAR 500,000 annually will be available. SAR 300,000 annual coverage is available for a premium of SAR 2,000 and SAR 100,000 coverage is available for a premium of SAR 1,000. Owners of the companies will get coverage of up to more than SAR 1 million for an annual premium of SAR 5,000.

To ensure compliance, the issuance of iqamas (residence permits) is linked to insurance. The Passport Department will not issue or renew iqamas if the holder is not covered by health insurance.

10. Mandatory Deductions from Salary

There is no income tax, VAT, or similar tax in Saudi Arabia on income earned by employees. There are no deductions required to be made for foreign national employees. However, Saudi employees are subject to the following deductions in favor of the General Organization for Social Insurance ("GOSI"). The total cost of GOSI insurance is 20%; 9% is paid by the employee, the remaining 11% is borne by the employer. As an example, where an employee earns SAR 100 per month:

- Employee's share: 9% of SAR 100 = SAR 9
- Employer's share: 11% of SAR 100 = SAR 11
- Total of employer + employee share = SAR 20 (20%)
- Net to employee: SAR 91 (SAR 100 –SAR 9 = SAR 91)

11. Transfer of Employees

The transfer of employees from one employer to another has become complicated and is subject to several restrictions. For a permanent transfer, an employee must obtain a "no objection" letter from his employer in order to commence work with a new employer. While the new law does not mention this requirement except for those employees who have access to trade secrets or confidential information, the Implementing Regulations continue past practice. The *nitaqat* system removed the requirement of consent from the previous employer where that employer has a red nitaqat status or is otherwise ineligible under the *nitaqat* system.

Non-compete clauses will be honored. However, such a clause must be in writing and cannot specify a period greater than two years. The law will not impose any non-compete restriction unless there is a specific non-compete clause in an employment contract.

An employee cannot be assigned duties other than those specified in the labor contract except in emergency cases and for no more than thirty days per year without his written consent (Article 60).

An employee who successfully completes his employment contract is entitled to a leaving certificate. The employer is prohibited from adding negative information to the certificate.

In the case of a company merger or acquisition, the employee's tenure is deemed to be continuous for the purpose of calculating the End of Service Benefit. The employee need not consent to employment by the merged or acquiring company. In such cases, the employment contract is terminated and the employee becomes eligible to receive the End of Service Benefit. *See*, Implementing Regulations Art. 18.

Additional contractual requirements for employee transfer are set forth in Implementing Regulation Article 15. Notwithstanding any other provision of law, an employee is permitted to transfer where the employer has failed to pay salaries for three months or where the employer is absent for three months.

12. Employment of Women

There are special rules which apply to the employment of women. In general "mixed" work environments are not the norm in the Kingdom. Furthermore, women are not permitted to work at night, though this provision does not seem to be rigorously enforced.

Women are entitled to maternity leave commencing four weeks before confinement and six weeks thereafter. The requirement that a woman work for one year prior to taking maternity leave has been abolished. A woman may take annual leave and maternity leave in the same year. Maternity medical care is an expense of the employer. Women who return to work following childbirth are entitled to additional breaks of up to one hour per day for the purpose of nursing. These periods are not deductible from her wages.

A woman may decide to leave employment due to pregnancy or childbirth and will owe no indemnity to her employer. However, the employer will nevertheless owe her the End of Service Benefit.

An employer who employs 50 or more women has to provide childcare for children under the age of six if there are at least ten children. An employer who employs 100 women must establish a childcare center in the vicinity, though the employer may cooperate with other employers in doing so.

Non-Muslim widows are entitled to fifteen days paid leave upon the death of the husband. In accordance with Islamic law, Muslim female employees are granted paid leave of four months and ten days following the death of a spouse. This paid leave may be converted to unpaid leave thereafter if the widow was pregnant. During this time the widow may not work for another employer.

13. Workers in Remote Areas

Under Articles 146 and 147, employees working in remote areas are entitled to:

- Housing;
- Camps;
- Meals;
- Transportation to the worksite;

- Shops selling food, clothing and necessary items;
- Suitable recreational, cultural and sports facilities;
- Suitable medical facilities including facilities for dependents if accompanied;
- Schools for dependents;
- Mosques or prayer places at worksites; and
- Training to eliminate illiteracy.

14. Termination of the Employer-Employee Relationship

Under Article 74 of the Labor Law, the employer-employee relationship can be terminated:

- By agreement of the parties,
- At the end of a definite term contract;
- At the request of either party in the case of indefinite term contracts;
- At retirement (age sixty for men and fifty-five for women); or
- Force majeure.

Article 75's requirement of a "legal reason" (i.e., just cause) for termination of an indefinite term contract employee has been eliminated. This is a major change. Notice of termination is required. Sixty day's notice is required for employees paid monthly and thirty days for all others. Failure to give proper notice requires the employer to pay an indemnity equal to the notice period's wages.

If there is no early termination clause in the contract, an employee is entitled to fifteen day's salary for each year of service if the employment contract is for (or has been converted to) an indefinite term. In the case of a definite term contract, the remaining salary owed under the contract must be paid despite the termination.

During the notice period, the employee is entitled to one day's leave (or eight hours) per week in order to seek new employment.

This leave will not be considered a break in service. An employee who does not renew an expiring contract is not considered to have resigned.

15. Retirement

The customary retirement age is found in Article 74 of the Labor Law and is fixed at age 60 for men and 55 for women.

The retirement provisions of Article 74 came into force on April 26, 2008. The parties to a labor contract can agree to permit an employee to work beyond that date. Where there is no agreement, the retirement age may be extended if the labor contract extends beyond the employee's sixtieth birthday. In case of an indefinite term contract, the employee's attaining the age of sixty or fifty-five is the triggering factor. Because of the difference in length between the Gregorian and Hegira year, labor contracts should specifically mention that calculation of age is based on one or the other.

The 2015 Implementing Regulations made it clear that professional or highly skilled employees are not subject to mandatory retirement at age 60. This exemption was continued in Article 15(9) of the 2016 Implementing Regulations.

16. End of Service Benefit

The End of Service Benefit (EOSB) was enacted so as to ensure that upon leaving his employment, a workman would be provided with a sum sufficient to satisfy his financial needs until new employment could be found.

The EOSB is calculated on the basis of the "basic wage." While the term "basic wage" is defined broadly under Article 2 of the Labor Law as "{e}verything the employee receives in return of his work according to a written or unwritten contract plus merit increases," not all payments or valuable items given to an employee will be considered part of the basic wage. Further, the Labor Law introduces the concept of "actual wages" and there is a good deal of overlap between the two concepts. In the past, Saudi Labor courts have classified certain kinds of payments as coming under the concept of "wages." Appendix 20 of this book contains a non-exclusive, but hopefully illustrative list of what payments may be taken into consideration in calculating the "wage" and which may not.

17. Calculation of End of Service Benefits

Severance pay is not payable before the end of the employment relationship. Thus, end of service benefits should never be paid until the employment relationship has terminated. This is because the regulatory severance pay is payable in full at the end of the employee's service regardless of any payments made prior to that point. To attenuate this right in any way would be to defeat the drafter's intent to safeguard the workman's financial security during the period in which he is actually unemployed.

According to Article 84, there is no longer any distinction between the ESOB for an indefinite term employee and a definite term employee. The benefit is calculated by adding one-half month's wage for each of the first five years and one month's wage for each of the subsequent years. For fractions of a year, the workman shall be entitled to severance pay which is proportionate to his service period during that year.

Examples:

Employee works three years and his wage is SAR 1,000 per month:

i. (1/2 x SAR 1,000) x 3 = SAR 1,500 EOSB.
ii. Employee works seven years and his wage is SAR 1,000 per month:
iii. (1/2 x SAR 1,000) x 5} + {(1 x US$ 1,000) x 2 = SAR 4,500 EOSB.

iv. Employee works 1 year and three months and his wage is SAR 1,000 per month:
v. Total: (1/2 x SAR 1,000) x 1.25 = SAR 625 EOSB.

In all cases, the employee must give the employer thirty days notice before leaving employment. The service period includes paid leaves, any probationary period but excludes unpaid leaves of absence. An employee who resigns because of serious illness or disability is entitled to end of service benefits. If an employee is called to military service, he is entitled to end of service benefits. If an employee cannot work because of force majeure he is entitled to end of service benefits. This obviously is a fact-driven question. Finally, female employees are entitled to end of service benefits if they resign their employment due to marriage or childbirth.

18. Disputes

Labor unions are illegal in Saudi Arabia. Worker's Committees or similar type organizations are also not permitted. Instead, the Ministry of Labor and the Labor Commissions have the tasks of safeguarding worker's rights. Workers may be represented by counsel, if appropriate, and many attorneys handle employment cases.

To adjudicate labor disputes, the Labor Law established specialized administrative tribunals called the Labor Disputes Settlement Commissions. The Commissions have two roles: insuring compliance with the law and settling disputes between employers and employees. There is a one year statute of limitations[2] or prescriptive period, which applies to disputes between employers and employees. This is important, because otherwise there are few legal statutes of limitations in Saudi jurisprudence. The Commission will investigate the complaint, take or development evidence as necessary, and make an

2. Article 297(c), Civil Transactions Law, Royal Decree No. M/191, dated 29/11/1444(18-6-2023.

award. Failure to honor the award or to otherwise violate the regulations will result in the imposition of additional penalties.

Labor disputes are currently subject to mandatory mediation. According to Royal Decree No. M/14 dated 22/2/1440 (31/10/2018) before filing a legal action, the dispute must be submitted to the labor office. This requirement was extended at least until August 14, 2026. [3]

Saudi law applies to the resolution of such disputes, even if the parties have chosen the laws of another country in their labor contract.

Article 15 of the Implementing Regulations sanctions employers who attempt to needlessly prolong labor court proceedings by failing to appear as long as the employee is not responsible for causing the absence.

III. Saudization

Both the Labor Law and its predecessor, the Labor Regulations, provide that employment is a right of the Saudi national and may not be exercised by others unless certain conditions have been fulfilled. The government recognizes that foreign workers comprise a large part of the workforce in Saudi Arabia. To insure that there would be jobs for the country's growing population, the government has taken steps to increase the percentage of Saudi nationals employed in any given business. This policy is known as "Saudization."

One of the first efforts to increase the percentage of Saudi nationals in the workforce was Cabinet Resolution No. 50 dated 4/21/1415 H (27 Sep. 1994). The Resolution set forth modest goals and remains in effect, though for practical purposes it has been superseded by new laws. The Labor Law does not address the Saudiuza-

3. The extension was authorized by a Council of Ministers decision announced on August 13, 2025.

policy. Among other things, Resolution No. 50 reserves certain employee categories to Saudi nationals. These are:

- Recruitment officials and personnel;
- Receptionists;
- Expeditors;
- Liaison personnel with government offices;
- Cashiers; and
- Security Guards.

Companies employing more than 20 employees must increase the number of Saudi employees by 5% annually. This percentage may be modified if a sufficient number of qualified workers are not available. Further, firms shall endeavor to employee Saudi nationals in different professional categories.

There are sanctions if the provisions of Resolution No. 50 are not complied with. In theory, the percentage of Saudi nationals employed by an employer should not be less than 75% of the total workforce. However, Ministry of Labor Resolution No. 1/1539 dated 1/8/1425 H reduced this requirement to 30%. It has not subsequently been increased.

In theory, the minimum percentage of employed Saudi nationals is 30% at the inception of a start-up company. This percentage has to increase in following years by 5% per year. The Minister of Labor can (and does) grant exemptions.

Saudi employees of an affiliated company cannot be considered as Saudi employees of another company for Saudization requirements. Based on Article 30 of the Labor Law, an employee is considered an employee of the company with whom they have a direct contractual relationship. The subcontracted employees are not are not employed by the contracting company and therefore are not counted for the parent company's percentage compliance needs. Furthermore, Article 39 provides that an employer may not allow his employee to work for another employer and an employee may not work for another employer. In the bidding for contracts, often times one of the key evaluation criteria for many tenders cover the level and degree of Saudi involvement in the project. In those instances, the number of Saudi employees working for an affiliated company is often of benefit to the bidder.

Note that there is no requirement that salaries paid to Saudi employees amount to a certain percentage of the total labor payroll.

In light of these policies, foreigners may not enter the Kingdom for the purposes of employment without first obtaining the approval of the Ministry of Labor and a work permit issued. Nevertheless, it is not uncommon for Muslims to come to the Kingdom on religious visas and stay in order to seek employment. [4]

Saudization-Government Contracts

Special rules apply with respect to government contracts. The Ministry of Labor has recently reduced the Saudization requirements for government contractors from 10% to 5%. This is with the objective of removing a major obstacle facing Saudi and foreign contractors in completing building and construction works for the government. This is viewed as a temporary measure caused by the Kingdom's current economic growth. In enacting the new regulations, the Minister nevertheless has stressed that government contractors must abide by the required Saudization percentage, as Saudization is a national obligation.

July, 2025 Update

Saudiization, now sometimes called "localization" continues apace. Rules concerning different professional sectors have been promul-

4. These immigration provisions have now changed. Tourist visas on arrival are freely available for travelers from most countries. A tourist visa holder may see employment in the Kingdom and later adjust status to reflect employment.

and are enforced by the Labor Inspectors. Engineering companies are required to have 25% Saudi national personnel. [5]

For the accounting profession, Saudi employee percentages shall be gradually increased until reaching 70%, starting on October 27, 2025.[6] Foreign accountants must also register with the Saudi Organization of Certified Public Accountants ("SOCPA"). Accountants who fail to qualify for SOCPA membership will be denied work permits. The following professions are targeted:

- Director internal auditing department, Cost clerk
- Accountant, costs
- Finance clerk
- Accountant, general
- Director. zakat & taxes department
- Internal auditor
- Manager, accounts and budget
- Senior Financial Auditor
- Director G.A of reviewing
- Director, financial and accounting affairs
- Auditor, accounts
- Accounts auditing technician
- Director. financial reports department
- Accounts technician General
- Chief of internal auditing programs
- Financial Auditing Supervisor
- Cost accounting technician
- Controller, financial

5. Ministerial Decree No. 99895, dated 09/07/1445 H. (21/01/2024 G., effective 15/01/1446 H, corresponding to 21/07/2024 G.This decree was established as a joint project between the HRSD and the Ministry of Municipal, Rural Affairs and Housing and should be considered an addition to but not a substitute for, existing Saudization directives.

6. Ministerial Resolution No. 103108, dated 26/01/2025.

. . .

Lawyers are no exception. Article 52 of the Law of the Legal Profession requires 70% Saudi national lawyers. Additionally, no more than 30% of advisory work can be conducted by firm lawyers in offices outside Saudi Arabia.[7] Pharmacists are also subject to localization rules, which prescribe the following percentage of local Saudis: 35% in community pharmacies and medical complexes, 65% in hospital pharmacy activities, and 55% in other pharmacy-related activities. The rules apply to firms with five or more employees. The prescribed minimum wage for pharmacists is SAR 7,000 per month.These percentages became effective on July 27, 2025. [8] Percentages for dentists were phased in starting in July, 2025. At first, the requirement is 45% from that date and 55% starting from January 1, 2026. The rule applies to firms with three or more dentists, The prescribed minimum wage for dentists is SAR 9,000 per month.[9] Engineering localization percentages of 30% apply to firms with five or more employees and are effective as of 27 January, 2025. The prescribed minimum wage is SAR 5,000 per month. Workers in retail and wholesale sales positions are subject to the Decision to Localize Sales Professions. [10]

- 122104 Sales manager
- 142001 Retail sales manager

---

7. Law of the Legal Profession, as amended by Royal Decree No. M/78 dated 29/11/1444 H (2023).
8. Ministerial Resolution No. M/103111, dated 26 January 2025 (17/6/1446 AH, corresponding to 26/1/2025), approving updates to the Procedural Manual for the Saudization Decree of Pharmacy Professions.
9. Ministry of Human Resources & Social Development, Ministerial Resolution No. 103107, dated 26 January 2025 (17/6/1446 AH, corresponding to 26/1/2025), approving the Procedural Manual for the Decree on Saudization of the Dental Medicine Profession.
10. Ministerial Decision No. 141713 dated 11/09/1444 AH (corresponding to 2/April/2023 G).

- 243106 Trade specialist
- 243109 Sales specialist
- 142003 Wholesale manager
- 243401 Information and communication technology equipment sales specialist
- 332201 Salesperson
- 332401 Future commodity broker
- 332402 Commodity broker

Project management is another area for which the HRSD has applied localization requirements of 35% for the initial first phase (first nine months) and 40% for the second phase (to be reached by January, 2026). [11] Procurement professionals are subject to a 50% localization requirement. [12] The targeted positions are the following:

- Purchasing Manager
- Procurement Representative
- Contracts Manager
- Tendering Specialist
- Procurement Specialist (also referred to as bidding or supply specialist)

Those who work for freight forwarding and freight brokering companies are subject to a 20% localization requirement. [13] The following positions with their profession codes in accordance with the Guide of National Classification of Economic Activities (ISIC4) are affected:

---

11. Ministerial Decision No. 141713 dated 11/09/1444 AH (corresponding to 2/April/2023 G).
12. Ministerial Decision No. 141612 dated 11/09/1444 AH (corresponding to 2/April/2023 G).
13. Ministerial Decision No. 141722 dated 11/09/1444 AH (corresponding to 2/April/2023 G).

- 522406 Freight brokers
- 522404 Sea freight brokers
- 522914 Stevedoring activities of containers
- 522402 Stevedoring of freight aircraft
- 521015 Other freight handling activities
- 522912 Activities of transport and freight agencies
- 522913 Certified air freight agencies
- 521012 Goods freight and dispersal services in general
- 522928 Air freight forwarding agencies
- 522927 Handling of air cargo and mail
- 522409 Other activities related to cargo handling
- 522923 Receiving and unloading goods and products from vessels, and lining and arranging them on the shelves
- 522401 Loading and unloading of cargo and passenger baggage, regardless of the means of transport
- 512009 Other activities for the air transportation of cargo

There is a good deal of Ministerial attention paid to this area and these percentages are subject to change at any time. Other professions may similarly face Saudiization percentage standards.

The *Nitaqat* System

The government's response to the private sector's failure to aggressively increase the number of Saudis in the workforce is the *nitaqat* (ranges) system. *Nitaqat* replaces the blanket 30% quota established under Resolution No. 50. Under this system, companies are assigned color codes based on the number of Saudi employees working for them. In the *Nitaqat* program, the labor market is divided into forty-one commercial activities. The employer's size is also taken into account.

There are four categories: Red, Yellow, Green and Blue/VIP. A company classified "green" is in full compliance; "yellow," nearly compliant and "red," non-compliant. Companies falling within the red category will not be able to renew their foreign workers' visas. "Yellow" firms will not be allowed to extend their existing foreign employees' work visas for more than six years.

Employees working for yellow or red companies will be able to transfer to "green" or "blue" companies without the consent of their employer. Non-Saudi employees working for a "red" company may change their employment to a new employer without obtaining the former employer's consent.

The success of these efforts is not yet clear. Some sectors of the economy are fully Saudized, such as the banking sector, with national employment in percentage terms reaching the high 90's. The task of nationalizing other sectors has been less successful. Several years ago there was a requirement to restrict taxicab companies from hiring foreign drivers. There was an outcry even though the taxicab companies are all Saudi-owned because of complaints of high cost.

After a while, the requirement was quietly abandoned. It is unclear whether the new system will be any more successful than the old one. One can expect that Saudi employers will continue to resist hiring their own nationals and that foreign companies will follow their example.

To help persuade recalcitrant companies, the Ministry of Labor has hired 1000 *nitaqat* compliance inspectors. While the program initially was to exclude small business, by October, 2012 the Ministry had removed the exemption to assist Saudis in finding employment in small business as well as discouraging what are called "commercial covering" businesses. Prior to Saudi Arabia's accession to the World Trade Organization, foreigners were prohibited from engaging in wholesale or retail business. A common but prohibited practice of paying a Saudi national for the use of his name so that a non-Saudi could commence business operations grew up.

Classification of companies under *nitaqat* rules vary based on the type of work performed, starting at 6% Saudi personnel for construction jobs, 30% for oil and gas extraction and over 50% for banks and financial institutions. Domestic workers are exempted from the program. Since its inception, the transportation sector has struggled considerably with the program, with only half of employers achieving compliance by August, 2012. 90% of gas stations are non-compliant. Companies that have failed to comply with the system face severe consequences. Sanctions include a prohibition on new work visas and the refusal of officials to approve new branch offices for Red companies.

As part of the initiative, the government has established a monthly allowance of SAR 2000 for Saudi job seekers. The effect of the allowance is to ensure that Saudi job seekers will not accept a job paying less than that amount. Foreign laborers in Saudi Arabia earn an average wage between SAR 700 and 1500 per month. Since 88% of the country's estimated 6.3 million workers comprise the private sector workforce, it is clear that major economic disruptions are likely. Complicating companies' search for qualified workers is the fact that only 30% of Saudis go on to higher education and many will not take jobs perceived as menial despite their lack of education.

Employing a Saudi woman for Saudization purposes counts as employing two men; employing a disabled Saudi counts as four Saudi employees for the purpose of Saudization statistics. An unintended consequence is the growing number of "no-show" jobs given to Saudis so that a company can better its *nitaqat* position.

In 2021, the HRSD added three amendments to the Nitaqat program.[14]

- 1. Simplifying Nitaqat by consolidating sectors.
- 2. Publishing a Saudization plan for the next three years to provide regulatory stability.
- 3. Removing fixed-size bands and moving to a smooth relationship between worker count and required Saudization.

---

14. Ministerial Decision No. 182495 dated 11/10/1442 AH (23/05/2021 AD)

The number of sectors has been reduced from 85 to 32. Nitaqat percentages are now to be calculated in accordance with the following formula:

Saudization Formula

The 2021 amendments to the Nitaqat program introduced a continuous, sector-sensitive formula to calculate the Saudization target for private sector establishments. The formula is defined as:

Where:

- is the required **Saudization percentage** for the establishment.
- is the **total number of employees** in the establishment.
- is a **sector-specific multiplier** assigned by the Ministry.
- is the **natural logarithm** of the total number of employees.
- is a **sector-specific offset** or baseline percentage.

Purpose

The formula allows for a smooth, non-linear increase in Saudization targets based on establishment size, ensuring fairness and scalability across different industries and company sizes.

Blue (Premium) Category Companies

- May recruit foreign workers without needing to apply for a visa once every two months.

- May transfer the visas of potential employees from other companies, without having them fulfil the condition of completing two years with the first employee.
- May recruit employees from companies within the Red or Yellow categories and transfer their visas without permission of their employer.
- Entitled to a one-year grace period if municipal and professional licenses or commercial registrations expire.

Green Category Companies

- May apply for new visas once every two months.
- May change the professions of your foreign workers, with the exception of positions restricted to Saudis.
- Entitled to a six-month grace period after the expiry of zakat and revenue certificates.
- May renew work permits of current foreign employees given that their residency visas are valid for at least three months.
- May recruit employees from companies within the Red or Yellow categories and transfer their visas without permission of their employer.

Yellow Category Companies

- May obtain only one visa upon the departure of two foreign employees.
- May not obtain new visas.
- May not transfer visas.
- Will not have control over employees as the employees would be able to move to Green or Blue category companies.

Red Category Companies

- May not obtain new visas.
- May not transfer visas.
- Will not have control over employees as the employees would be able to move to companies under Green or Premium categories.
- Will be deprived of basic ministry services such as renewal of employees' working permits, change of profession, transfer of visas, issuance of new visas and opening files for new business branches.

Foreign Employee Fee

The Ministry of Labor now imposes a fee of SAR 2500 per foreign employee imposed on any company which has less than 50% Saudi national employees regardless of its *nitaqat* compliance status. Companies have complained that this fee is an illegal tax but the Ministry has insisted on compliance. The imposition of such a fee within such a short time after the inauguration of the *nitaqat* system shows how aggressive the government will be in seeking employment opportunities for Saudi nationals.

The government hopes that its efforts will result in the nationalization or creation of 3 million new jobs to be occupied by Saudi nationals by 2025. The *nitaqat* system is expected to result in increasing the percentage of Saudi workers from 10 to 50% over the next three years.

Secondment of Employees

Secondments are common in Saudi Arabia but legally problematic. On the one hand, rules prohibiting the transfer of employees, the prohibition against cover-up businesses and the requirements of Articles 30 and 39 would seem to prohibit the practice. Nevertheless, employers second employees frequently. Under Article 58 of the Labor Law, the employee must agree to any transfer.

Article 60 requires the new duties to be substantially similar unless the secondment is for a period of less than 30 days. Article 39(1) provides that without following the established rules and procedures, an employer cannot permit an employee to work for another employer. "Established rules and procedures"refers to sections 16 and 17 of the Implementing Regulations which bind an employee to his job title or description as well as employer. One employer who is ineligible to import foreign labor cannot circumvent the restrictions by accepting secondees from an eligible employer.

Moonlighting for another employer without the consent of the employer-sponsor is not permitted in Saudi Arabia, but is nevertheless commonplace.

Employees may not work for their own account. The so-called "gig economy" is not recognized by the Labor Law. In all cases, a worker must be tied to an employer.

Government employees who are seconded to the private sector are included in the private sector's head count for the calculation of localization percentages under the Nitaqat system. [15].

Recurring Issues

Employee Transfer

Employees often either seek to a better job within the organization or to move to a more advantageous position with another employer. They are usually very surprised to find out that such transfers, routine in their home countries, are far from trivial in Saudi Arabia. An employee leaving on bad terms is usually shocked to find out that a transfer requires the approval of his original employer.

15. Ministerial Decision No. (4074) dated 28/11/1436 AH (29-4-2025G)

One way to deal with the problem in advance is to put a provision in the employment contract that the employer will cooperate in the transfer of the employee and consents to the transfer. While it is impossible to guarantee the success of this tactic, in some cases the signed contract may substitute for the transfer consent letter.

Probationary Period

Employees are usually surprised to find out that the right of dismissal during the probationary period is one-sided in favor of the employer unless the employee is specifically given the right to resign for no reason during the probationary period. An employee who attempts to resign without the right may find himself in a good deal of difficulty. Without the employer's assistance it will be difficult to obtain an exit permit if one has not been obtained already. Moreover, the employer has the right to claim contract damages from the employee. These will include, at a minimum, the costs of transportation and lodging during the time the employee has been in service.

Many employees starting a new position are seldom in a position to make what for them are substantial payments. The employee then feels trapped and calls upon his Embassy for assistance. Unfortunately, there is little that the Embassy can do. A threat to prohibit the employer from future recruiting is a toothless one and there are other countries that will happily send their citizens. The predominant theme of Saudi dispute resolution is compromise, so the Embassy may be able to act as mediator and arrange for a meeting with the employer. But given the press of diplomatic duties, the employee who wishes only to leave will often be upset, if not frantic, because of the pace of the dialogue.

Employees in this situation will feel trapped and may become desperate. Unfortunately there are no good answers. An appeal to the local *majlis,* that is, the Office of the Prince with specific responsibility for the geographical region, has been known to be helpful in extreme cases.

The probationary period shall not exceed 180 days.

Passport Confiscation

It is still a common practice in Saudi Arabia for the employer to insist that the employee surrender his passport during his term of employment. Saudi Arabia has been subject to a great deal of criticism on this subject. Many Western governments insist that the practice is illegal but nevertheless it tends to be the norm. Since the employer will require the employee's passport in order to get the residence permit, the employee often finds himself in the position of having already surrendered his passport when he learns his employer will not give it back. A sentence along the lines of "the employee's passport will remain in his custody at all times during the period of his service except when required by agencies and instrumentalities of the government of Saudi Arabia" is a sentence that should be in every labor contract.

The new Implementing Regulations provide that the employer is not to retain the employee's passport "unless requested" by the employee. The Ministry has issued a form request letter. Is passport theft so rampant that the only way to combat the practice is by surrendering passports to employers for safekeeping? Or is this a vestige of servitude? Unfortunately, it is likely that the employee will be handed the form request, told to sign, and not told that there is no requirement that the employer hold the employee's passport. As as result, it will become routine for employees to "request" that their employer hold the passport and the problem of de facto passport confiscation will remain. Saudi Arabia is frequently criticized in the West for this practice. There really is no good reason to continue this practice.

Freezing Bank Accounts

When moving to a new city, it is common for an employee to obtain a local bank account at least for the purpose of dealing with local businesses, if for no other reason. Unfortunately, in Saudi Arabia a worker's bank account is tied to his immigration status which is in turn tied to his employment status. A worker who quits his job will find that his bank account has been frozen. This can also happen because of a data entry mistake, or a faux pas in the personnel office. In any case, fixing the problem is very, very difficult because the bank will defend its actions on the basis of a notification from the Saudi Arabian Monetary Agency (SAMA) which has acted based on information received from the Labor Ministry. There are four entities that must get involved to resolve the "problem" the employer, the Labor Ministry, SAMA and the employee's bank. Each will deny responsibility and there is no coordinating committee to facilitate communication amongst all of them. An accidental funds freeze can come without warning at any time.

To make matters worse, the freezing of an employee's funds usually comes at a time when the employee needs funds to leave the country. This problem lacks a legal solution because there is no language that can be put into a labor contract that would bind nonparties to the contract. Until SAMA, the country's central bank, establishes procedures to deal with accidental account freezing, the only solution is to not leave any significant sums in Saudi bank accounts.

Lay-offs or Redundancies

Lay-offs or redundancies need the permission of the Labor Ministry. Otherwise employers must comply with the obligations as stated in the various labor contracts. An employer may purchase the employee's contract by paying those wages that would have been earned had the employee continued to work for the duration of the contract. The

End of Service Benefit is owed as well. Employees with indefinite terms contracts are not in this position. Employers should carefully consider whether it is appropriate to attempt to make an employee with an indefinite term contract redundant without Ministry approval, since such a wrongfully terminated employee may obtain an injunction requiring reinstatement with back pay.

Transfers

An employee must consent to any transfer other than a temporary one, that is, a transfer for a period of thirty days or less. Similarly, an employer may not demote an employee or give him duties which are inferior to those stated in the contract. The remedy is reinstatement in the position and if the employer lowered the salary, back pay as well.

Late Salary Payment

Despite the fact that the Qu'ran prohibits withholding what is due to another (7:85) and the existence of a hadith of the Prophet Mohammad which commands that a worker be paid before "the sweat of his brow dries" late payments by Saudi employers to workers is a chronic problem. It is not clear whether this is due to an economic system that prohibits the payment of interest or for other cultural reasons. The problem exists in all labor sectors and among all classes of society, from the poor to the excessively wealthy. In any event, Saudi media outlets regularly contain stories about workers who have not been paid for months. In the past, these workers have had little recourse, but now the Labor Ministry has commenced collecting data on employers who fail to pay their workers promptly. Employers who fail to pay their workers on time will be sanctioned by the Ministry and prevented from recruiting any foreign workers. The Ministry has encouraged workers to complain, even anonymously.

Unfunded End of Service Benefit

Another recurring problem is the employer who cannot or will not pay the End of Service Benefit as required by law. Part of the problem is that employers are required to maintain relatively low bonds to cover payments to workers. For regulated recruitment companies that lend labor to other employers, the amount of the bond is only 300,000 SAR. Other types of employers in the private sector need submit no bond at all. If an employer has not specifically budgeted for and funded the End of Service Benefit payment, at the time of an employee's departure there will be no funds to pay him.

Suing the employer in the Labor Ministry's Disputes Resolution Committee is an expensive proposition. The proceedings are in the Arabic language and the cost of counsel and interpreters are not insignificant. Furthermore, if an employee returns to his country he must return in case any hearings are set. Saudi judicial practice permits several continuances before a matter is adjudicated. Obtaining a visa in order to attend court proceedings may be difficult. For many, the costs of securing rights under Saudi law are simply too high. The Labor Ministry could take steps to resolve the issue by requiring all those who recruit labor to submit a bond and not just regulated recruiting companies.

Unfair Competition

Employees may find themselves caught up in a dispute between their employer and his Saudi distributor. This can occur when foreign employees are sent by the home company to Saudi Arabia to work under the sponsorship of a Saudi distributor. As long as the relationship is a harmonious one, problems rarely come up. But from time to time foreign manufacturers decide to change their local distributor and these employees are caught in the middle. Without proper planning, the foreign manufacturer may find that these employees have had their visas cancelled, their bank accounts frozen and been given one-way ticket out of the country. Their sponsor will claim that they have had access to confidential information, that is, the trade secrets of the Saudi distributor. He can blacklist these employees from returning to the Kingdom for a period of two years. The fact that these employees were only nominally the Saudi distributor's employees does not matter for the purposes of Saudi law, they were under his sponsorship and he has this right.

In other cases, the Saudi distributor can simply refuse to consent to the transfer of the foreign manufacturer's employees to the new distributor. Unless the Saudi distributor is in a red or yellow *nitaqat* status, he has this right. The foreign manufacturer's sole option may be to hire or transfer new employees who lack the local knowledge gained by their predecessors over a period of time.

This kind of problem is normally resolved between the manufacturer and his agent. Anticipating the problems means including provisions in the seconded employee's labor contracts to avoid any retaliation against them. For those foreign companies that have not anticipated this problem, the impact on their employees can be harsh indeed.

The Labor Law makes it clear that employees who have access to an employer's trade secrets "which include business practices" may be barred from returning to the Kingdom after completion of the employment contract for a period of up to two years.

CHAPTER 3
APPENDIX THE LABOR LAW

APPROVED by Ministerial Council Decision No. 219 dated 22.8.1426H (Note: titles given to Articles do not form part of the law and are provided for the reader's convenience.)

(As amended by Royal Decree No. M/51 dated 23/8/1436H, published in the Umm al-Qura, Issue No. 4563 on April 24, 2015)

Chapter I—Definitions and General Provisions

Article 1-Designation

This law shall be called the Labor Law.

Article 2-Definitions

~~Wherever the following terms and expressions are mentioned in this Law, their meanings would be as set forth below unless otherwise stated.~~ The following terms and expressions, wherever mentioned in this Law, shall have the meanings assigned to them unless the context otherwise requires. **The Ministry**: ~~The Ministry of Labor.~~ The Ministry of Human Resources and Social Development. **The**

Minister: ~~The Minister of Labor.~~ The Minister of Human Resources and Social Development. **Labor Office**: ~~The administrative department responsible for the Labor Affairs in the place specified by the Minister's decision.~~ The administrative body responsible for labor affairs within a spatial scope defined by a ministerial decision. **Employer**: ~~Every natural or juristic person who employs a workman or more in return for payment.~~ Any natural or legal person who employs one or more workers in exchange for wages **Worker**~~man~~: ~~Every natural person who works for the interest of the employer and under supervision in return for payment even if the workman is not under the direct supervision of the employer.~~ Any natural person – male or female – who works for the benefit of an employer, under their management or supervision, in exchange for wages, even if away from their direct oversight. **Juvenile**: A person who is at least 15 years old but has not reached his 18th birthday. **Work** ~~The Labor (sometimes, the "Work")~~: ~~The effort exerted in all the human activities in performing a labor contract (written or otherwise) regardless of their nature or being industrial, commercial, agricultural, technical, whether muscular or mental.~~ The effort exerted in all human activities in the implementation of an employment contract (written or unwritten), regardless of its nature or type, whether industrial, commercial, agricultural, technical, or otherwise, whether physical or mental. **Original Work** ~~Labor~~: **For individuals**: ~~Their ordinary activity.~~ The subject of their usual activity and as for establishments: the work for which the establishment was created to perform and **For corporations**: The labors for which the corporation was established and which are stated in their articles of incorporation if they are franchise companies or registered in the Commercial Register. **Temporary Work** ~~Labor: The labor which, by its nature, is part of what is practiced by the owner of the enterprise, and the execution of which requires a limited period, or concentrates on special labor and finally ends, and which usually does not exceed 90 days in both cases.~~ Work that, by its nature, falls within the employer's activity and requires a specific duration to complete, or focuses on a specific task and ends with its completion, and in both cases does not exceed ninety days. **Occasional Work**: ~~Incidental Labor: The labor which is not included in the usual activities of the owner, and its execution does not take more than 90 days.~~ Work that is not part of the usual activity of the employer and does not take more than ninety days to complete. **Seasonal Labor**: ~~The labor which is executed in conventional periodic seasons.~~ Work that is performed during established periodic seasons. **Part-time Labor**: ~~The labor performed by a part-timer, for an employer, for labor hours less than half the usual daily labor hours whether this workman performs this labor on a daily basis or on some days of the week.~~ Refers to work performed by an employee who is not fully dedicated to the employer and works fewer than half of the standard daily working hours at the establishment, whether the employee works daily or only on certain days of the week. **Continuous Service**: ~~The continuous service of the workman with the employer himself or his legal representative from the date of commencing the service. The service is considered continual in the following cases:~~ Refers to the uninterrupted service of an employee with the same employer or their legal successor, starting from the commencement of service. The service is considered continuous in the following cases:

- ~~Regular vacations and holidays according to the Law.~~ Statutory holidays and leave.
- ~~Absence for performing examinations in accordance with what is stated in this Law.~~ Periods of absence for exams as stipulated in this Law.
- ~~Leave without pay, which is not more than casual 20 days during the work year.~~ Cases of employee absence without pay, provided the total duration does not exceed twenty intermittent days during the work year.

Assignment: The service of providing a worker to work for someone other than the employer, through an establishment licensed for this purpose. [textitEd.note: New Definition]

Resignation: The worker's written declaration of their desire, without coercion, to terminate a fixed-term employment contract without any condition or stipulation, and the employer's acceptance of it. [textitEd.note: New Definition]

Basic Salary: ~~Every salary given to the workman in return for his labor according to a written or not written labor contract whatever the kind of salary or the way the labor is performed in addition to the periodic allowances.~~ Everything given to the worker in return for their work, based on a written or unwritten employment contract, regardless of the type of wage or method of payment, in addition to periodic allowance **Actual wage**: ~~The basic salary in additional to all other due allowances fixed for the workman in return for the effort he has exerted, or hazards he faces during the performance of his labor, or those fixed according to the contract or regulations such as~~: The basic wage plus any other due increments granted to the worker in return for effort exerted in the work, risks faced in performing the job, or as stipulated in the employment contract or work regulations, including the following:

- ~~Commission percentage of sales or profits paid in return for marketing, production, collection or the increase or improvement which the workman achieves.~~ Commission, or a percentage of sales, or a percentage of profits, paid in return for what the worker markets, produces, collects, or achieves in terms of increased production or improvements.
- ~~Due allowances in return for hard work or hazards he faces during the performance of his labor.~~ Allowances that the worker is entitled to receive in exchange for the effort exerted or risks encountered while performing their work.

- ~~Allowances which might be awarded in accordance with the living standard or for fulfilling the family obligations.~~ Increases that may be granted based on the cost of living or to meet family burden
- ~~Bonus or premium which is awarded by the employer for honesty, competence and the like, if this bonus or premium is stated in the contract or the corporation regulations or that they are usually awarded so that the workmen consider this part of their salary and not donation.~~Grant or Bonus that refers to payments made by an employer to an employee in recognition of their honesty, efficiency, or similar qualities, provided such payments are specified in the employment contract, the establishment's work regulations, or are regularly provided as a customary practice, such that employees regard them as part of their wages rather than a voluntary gift.
- ~~Material benefits: The benefits given by the employer to the workman in return for his labor which is stated in the contract or the labor regulations. This is estimated as a maximum of the basic salary for a period of two months yearly unless estimated in the contract or regulations in not more than the same.~~ Benefits in kind: Refers to benefits that the employer is obligated to provide to the worker in exchange for their work, as specified in the employment contract or the establishment's work regulations. They are valued at a maximum equivalent to two months' basic salary for each year unless the employment contract or the work regulations specify a higher value.

Wage~~Salary~~: ~~The Actual Salary.~~ Means the actual wage **Establishment**: ~~Every project managed by a natural or juristic person, and which employs one workman or more in return for whatever~~

~~salary.~~ Any project managed by a natural or legal person who employs one or more workers in return for a wage of any kind. **Month**: ~~30 days unless otherwise stated in the contract or regulations.~~ Thirty days unless otherwise stipulated in the employment contract or the establishment's work regulations. **Regulation**: ~~The executive regulation of this Law.~~ Implementing Regulations of this Law.

Section 2 General Rules

Article 3–Employment is a Right

Labor is the citizen's right and should not be practiced by others unless the conditions stated in this Law are prevailing, and the citizens are equal in the right to work.

Article 4–Shari'a to be Observed

The employer and workman should observe the provisions of the Islamic Shari'a when applying the provisions of this Law.

Article 5–Scope

Article 5: *Provisions of this Law shall apply to the following:*

- Any contract whereby a person commits himself to work for an employer and under his management or supervision for a wage.
- Workers of the government and public organizations and institutions ~~including those who work in pastures or agriculture.~~
- Workers of charitable institutions.
- Qualification and training contracts with workers other

than those working for the employer within the limits of the relevant provisions provided for in this Law.

- Part-time workers with respect to safety, occupational health and work injuries, as well as decisions issued by the Minister.

Previous Article 5: The provisions of this Law are valid for:

- Every contract according to which any person is bound to work for the interest of the employer under his supervision in return for salary.
- Government organizations and public institutions' employees including those working in pastures or agriculture.
- Workers of charitable establishments.
- Workers of the agricultural and pasture establishments which employ 10 or more workers.
- Workers of the agricultural establishments which manufacture their own products.
- Workmen who permanently operate or repair the mechanical equipment necessary for agriculture.
- Qualifying and training contracts with other workers who do not work for the employer according to the special provisions stated in this Law.
- Part-time workers with respect to matters of safety and professional health, workplace accidents and any other matter as is decided by the Minister.

Article 6–Application to Seasonal or Part-time Workers

The special provisions related to duties and discipline, maximum working hours, daily rest breaks and weekly holidays, overtime, official holidays, the rules pertaining to safety, professional health, work place accidents and compensation for the same, as well as what is decided by the Minister in this respect, are also valid for incidental, seasonal and part-time workers.

2025 Implementing Regulation Article 1

Subject to Article (6) of Labor Law:

1. If both parties to the temporal or incidental employment contract continue the contract enforcement for a period exceeding (90) ninety days, the temporal or incidental employment contract shall be deemed as a permanent employment contract subject to all provisions of the Labor Law. Neither the job title indicated in the work permit submitted by the worker- if expatriate-, nor the residence period granted thereunder is considered.

2. The Labor Courts shall have the jurisdiction to consider the disputes arising between the parties over the incidental, seasonal and temporal employment contract.

Article 7-Exclusions

Article 7 [Ed. Note: 2024 revision] 1. The following are exempt from the application of the provisions of this Law:

- A. The family members of the employer, including the spouse, parents, and children, who work in the establishment and who are the only employees there.
- B. Players and coaches of sports clubs and federations.
- C. Domestic workers and those considered as such.
- D. Agricultural workers, private herders, and those in similar roles.
- E. Sea workers who work on ships of less than five tons. [textitEd.note: not changed by the 2024 revision]
- F. Non-Saudi workers who come to perform a specific task for a period not exceeding two months.

2. The minister, in coordination with the relevant authorities, shall issue one or more regulations for the categories mentioned in

paragraphs (A), (C), (D), and (E), of paragraph (1) of this Article, outlining the rights, duties, and other relevant provisions specific to each category. Notwithstanding the provisions of paragraph (1) of this article, the penalties specified in Article 229 of this law shall apply to violations of the provisions of those regulations.

3. The regulations issued for the two categories mentioned in subparagraphs (c) and (d) of paragraph (1) of this article should include clear procedures and mechanisms to improve the performance of the labor market for these categories. They should also regulate the movement of workers, define the responsibilities of employers, and outline the duties of offices and companies involved in mediating their recruitment.

Old Article 7:

The following are excluded from the application of the rules of this Law:

- Family members of the employer: his wife, and relatives, who work in the establishment, which does not including anyone else.
- House servants and the like.
- Sea workmen who work in boats of loads less than 500 tons.
- Agriculture workers who are not mentioned in Article 5 of this Law.
- Non-Saudi workers who are employed for one limited job for a period not more than two months.
- Sports club players, members of sports teams and coaches.

The Ministry is to coordinate with the concerned authorities for the preparation of special regulations dealing with house servants and the like governing their relations with their employers, which would specify the rights and obligations of each party and submit the same to the Council of Ministers.

2025 Implementing Regulation Article (2)

Subject to the provisions of sub-paragraph (d) of paragraph (1) of Article (7) of the Law: The agricultural workers, shepherds and the like shall mean agricultural workers, shepherds and the like who work in individual's houses, farms, livestock farms, laying aside those working in establishments.

Article 8-Precedence of Law

Every term or a condition which contradicts the rules of this Law will be invalid, and any modification of the rights of the worker during the validity of the contract, will be invalid according to this Law, unless they are more beneficial to the worker.

Article 9-Arabic Language

The Arabic language must be used in the statements, records, files, labor contracts and other documents stated in this Law or in any decision issued to be applied, as well as the instructions issued by the employer to this workers. If the employer uses a foreign language beside the Arabic language in any of the said cases, the Arabic text would be the approved text.

Article 10-Hijra Calendar

All the periods and dates stated in this Law are to be considered from the Muslim calendar (Hijra) unless otherwise stated in the labor contract or rules of work.

Article 11-Subcontracting

Article 11: 1. *An employer who subcontracts any part of the work to a natural or corporate person must give the workers all the rights and benefits called for under the original contract of employment.*

2. *Without prejudice to the provisions of this law and relevant laws, the Minister may take action to secure the improvement of labor market performance and regulate the movement of the labor force.*

Old Article 11:

1. If the employer subcontracts his original work, or part thereof to any natural or juristic person, the latter must give the workers all the rights and benefits which are given by the original owner to his workers, for which both of them will be jointly responsible.

2. If there are several employers, they will be jointly responsible for the discharge of the obligations stated in this law and the labor contracts.

Article 12–Work Rules

New Article 12:

1. *The Ministry of Labor shall establish one or more consolidated forms for work organization policy, provided that the form shall include the rules of labor regulation and related provisions including those provisions related to violations and disciplinary penalties.*

2. *The Ministry shall establish controls and mechanisms for the approval of labor regulation rules.*

Old Article 12:

The employer and the worker must know the rules of the Labor Law in all its contents so that each of them will be acquainted with his rights and obligations. The employer who employs more than 10 workers must submit, to the Ministry, within a year from this Law coming into effect, rules for organizing work including the internal rules of their work.

These rules should cover organization of work, including rules related to benefits, and any special instructions pertaining to violations and disciplinary penalties, which do not contradict the rules of this Law.

2025 Implementing Regulation Article (3)

Subject to the provisions of paragraph (1) of Article (12) of the

Law, the unified form of the work regulations shall be approved as per the form attached hereto (Annex No. 1). (*Also see the Implementing Regulation of Article 13, below*)

Article 13–Approval of Work Rules

Article 13: 1. *Every employer shall prepare work rules for regulating the work in his organization pursuant to a form prepared by the Ministry of Labor. The Minister of Labor may make exceptions to this provision.* 2. *The employer may include additional terms and conditions in the work rules provided that they do not contradict the provisions of this Labor Law and those rules issued for its implementation.* 3. *The employer must post the work rules and any amendment at a conspicuous place in the work place or through any other means designed to communicate its contents to employees.* Old Article 13: The Ministry is to ratify the rules for organizing work and their amendments within 60 days from submission to the Ministry. If this period expires without agreement or objection, the said rules will be considered valid and ratified, from the date of the expiry of the 60 days period. The employer should declare these rules after their ratification in a conspicuous place in the establishment or by any other means that enables the laborers to note it and become acquainted with it.

2025 Implementing Regulation Article (4) Subject to the provisions of paragraph (2) of Article (12) and paragraph (2) of Article (13) of the Law, the establishment's work regulations shall be approved according to one of the following procedures:

- 1. The establishment may select the online unified form of the work regulations, in order to regulate the establishment's work without any amendments or additions, through the Ministry's e-services portal, and to follow-up the required steps pending the final approval, by issuing relevant e-certificate.

- 2. If the establishment desires to prepare a special work regulation rather than selecting the unified form regulations, such regulations shall be audited and approved by the law firms certified by the Ministry of Human Resources and Social Development. Relatedly, the law firm shall ensure that no contradiction with the provisions of Labor Law, its Implementing Regulations or enforcement decisions is established. Consequently, such regulations shall be referred to the competent authority determined by the Ministry in order to be approved as per the applicable procedures.

Article 14-Model Work Rules—Repealed. See New Art. 12(2)

Repealed.

Article 15-Data Collection

When commencing work at any enterprise, the employer should notify the concerned labor office in writing of the following information:

- The name, type, and center of the enterprise, the correspondence address and any information which makes the contact with the enterprise easy.
- The licensed economic activity, the commercial register number, the license, its date, the issuing authority and a copy thereof should be attached.
- The number of workers that would be working in the enterprise.
- The name of the executive manager of the enterprise.
- Any other information required by the Ministry.

Article 16–Appointment of Manager

1. If the employer could not run the labor by himself, he should appoint a person to represent him. In case the partners or managers are several, one of whom who stays at the site of the enterprise is to be named as a representative of the employer and would be responsible for any violation of the rules of this Law. 2. The employer should notify the concerned labor office in writing the name of the partner or manager. In case of his replacement, he should notify the labor office name of the partner or the new manager within seven days of the taking over of the replacing person. 3. If there is no specific person working as the office manager, or if the appointed person has not started his job,then the person who actually conducts the job of the manager or the owner himself is considered a manager in charge of the enterprise. In all cases the responsibility of the employer remains the main one.

Article 17–Record Retention

The employer should keep the records, statements of account and their related files and the information pertaining to the rules. The employer should display at a prominent place a time table for the dates of work, break times, the weekly rest day, the starting and ending times of every shift in case of rotation of workers.

2025 Implementing Regulation Article 5 Subject to Article (17) of the Law, the employer shall incorporate under the statements, records and files maintained in the workplace- whether in hard or soft copies- the following details:

- 1. Workers' Name Statement: including names, occupations, ages, nationalities, and identifications numbers of workers, and numbers and dates of work permits in case of non- Saudis.

- 2. Workers' Wage Payroll: including wages of workers, dates of receipt, deducted amounts and deduction reason.
- 3. Fine Record: including the name and wage of worker, and the amount, reason and [the] effective date of fine.
- 4. Attendance Record: including the attendance and departure to/from the workplace as well as any other statements specified by the employer.
- 5. Saudi Training Record: including the training program's title, category, duration, year, enrolled workers and their percentage out of total workers.
- 6. The medical examination record for the establishment's workers who are likely to be infected with occupational disease: including the workers names who were examined as well as the date and result of examination.
- 7. Work file for workers: including data, address, copy of the employment contract and any certificates or documents submitted to the employer.

Article 18–Employment and Merger or Sale of Enterprise

If the ownership of the enterprise is transferred to a new employer, or its form changes due to amalgamation or break up, the labor contract remains valid in both conditions and the service is considered continuous. As for the rights of the workers prior to the period preceding this change, pertaining to wages or the dues of end of service benefits, as they stood on the date of the transfer of ownership or other rights, the successors and predecessors will be jointly responsible for the same. In case of the transfer of the individual enterprise for whatever reason, the agreement of the successors and predecessors is allowed for the transfer of all the previous rights of the workers to the new owner by the written agreement of the workers. In case the worker refuses to agree, his contract will be cancelled and all his rights are received from the predecessors.

Article 19–Bankruptcy of Employer

The due rights of the worker or his heirs are considered by this Law preferred debts of first class. To receive these due rights, the worker and his heirs have priority on all the monies of the employer. In case of the owner's bankruptcy or the liquidation of his enterprise, the said due rights are to be registered as preferred debts and are to be paid to the worker expeditiously in an amount equal to one month salary. This is to be done before the settlement of any other dues including the judicial expenses, bankruptcy payments or liquidation expenses.

Article 20–Misuse of Law, Prohibition on Collective Action

The employer or the worker is not allowed to do any action that misuses this Law or the rules and the decisions or regulations issued for the execution of its provisions. Either of them is not allowed to force the other party or the other workers or employers in order to achieve interest or the adoption of a point of view which contradicts the freedom of labor or the function of the concerned authority for the settlement of disputes.

2025 Implementing Regulation Article (6)

Subject to Article (20) of Labor Law:

The employer may not withhold the passport, residence or medical insurance card of non-Saudis.

Article 21–Coordination with other Authority

To execute the requirements of this Law, the Minister should coordinate with the concerned authorities whenever necessary.

Chapter II—Workplace Organization

Section 1 Employment Departments

Article 22-Labor Offices

Ed.note: 2024 revision ~~The Ministry is to provide free employment departments in places accessible to the employers and workers. These departments carry out the following:~~ The ministry provides free employment channels that perform the following:

- ~~Helping the workers in obtaining suitable work and assisting employers in finding suitable workers.~~ Assisting workers in obtaining suitable employment and assisting employers in finding suitable workers.
- ~~Collecting necessary information on the labor market, its development and the analysis of this information made available to different public and private organizations dealing with the economic and social planning affairs.~~ Gathering the necessary information about the labor market and its development, and analyzing it, to make it available to various public and private bodies concerned with economic and social planning.
- ~~Carrying out the following duties:~~ Performing the following duties:
- ~~Registration of applicant workers.~~Registering job seekers,
- ~~Obtaining information related to job vacancies from employers.~~ Obtaining data on job vacancies from employers,
- ~~Referring workers' applications for suitable jobs.~~Matching job seeker applications with job vacancies according to their qualifications.
- ~~Offering advice and assistance relating to qualifications, vocational training or retraining necessary for obtaining~~

~~vacant job.~~ Providing advice and assistance to job seekers regarding vocational qualification and training, or the necessary retraining to obtain job vacancies,

- ~~Other issues decided by the Ministry.~~Other matters determined by the ministry.

2025 Implementing Regulation Article (7)

Subject to the provisions of Article (22, 23, 24 and 25) of the Labor Law, there shall be mutually coordination between the Ministry and the Human Resources Development Fund (HRDF) in order to activate and support those employment units affiliated with HRDF to employ, qualify and train national workers to replace expatriate labor.

Article 23-Labor Office Duties

Ed.note: 2024 revision ~~Every citizen who is capable of and interested in work has to ask for the registration of his name in the employment department stating his date of birth, qualifications, his previous jobs, interests and address.~~ Every citizen of working age who is able and willing to work has the right to register their name in the employment channels, stating their date of birth, qualifications, previous work experience, preferences, and address.

2025 Implementing Regulation Article (7)

See Article 22 above for the corresponding Implementing Regulation.

Article 24-Regulations for Labor Offices

Ed.note: 2024 revision ~~The regulations are to specify the rules and procedures of work in the employment departments, records forms, notices and papers used. Also the job description tables in accordance with the approved job description.~~ The regulations specify the rules and procedures of work in employment channels, the forms of records, notices, and documents used in their work, as well as job classification tables according to the approved occupational classification, and serve as the basis for organizing employment operations.

2025 Implementing Regulation Article (7)

See Article 22 above for the corresponding Implementing Regulation.

Article 25–Data Collection

Ed.note: 2024 revision ~~Every employer should send the following to the concerned labor office:~~Every employer must send the following to the Ministry:

- ~~Statement of vacant and new jobs, their type, place, salary and conditions within a period of time not exceeding 15 days from the date of being vacant or new.~~ A statement of vacant and newly created jobs, their types, location, assigned wages, and the necessary conditions for filling them, within a period not exceeding fifteen days from the date of vacancy or creation
- ~~Notification of what he has decided about employing the citizen nominated by the employment department within seven days from the date of receiving the nomination letter.~~A notification of the action taken regarding the employment of the citizen nominated by the employment unit, within seven days from the date of receiving the nomination letter.
- ~~Information of the names, jobs, profession, salaries, ages, nationalities of his workers and the numbers of work permits of the non-Saudi workers, their dates and other information to be specified by the regulations.~~ A statement of the names of their workers, their jobs, professions, wages, ages, nationalities, work permit

numbers for non-Saudis and their dates, and other data specified by the regulations.

- ~~A report on the conditions and nature of work, as well as expected shortage and excess in potential business during the year following the date of the report.~~ A report on the state of work, its conditions and nature, and the expected increase or decrease in work during the year following the report date.
- ~~The information stated in the two clauses 3 and 4 of this Article must be sent during the month of Moharram of each year.~~The data referred to in paragraphs 3 and 4 of this Article shall be submitted during the month of Muharram of each year.

2025 Implementing Regulation Article (7)

See Article 22 above for the corresponding Implementing Regulation.

Article 26–Preference for Saudi Employees

- All enterprises in their different fields of activities, and whatever the number of their workers is, should employ Saudi citizens and encourage them to continue in their jobs by instructing, training and qualifying them for the work they are entrusted to do.
- The percentage of the Saudi workers employed by the employer should not be less than 75% of the total number of workers.

In case of non-availability of technical abilities or academic qualifications to occupy the jobs by citizens, the Minister has the right to reduce this percentage temporarily.

2025 Implementing Regulation Article (8)

Subject to the provisions of paragraph (2) of Article (26) of Labor Law, the obligatory Saudization rates for establishments shall be determined through programs set out by the Ministry. Through such programs, the Saudization rates for each activity of the private sector shall be followed-up. Furthermore, all or part of the Ministry's services provided for establishments failing to achieve the specified Saudization percentage shall be ceased, such as the Program for Incentivizing Establishments to Saudize Jobs (Nitaqat); provided that the Ministry periodically updates these programs whenever necessary.

Article 27-Registration of Employees

Ed.note: 2024 revision ~~When necessary, in some activities and professions and in some regions and governorates, the minister has the right to force the employers not to employ workmen without registering them in the employment departments in accordance with terms and conditions specified by his decision.~~ When necessary, the Minister may require employers – in certain activities, professions, and certain regions and governorates – not to employ workers unless they are registered in employment channels, under the conditions and circumstances specified by a decision from him.

Section 2 Employment of the Handicapped

Article 28-Disabled Employee Percentage Targets

Ed.note: 2024 revision ~~Every employer who employs 25 workers or more, and that the nature of his business enables him to employ the handicapped who were professionally rehabilitated, must employ at least 4% of the total number of handicapped workers who are professionally rehabilitated whether through nomination of the employment departments or otherwise. He should send information to the concerned labor office about the number of jobs and work~~

~~positions occupied by professionally rehabilitated handicapped and the salary of each.~~ Every employer who employs twenty-five workers or more, and whose nature of work enables them to employ professionally qualified persons with disabilities, shall employ at least 4

2025 Implementing Regulation Article (9) Subject to Article (28) of Labor Law,

- 1. A person with disability means every person proven under a medical report issued by the Ministry of Health or Hospitals of other governmental sectors or under one of the identification cards issued by the Ministry of Labor and Social Development (MLSD) that he has one or more permanent disability as in the following forms: Visual, hearing, mental, physical, and motor impairment, learning disability, speech disorder, behavioral and emotional disorders, autism, or any other disability requires one form of the facilitating measures and services.
- 2. The facilitating measures and services:mean the engineering modifications and provision of appropriate work conditions and environment according to the standards stated under Chapter (2) of architectural requirements folder, under Saudi Building Code and any of the arrangements indicated under the guiding list attached hereto (Annex No. 2) that might be required to enable the person with disability to perform the assigned tasks.
- 3. The ability to work means that the person with disability has fulfilled the vacancy requirements, or the work applied for, including the science, vocation, skill and/or other requirements that help him perform his work.
- 4. In order to consider the person with several disabilities

according to [the] (Nitaqat) program, the following requirements shall be applicable:

- a. The person with disability shall obtain the identification card from MLSD indicating the type and degree of disability.
- b. The functions and employment nature held by the worker as well as the type and degree of disability.

- 5. Each and every worker shall benefit from the necessary facilitations and measures in order to perform his work if proven according to a medical report issued by the authorities stipulated under clause (1) of this Article that he suffers from an illness or disability that does not require a leave for a period exceeding 120 days after the date of disability.
- 6. Workers with disability shall have all rights and benefits provided for others, specified under the Labor Law, these Regulations or the establishment's work regulations.
- 7. The disability may not be regarded as a main reason to reject the person-with-disability employment, promotion, or the provision of professional trainings if the ability to work is fulfilled under the definition included in clause (3) of this Article.
- 8. There may be no wage discrimination among workers based on disability, which shall be deemed as a misconduct.
- 9. The establishment shall keep the data, work nature, wages, and types of measures and facilitations of the workers with disability. Such data shall be disclosed to the work inspectors upon request.
- 10. The job applications submitted by persons with disability shall be in accordance with the forms and controls applicable by HRDF.

- 11.The establishment recruiting persons with disability shall maintain the place-based requirements and explanatory services stipulated under the guide attached hereto (Annex No. 2).
- 12. The work inspectors shall, upon paying an inspection visits for establishments, examine the persons-with-disability number, work nature, arrangement types and explanatory services.

Article 29–Status of Employee after Work-Related Accident

If any workman suffers a workplace accident, which resulted in a loss of his normal capabilities but does not inhibit him from performing another job, the employer should employ him in a suitable job for the salary specified for such job and this does not violate the compensation he deserves for his workplace accident.

Section 3 The National Offices for Employment of Citizens and the National Recruitment Offices

Article 30–Recruitment Offices

Ed.note: 2024 revision ~~No natural or legal person may engage in the recruitment of Saudis or the recruitment of employees unless licensed by the the Ministry of Labor. The [Implementing] regulations shall specify the scope of each of these [recruitment] activities, the conditions of license issuance and renewal, the rules for non-renewal or cancellation of the license and the consequences thereof, and other conditions and controls to ensure proper administration.~~

- 1. No natural or legal person may engage in the activity of employing Saudis, recruiting workers, or subcontracting unless licensed to do so by the Ministry. The regulations shall specify the controls for practicing each of these activities, the conditions for granting and renewing the license for each, the obligations of the licensee, the rules for non-renewal or revocation of the license, the consequences thereof, and other necessary conditions and controls to ensure the proper conduct of work thereunder.

- 2. The Ministry proposes the value of fees for practicing the activities referred to in paragraph (1) of this Article, and their disbursement channels, in preparation for completing the regulatory procedures in this regard.

2025 Implementing Regulation Article (10)

Subject to Article (30) of Labor Law, the licensing requirements of Saudization activity, recruitment activity, renewal and termination of licenses, and Saudis' tasks, as well as their implications shall be determined through the following:

- 1. Controls and rules of Saudization as per the format attached hereto, which shall be deemed an integral part hereof (Annex No. 3).
- 2. Controls and rules of practicing the outsourcing activity for recruitment and provision of the labor services as per the form attached hereto which shall be deemed an integral part hereof (Annex No. 4).

Article 31–Employer of Recruited Employees

Ed.note: 2024 revision ~~The Saudi workers, whom the labor offices have assisted in their employment, and the workers whom the recruiting offices have recruited on behalf of employers are considered workers for the owners of the enterprise employing them and shall execute employment contracts with the employers.~~ Saudi workers employed through the assistance of offices or companies, and workers recruited on behalf of employers, are considered employees of the employer and have a direct contractual relationship with them.

Chapter III—Employment of Non-Saudis

Article 32-Approval from Ministry Required to Hire Foreigners

Recruitment of foreign workers is only allowed after obtaining the approval of the Ministry.

Article 33-Work Permit Required

A non-Saudi is not allowed to practice work but only after obtaining a work permit from the Ministry in accordance with the form prepared for such purpose. The following are the conditions for granting the permit:

- The laborer shall have entered the country legally with an appropriate work visa.
- He should be qualified for professions needed in the country, and that there are no citizens who have the same qualifications or that the number of the qualified citizens is not enough, or that he is a normal worker needed by the country.
- He should be under contract with the employer and under his sponsorship.

In this Article, the word "work" means every industrial, commercial, agricultural, financial or other endeavors and any service including domestic service.

Article 34–Work Permit in Addition to other Licenses

Any permit or license required by another authority to practice work or profession cannot substitute for the work permit referred to herein.

Article 35–Lack of Eligible Saudi Candidates a Condition of Iqama Renewal

Ed.note: 2024 revision ~~The Ministry of Labor may refuse to renew a work license whenever the employer violates the Saudization criteria established by the Ministry of Labor.~~ For reasons it deems appropriate, the Ministry may refuse to renew the work permit if the employer violates the standards for nationalizing jobs set by the Ministry, or any other conditions or regulations mentioned in the regulations. The regulation outlines procedures to ensure that the worker is not negatively impacted by the non-renewal of the work permit, including the possibility of transferring the worker's service to another employer without the approval of the violating employer.

[1]

Article 36–Regulations concerning Professions Reserved to Saudi Nationals

The Minister should specify by his decision the professions and works which foreigners are prohibited to practice.

2025 Implementing Regulation Article (11) Subject to Article (36) of the Labor Law: I: The non-Saudis may not be recruited for any of the following occupations:

- 1. Senior HR Manager.

---

1. Pre-2016 version of Article 35: Before the renewal of the work permit, it should be ensured that there is no applicant among the Saudis applying for work who fulfills the required conditions.

- 2. Director of Personnel Department.
- 3. Director of Labor Affairs
- 4. Director of Personnel Relations Department
- 5. Personnel Specialist
- 6. Personnel Affairs Clerk
- 7. Recruitment Clerk
- 8. Staff Affairs Clerk
- 9. Attendance Clerk
- 10. General Reception Clerk
- 11. Hotel Reception Clerk
- 12. Patient Reception Clerk
- 13. Complaint Clerk
- 14. Treasurer
- 15. Private Security Guard
- 16. Expediter (Government Relations Officer)
- 17. Key Smith
- 18. Customs Broker.

Furthermore, any of the functions included under the above-mentioned occupations and employments may not be assigned to a non-Saudi worker - directly or indirectly - under any other job title.

II: Working in any activity, occupation or jobs may be reserved for Saudis as determined by the Ministry.

Article 37–Definite Term Employment Contracts

Ed.note: 2024 revision ~~The contract for a non-Saudi worker should be written and should be for a limited period. If this is not mentioned in the contract, the period of the work permit is to be considered the contract period.~~ The employment contract for a non-Saudi worker must be written and of a fixed term. If the contract does not specify its duration, it is considered to be one year starting from the worker's actual commencement date. If the work continues after this period, it is considered renewed for a similar duration.

2025 Implementing Regulation Article (12) Subject to Article (37) of the Labor Law, the non-Saudi employment contract shall have a definite term regardless of any extended terms. In any event, the contract may not be amended to have an unspecified term even if agreed to by the parties.

Article 38–Approval Required for Employee Profession Change

The employer has no right to employ the worker in a profession other than the one written in the work permit and the worker is prohibited to practice another type of work before finishing the regular procedures for changing his profession.

Article 39–Secondments

Ed.note: 2024 revision

- ~~Unless he has followed the stipulated legal rules and procedures, an employer may not allow his worker to work for others, and a worker may not work for other employers. Similarly, an employer may not employ the workers of other employers. The Ministry of Labor shall inspect firms, investigate violations of this paragraph detected by its inspectors, and refer them to the Ministry of Interior for the imposition of prescribed penalties.~~
- ~~An employer may not allow a worker to work for his own account and a worker may not work for his own account. The Ministry of Interior shall be in charge of detection, detention, deportation, and imposition of penalties on violators working for their own account in streets and squares, as well as absconding workers and persons employing, hiding, or transporting them as well as any person involved in such violation, and shall impose the prescribed penalties against them.~~

An employer may not allow their worker to work for another employer or their account, nor may a worker work for another employer or their account, unless in accordance with the prescribed rules and procedures. An employer is also prohibited from hiring another worker. The Ministry is responsible for inspecting establishments, identifying violations of this regulation, and taking necessary actions to enforce the prescribed penalties. Any violations falling under the jurisdiction of the Ministry of Interior will be referred to it for appropriate action in accordance with the applicable legal provisions. If the Ministry of Interior detects violations related to the provisions under its jurisdiction, it shall refer the details of the violating employers to the Ministry of Human Resources and Social Development for the enforcement of the penalties prescribed by this regulation.

2025 Implementing Regulation Article (13)

Subject to Article (39) of the Labor Law, the non-Saudi part-timers shall be subject to its provisions; except those excluded by the Ministry and included under the Ajeer Program.

Article 40–Responsibility for Fees

Ed.note: 2024 revision

- ~~The employer bears the recruitment fees of the non-Saudi worker, the residence permit fees, the work permit fees and its renewal fees and the fines due to the delay of such, as well as fees for change of profession, exit and re-entry visa fees, and a return ticket in the event of a final exit.~~ The employer shall bear the costs of recruiting the foreign worker, the residence nd work permit fees and their renewals, along with any penalties resulting from delays in such renewals, the fees for changing the profession, exit and re-entry fees, and the cost of the worker's return ticket to their home country after the termination of the relationship between the two parties.

- ~~The worker bears the costs of his return to his home country in case he is not found fit for the work or if he wishes to return home without a legal reason.~~ The worker shall bear the costs of his return to his home country if he is unfit for work or if he wishes to return without a legitimate reason.
- ~~The employer bears the fees of transferring the sponsorship of the worker to work for him.~~ The employer shall bear the costs of transferring the services of the worker who wishes to transfer his services to them.
- ~~The employer should pay the costs for the repatriation of the worker's remains to the place where the contract was signed or the place of recruitment unless the worker's family agrees to his burial in the Kingdom. The employer is exempted in case the General Organization for Social Insurance made a commitment, in this regard.~~ The employer shall be responsible for the costs of preparing the worker's body and transporting it to the location where the contract was concluded or where the worker was recruited from unless the worker is buried with the consent of their family within the Kingdom. The employer shall be exempted in case the General Organization for Social Insurance assumes this responsibility.

Article 41–Reference to Implementing Regulations

The regulations under this Law specify the conditions of recruitment, transfer of services, change of profession, as well as the rules and procedures for the same.

2025 Implementing Regulation Article (14) Subject to Article (41) of the Labor Law, there shall be determined:

I. Requirements, controls and procedures of recruitment as follows:

- 1. The recruitment process shall not lead to a competition among Saudis or excluding from an occupation, or a number of occupations, crafts, or activities.
- 2. The employer failure to recruit Saudis may not be deemed as a reason for recruiting non- Saudis.
- 3. The establishment wishing to carry out the recruitment shall achieve the Saudization percentage in order to carry out the recruitment process established under (Nitaqat) Program.
- 4. Any recruitment visas granted to the non-Saudi applicants that may decrease the Saudization percentage below the standards of the Ministry may not be issued.
- 5. The workers recruited for the establishments shall be determined according to [the] Nitaqat program.
- 6. Codes and titles of occupations shall be strictly adhered to as per Saudi vocational Classification Guide upon request for recruitment visas.
- 7. The non-Saudis recruitment and employment shall be limited to the activities indicated under [the] Nitaqat program.
- 8. No workers may be recruited for occupations reserved for Saudis.
- 9. Workers under the age of 18 or above the age of (60) may not be recruited for work. Meanwhile, the experts, physicians and others determined by the Minister shall be exempted from the maximum limit for working age.
- 10. The recruitment applications shall be submitted through [the] e-services website of the Ministry as per [the] Nitaqat program.

- 11. An approval letter sent by a governmental or private agency, supporting the need of the establishment to a number of workers, may not be deemed as an approval by the Ministry to recruit those workers. Such approval shall subject to the standards stated under [the] Nitaqat program or to the decisions of the Ministry.
- 12. The Ministry may reject the recruitment application in the following cases:
  - a. If there is a collective delay of wages, a commercial concealment is established or there has been proven that the employer allows all or part of his workers to illegally work for third parties or work for their own account.
  - b. If the establishment fails to achieve the minimum limit of the required Saudization percentage.
  - c. If the establishment submits or has submitted to the Ministry or the Labor Office, incorrect data, information or confirmations. Consequently, all procedures related to the recruitment shall be suspended for a period of at most five years. In addition, the visas issued for the establishment shall be canceled. Nonetheless, no work permits may be issued for the establishment based on such recruitment visas. The statutory procedures shall be enforced for the implementation of Anti-Forgery Law and other relevant laws stated under [the] Nitaqat program.
  - d. If the establishment was proven to have sold the obtained work permits. Consequently, all relevant procedures for recruitment shall be suspended for five years.
  - e. If the establishment failed to renew the work permits or residence of its workers.

- f. Any other cases stated under [the] Nitaqat program.

- 13. Whosoever obtaining one or more visas may request termination. In such case, he may not be granted an alternative visa. Any request for an alternative visa shall be deemed as a recruitment request that shall be subject to the requirements of approving the visas stated under [the] Nitaqat program.
- 14. An alternative visa replacing the terminated one may be issued if it has a governmental accreditation, with no need for a new governmental endorsement, provided that the alternative visas application shall be conducted within (6) six months after the date of previous visa's termination. In addition, the remaining term of the governmental contract may not be less than (6) six months.
- 15. In case of visas termination or expiry, the applicant shall be refunded the paid fees.

II. Terms, controls and procedures for employing expats for others as follows:

- 1. No specific term for the expats working for a specific employer is required to be realized in order to be employed to another employer; unless the controls stated under (Nitaqat) program otherwise stated.
- 2. Transferring the employment of a worker to another establishment shall be rejected if the establishment, to which the transfer occurs, has an expatriate worker holding an expired work permit or residence that were not renewed, or if such expatriate had entered [the Kingdom of Saudi Arabia] [and remained for] (3) three months ago without obtaining [a] work permit or residence. The following expats shall be excluded: the one reported as absent from

work for a period exceeding (15) fifteen days; the one who has an employment transfer application under review by the Ministry and the one who obtained [a] final exit visa.

- 3. The services of workers, of nationalities that prohibit their services transfer, may not be transferred according to laws.
- 4. The services may not be transferred to an employer who was reported for a collective delay of wages or proven to have committed a commercial concealment or to allow all or part of his workers to illegally work for third parties or work for their own account.
- 5. The services of the new expat for whom no work permit was issued may be transferred without the consent of his employer according to the controls stated under [the] Nitaqat program.
- 6. The expat services may be transferred if his authorized contract, work permit or residence was expired without the consent of the current employer according to the controls stated under [the] Nitaqat program.
- 7. The Minister or his deputy may approve transfer of the expat's services to another employer without the consent of the worker's current employer in the following cases:
    - a. If there is a claim between the worker and the employer considered before a court, while the employer caused the extension of the case consideration. This shall be established by any of the following cases: • If the employer or his representative do not appear before the court in two hearings of the same judicial degree without legal justification accepted by the judiciary. • If the court establishes that the employer or his representative cause the extension of the case in a way differs from the above-mentioned case. The above two cases

require the worker to never causes or contribute to extension of the claim consideration.

- b. Based on a recommendation by the court during the proceedings in order to avoid any damages that might affect the worker.
- c. If the establishment do not pay the worker's wages for three successive months or delays the remuneration beyond the maturity date on the third month, provided that the worker may not have caused such actions based on a request submitted by the worker within the Hijri year effective from the maturity date on the third month.
- d. If the employer is absent due to travel, imprisonment, death or any other reason which leads to the establishment's inability to fulfill its obligations towards its workers for 3 months without appointing an official to be responsible for the establishment and personnel affairs.
- e. Some categories or nationalities of workers who have special instructions regulating their conditions, if the employment contract is expired or terminated by the employer.
- f. The expat whose services are transferred to work for any establishment after the expiry of the work relation as per the controls and arrangements set out by the Ministry.
- g. Family reunification: • If one of the spouses entered into a valid contract inside KSA, provided that the employment contract is expired or terminated by the employer. • If one of the spouses was a Saudi national.
- h. If the worker reported a commercial concealment against the employer while providing the supporting

proof, provided that the worker may not be involved in such case.

- i. Any other cases required for the public interest and determined by the Minister or his authorized representative.

- 8. The services of the expat residing in KSA may be transferred under the statutory measures to the establishment that fulfills the recruitment terms stipulated under Article (14) herein. In order to transfer the service, the following conditions shall be fulfilled:
  - a. The expat shall be (18) years old or above.
  - b. The services transfer requirements indicated in this Article shall be fulfilled.
  - c. The occupation requirements stated under paragraph(2) of clause(III) herein shall be fulfilled except [for]the paragraphs (a, c and d).
- 9. The establishment requiring the services to be transferred shall achieve the Saudization percentage for the activity or entity according to [the] Nitaqat program.
- 10. The services transfer requests shall be submitted for the purpose of online working through the e-services website of the Ministry.
- 11. The Ministry may coordinate with HRDF in order to ensure that there is no Saudis available to the occupations for which the services required to be transferred.
- 12. The Ministry may ensure the coordination between the activity and occupations for which the services required to be transferred.
- 13. The previous and current employers shall maintain a written consent of the worker, for transferring his services to the new employer before conducting the relevant procedures.
- 14. An e-consent by the employer for the request of transferring the worker's services or a hard copy for the

unconditional waiver for the worker's services by his employer addressed to the applicant of service transfer, endorsed by an official authority. Such e- consent or hard copy waiver shall exempt the followings:

  - a. Cases of transferring services without the employer's consent stated under such regulations and [the] Nitaqat program.
  - b. Cases of transferring the workers' services for the new contractor in the ongoing Management, Operation and Maintenance contracts (OMM) concluded with the governmental agencies; if they were recruited or their services transferred in order to execute such contracts.

- 15. If no consent is obtained for the worker's services' transfer after the e-consent or the hard copy waiver is endorsed by the previous employer had been issued, for whatsoever reason, the worker shall remain in service of the principal employer.
- 16. Prior to conducting the transfer procedures, no contradicting decision or final judgment may have been issued.
- 17. If no consent was obtained for transferring the worker's services for any of the cases stated in paragraph (7) of this clause, the Minister or his authorized representative shall authorize the worker to work for another employer. The authorization terms shall be determined as part-time work for (six months). It shall be regularly renewed until the full achievement of the authorization's purpose.
- 18. The following cases may not be deemed as services transfer cases, rather, job retitled cases:
  - a. Desire by one or some of the heirs to continue the activity of their decedent, as long as an authorization from the heirs to the appointed heir who would

continue the business is obtained, the business status changed to be a company managed by all or part of inheritors, or an approval by the Ministry of Commerce and Investment obtained.

- b. Change of the establishment's name, purposes, all or part of the partners, business status while maintaining the commercial register, obtaining an approval by the Ministry of Commerce and Investment (MOCI).
- c. Merger of two or more establishments whether by changing the legal status or not, save the change status shall be specified in the Articles of Association and an approval by the Ministry of Commerce and Investment issued.
- d. Separation and independence of one or more partners with their individual shares; provided that such procedure shall be specified in the company's amendment contract or company's splitting up contract and an approval by the Ministry of Commerce and Investment shall be obtained.
- e. Transformation of the sole proprietorship to a partnership through one or more partners.
- f. Transfer of establishment ownership to another owner while maintaining the same workers and commercial register and obtaining an approval by the Ministry of Commerce and Investment.
- 19. The following cases may not be deemed as service transfer cases, rather, workers' registration transfer ones:
    - a. Transferring the expats' registration among branches in the same entity for more than once with no restrictions according to the provisions of [the] Nitaqat program.

- b. Transferring the expats' registration among entities of the same establishment according to the provisions of [the] Nitaqat program.

III. Terms, controls and procedures for occupation change as follows:

- 1. The occupation change means the authorization of the non-Saudi worker to work in another occupation other than the one he was authorized for.
- 2. In order to change the occupation, the following conditions shall be fulfilled:
- a. The employer of the worker shall have a valid business license or valid commercial register registered with the Labor Office and the business shall be existing.
- b. The occupation required to be changed shall be specified as per the Saudi vocational Classification Guide.
- c. The worker shall have the supporting academic qualifications and experience required for the occupation. Such academic certificates shall be certified by the competent authorities in the worker's home country and the Saudi Embassy, if it was issued outside KSA. Such condition may not include the following cases:
- • If the occupation change was resulted from a gradual promotion achieved by the worker.
- • If the occupation change does not require academic qualification, training or experience.
- d. The establishment shall achieve the required Saudization percentage according to [the] Nitaqat program.
- 3. The occupation change may not be applied to occupations reserved for Saudis.

- 4. The occupation change may not be applied to occupation prohibited under regulatory instructions.
- 5. The occupation change request shall be applied via the e-services website of the Ministry.
- 6. If change of specific occupation requires obtaining prior work permit, consent or work permit certificate in accordance with laws or the instructions of other official authorities, the approval of the relevant authorities, that is, Saudi Council of Engineers and Saudi Commission for Health Specialties, shall be obtained in order to change the occupation category to engineering or medical field occupation, etc.

Chapter IV—Training & Orientation

Section 1 Training & Orientation of Workers

Article 42-Training Required

Ed.note: 2024 revision ~~Every employer should prepare Saudi workforce and improve their standards in the technical, administrative and professional fields in order to gradually employ them in the jobs occupied by the non-Saudi workers. He should prepare a register in which records the names of the Saudi workers who replace the non-Saudi workers according to the terms and conditions specified by the regulations.~~ Each employer shall establish a policy for training and qualifying their Saudi workers to enhance their skills and improve their performance in technical, administrative, professional, and other fields. The regulation shall specify the provisions related to this matter.

2025 Implementing Regulation Article (15) Subject to Article (42) of the Labor Law, each and every employer shall in order to replace the non-Saudis by the Saudis, observe the following terms and rules:

- 1. Preparation of job description for the tasks and functions of the employment according to the adopted Saudi vocational Classification Guide, and, accordingly, determination of the relevant job requirements.
- 2. Identification of the relevant career paths of employments for the workers.
- 3. Provision of the required training and qualifying programs for jobs, according to paragraph(1) of this Article. Employer shall also seek to be updated of the new techniques, within his tasks and functions and to enable the Saudis to receive the relevant training and qualifying programs.
- 4. Generation of timelines as per the vocational categories and classifications for all posts held by non-Saudi workers; through which the employer shall provide the appropriate means for qualifying and training the Saudis replacing the non-Saudis.
- 5. Provision of the opportunities for Saudis to occupy the vacancies of non-Saudis enabling them to acquire experience and on-the-job-training so as to observe paragraphs (2) and (3) of this Article.
- 6. Preparation of a report for the Saudis replacing the non-Saudis.

Article 43–Large Employers to Train Saudi Nationals

Ed.note: 2024 revision ~~Without prejudice to the conditions set forth in franchise and other agreements regarding training and qualifications, every employer employing 50 or more workers shall annually train, in his business, a number of his Saudi workers not less than 12% of the total number of his workers. This percentage shall include Saudi workers who are pursuing their studies if the employer is covering their tuition fees. The Minster may raise this percentage in certain firms pursuant to a decision by him.~~

This is without prejudice to the provisions of franchise agreements and other agreements that specify particular conditions and rules for training, qualification, and skill development. Every employer must provide training or qualification for his workers in accordance with these requirements. The employer must train or qualify a percentage of his Saudi workers, which is determined by a decision from the Minister. This percentage includes Saudi workers who continue their studies, provided the employer bears the costs of their education. The regulation shall define the standards and general provisions related to this matter.
[2]

Article 44–Details of Required Training

Ed.note: 2024 revision ~~The training program should contain terms and conditions which should be followed in training, its period, the number of hours, the theoretical and practical training programs, the method of examination and the certificates granted in this respect. The regulations specify the criterion and the general rules which should be followed in order to promote the standard of performance of the worker in skill and productivity.~~ The training program must include the skill that the worker is being trained on, the rules and conditions followed in the training, its duration, the number of hours, the theoretical and practical training programs, the method of assessment, and the certificates awarded in this regard. The regulation shall define the standards and general rules to be followed in this regard to enhance the worker's performance in terms of skill and productivity.

2025 Implementing Regulation Article (16) Subject to Article (44) of the Labor Law: I: The establishment requiring training shall observe the following standards and rules:

2. The previous version of this Article was amended by Royal Decree No. M/51 dated 23/8/1436H.

- 1. Various training programs shall be prepared for all occupations required by the establishment, since such programs boost the worker's efficiency and skills that are required for the employer's objectives.
- 2. The establishment shall direct the training programs to focus on the most needed occupations, crafts and works needed, especially those occupied by non-Saudis, in order to gradually replace the non-Saudis by Saudis.
- 3. Whenever professional standards or aptitude tests in any sector is adopted by the competent governmental agencies such as Saudi Commission for Health Specialties or other, the training standards set forth by the establishment shall be compatible with the very standards and tests.
- 4. The training program duration may not be less than 16 hours.
- 5. The employer shall determine the worker's employment term after the completion of training, provided that such duration may not exceed the duration of the training program for which the worker has undergone. Furthermore, he shall determine the employment term if the employment contract term is undetermined or if the remaining employment term in undetermined contract is less than the period required for the training program.
- 6. The programs shall include theoretical and practical training with single or multi-levels scaled according to the skills and productivity of the worker, so as to increase the worker's skills and efficiency.
- 7. The training programs shall have direct or indirect relation with the trainee's work.
- 8. In case the trainee passes the course's examination, the establishment shall provide the Ministry with a the course completion certificate, including the trainee's

name, title, type, duration and year of the program via the Ministry's e-portal.

- 9. The training fees shall be on the employer's account. The establishment shall conduct the training in the workplace if it was certified by the Technical and Vocational Training Corporation (TVTC) or it may assign the training to any training centers or institutes certified by the competent authority or e-training platforms. The training may be conducted inside or outside KSA.
- 10. The establishment shall notify each Saudi worker of the training data including the title, type and duration of training, the entity conducting the training, training mechanism and method and the examination result in case the trainee passes the examination within one month of the training date.

II. The employer may charge the training and qualifying fees to the worker in the following cases:

- a. If the worker decides to terminate the training or qualifying program before the due date without an acceptable justification.
- b. If the employment contract is terminated according to the cases specified under Article (80) of the Labor Law, except for paragraph (6) therein, during the training and qualifying term or within the period determined by the employer after the completion of the training or qualifying program term in proportion with the remaining period.
- c. If the worker resigned or abandon the job for reasons other than those specified under Article (81) of the Labor Law during the training and qualifying program term or within the period specified by the employer after the

completion of the training or qualifying program term in proportion with the remaining period.

III: Meeting the determined training percentage is not a requirement for the establishments recruiting more than 50 workers, while their Saudization percentage determined in [the] Nitaqat program required is less than (12 %) of their total workers. In such case, it is only required to train all Saudis annually.

Section 2 Qualification and Training Contract with the Workers not Working for the Employer

Article 45–Apprenticeships

The qualification and training contract is a contract according to which the employer undertakes to qualify or train a person to prepare him for a certain profession.

Article 46–Need for Written Contract

Ed.note: 2024 revision ~~The qualification or training contract should be written, stating the type of profession for which the person has been contracted, the period of training and its successive stages, as well as the amount of the reward to be given to the trainee in each stage. The reward should not be specified on the basis of any piece or production.~~ The training or qualification contract must be in writing, specifying the type of profession for which the training is being undertaken, the duration of the training, its successive stages, the skill to be acquired, and the amount of compensation provided to the trainee at each stage, ensuring that compensation is not based on piecework or production. The contract must also outline the rights and obligations of both the trainee and the employer and indicate whether the training or qualification will take place within the employer's establishment or at another facility.

Article 47–Employer's Obligation to Accept Apprentices

Ed.note: 2024 revision ~~The Minister should compel the establishments — which he specifies by his decision — to accept a number or specified percentage of the students of colleges, institutes and centers and their graduates for the purpose of training and [providing] practical experience in accordance with the conditions, term and the trainees' compensation as stated in an agreement made between the Ministry and the management of the concerned establishment.~~ The Minister may require establishments to accept a specified number or percentage of students from universities, colleges, institutes, centers, and their graduates for training and to complete practical experience, in accordance with the conditions, terms, and durations set out in the regulation. A training contract must be concluded between the trainee and the employer, and the provisions of this chapter shall apply. The establishment may provide the trainee with an allowance.

Article 48–End of Apprenticeship

Ed.note: 2024 revision ~~1. The employer has the right to cancel the qualification or training contract if he finds that the trainee is unable to complete the training programs effectively. The trainee or his guardian have the same right. The party who wishes to cancel the contract should notify the other party of such intention at least a week before the date of suspending the training. 2. The employer shall, after completion of training or qualification period, oblige the trainee or a person who is subject to the training program to work with him for a period similar to the period of training or qualification.~~ ~~*If the trainee or the person who is subject to the qualification program refuses to work for such period, he must pay to the employer those costs of the training or qualification incurred by the employer.*~~ ~~[Note: new compensation requirement. Obligation to work for double the training period repealed.~~

1. The employer may terminate the training or rehabilitation

contract if it is proven that the trainee or rehabilitee is not capable or able to complete the training or rehabilitation programs beneficially. Similarly, the trainee, rehabilitee, or their guardian or custodian has the right to exercise this option. The party wishing to terminate the contract must notify the other party of their intention at least one week prior to the specified termination date. Neither party may demand compensation from the other unless the contract includes a provision stating otherwise.

2. The employer, after the completion of the training or rehabilitation period, may require the trainee or rehabilitee to work for a period equal to the duration of the training or rehabilitation. If the trainee or rehabilitee refuses or fails to work for the equivalent period or part of it, they must compensate the employer for the costs of the training or rehabilitation incurred by the employer, or a proportionate amount for the remaining period.

Article 49-Application of Law to Apprentices

The qualification and training contract is subject to the rules stated in this Law pertaining to annual vacations and official holidays, the maximum working hours, the daily and weekly rest periods, the rules for safety and occupational health, work related injuries and their conditions, and what the Minister decides.

2025 Implementing RegulationArticle (17) Subject to Article (49) of Labor Law, the Labor Courts shall have jurisdiction to consider disputes arising out of the training and qualification Contracts.

Chapter V—Labor Relations

Section 1 The Work Contract

Article 50-The Employment Contract

A work contract is a contract concluded between an employer and a worker, whereby the latter agrees to work under the direction or control of the employer for a wage.

Article 51-Contract Must be in Writing

Ed.note: 2024 revision

~~The employment contract must be written in two copies, with each party retaining one copy. The contract shall be considered valid even if it is not written. In this case, the employee alone may prove the contract and the rights arising from it using all methods of proof. Either party has the right to request the written contract at any time. As for government employees and public institutions, the decision or appointment order issued by the competent authority shall serve as the contract.~~

The employment contract must be written in two copies, with each party retaining one copy. It must be documented in accordance with the relevant regulatory provisions and as specified by the regulations. The contract is considered valid even if it is not written. In this case, the worker alone may prove the contract and the rights arising from it using all means of proof. Either party has the right to request a written contract at any time. As for government employees and public institutions, the decision or appointment order issued by the competent authority shall serve as the contract.

Article 52–Identification of the Parties

Ed.note: 2024 revision ~~1. Subject to Article (37) of this law, the Ministry of Labor shall establish a standard form of employment agreement that contains the following:~~

- employer's name
- employer's address
- employee's name
- employee's nationality
- employee's ID number
- employee's residence address
- wages agreed to including benefits and allowances
- date of joining the organization
- term of the agreement if the period is specified

2. *The employment agreement shall be in the form referred to in paragraph (1) of this Article. The contracting parties agreement may add further provisions provided that such provisions are not inconsistent with the provisions of this law, regulations and the implementing resolutions.*

[3] 1. Taking into account the provisions of Article (37) of this Law, the ministry shall provide a unified model for each type of employment contract. The model shall include, as a minimum, the employer's name and location, the worker's name and nationality, the necessary details to verify their identity, their residence address, the agreed-upon salary including allowances and benefits, the type of work and its location, the starting date of employment, the contract's duration if it is for a fixed term, and the basic rights and obligations of

3. The previous version of Article 52 read: The work contract must essentially contain the name of the employer and his place, name and nationality of the worker, his identification, the wage agreed upon, type and place of work, date of appointment, period of employment if specified, in consideration of what has been stated in Article 37 of this Law.

each party. 2. The employment contract shall be in accordance with the model referred to in paragraph (1) of this Article. Both parties to the contract may add other clauses, provided they do not conflict with the provisions of this Law, its regulations, and the decisions issued for its implementation.

2025 Implementing Regulation Article (18) Subject to paragraph (1) of Article (52) of the Labor Law, the employment contract shall be approved as per the attached form hereto as a unified form for the employment contract (Annex No. 5). The employer shall conclude an employment contract with the worker, provided that the employment contract shall at least include the obligatory clauses stated under the unified form. Other clauses may be added to the contract, without prejudice to the provisions of this Law, Regulations and decisions issued for its implementation.

Article 53–Probation to be Clearly Stated

Ed.note: 2024 revision ~~If an employee is subject to a probationary period, such period must clearly be mentioned and identified in the employment agreement but shall not exceed ninety days. With the written consent of both employer and employee, the probationary period may be fixed at a period not to exceed *one hundred eighty days.* [Note: amended from 90 days.] The holidays of *Eid al Adha, Eid al Fitr* and any employee sick leave shall not be included in the calculation of the probationary period. Either party has a right to terminate the employment agreement during this period unless the employment agreement includes a text reserving the right of termination to one of the parties.~~ If the worker is subject to a probationary period, this must be explicitly stated in the employment contract, with the duration specified, provided that the total duration does not exceed one hundred and eighty days in all cases. The regulations shall specify the provisions related to this, including those concerning the leave that does not count toward the duration of the probationary period. Both parties have the right to terminate the contract during this period

2025 Implementing Regulation Article (19) Subject to Article (53) of the Labor Law, if both parties agree to extend the probationary period, such period shall be extended after the commencement of the employment contract, within the valid probationary period. Such extension may carry out once or more times; provided that it shall be conducted based on a prior written agreement per each time. In any event, the original probationary period along with the extension periods may not exceed 180 days.

Article 54–Only One Probation Period except by Agreement

A worker may not be placed on probation more than once by the same employer. As an exception, the worker may, with the approval of contract parties, in writing, be subjected to another probation period provided that such period involves another profession or work, or if no less than six months have elapsed since the termination of the work relationship between the worker and the employer. If the contract is terminated during the probation period, neither party shall be entitled to compensation nor shall the worker be entitled to an end-of-service award. [Note: as amended.]

Article 55–Term of Employment Contract

1. A limited period employment contract terminates upon expiration of its term. If the two parties continue the execution of the contract after expiration, then such contract shall be considered renewed for an unlimited period in consideration of what has been stated in Article 37 of this law in respect of non-Saudi workers.

2. If a limited period employment contract provides for renewal for a similar or specified period, the contract may be renewed for the agreed upon term. If the contract is renewed for *three* ~~two~~ consecutive periods, or if the initial contract term plus the renewal periods

reaches *four* ~~three~~ years or whichever is less, and the two parties continue to execute the agreement, the employment contract is then converted into an indefinite term contract. [Note: as amended.]

Article 56–Renewal of Employment Contract

In all cases in which the contract is renewed for a limited period, the renewal period is considered an extension to the original period for the determination of the worker's rights for the calculation of his service period.

Article 57–Project Employment Contracts

If the contract is for the performance of a certain work, it expires after the execution of the work agreed upon.

Article 58–Prohibition on Transfer of Employees

Article 58:

1. *An employer may not transfer an employee, without an employee's written consent, from his original work place to another place that requires change of his place of residence.*

2. *An employer may, when the circumstances require, but not for a period not exceeding thirty days in a year, require the employee to work at a place different from the place agreed to without his consent provided that the employer shall incur the costs of transfer and housing the employee during that period.* [4]

2025 Implementing Regulation Article (20) Subject to Article (58) of Labor Law, if the employment contract included a condition specifying the workplace of the worker within KSA or allowing the

4. The previous version of this Article read as follows: The employer has no right to transfer the worker from his main place of work to another place which requires change of his place of residence or if such transfer may cause bodily injury to the worker, while there is no legal reason required by the nature of work.

employer to transfer the worker from his original workplace to another one which requires the worker to change its residence per work requirements, this condition, then, shall be deemed as a written consent by the worker to be transferred to another place requiring the residence change per the above-mentioned Article.

Article 59–Prohibition on Change of Payment Schedule

It is not allowed to transfer a worker whose wage is paid monthly to the category of the daily, weekly paid workers or to the category of piecemeal or hourly paid workers unless the worker agreed to such transfer in writing and without prejudice to the rights earned by the worker during the period he spent in the monthly wage category.

Article 60–Prohibition on Change in Duties

Without prejudice to what is contained in Article 38 of this Law, it is not allowed to charge the laborer with a labor substantially different from the labor agreed upon without his written agreement but in cases required by emergency and for a period not exceeding 30 days in the year.

Section 2 Duties and Rules for (*the imposition of*) Penalties

First: Duties of Employers

Article 61–Duties of Employer

Ed.note: 2024 revision

~~In addition to the duties stated in this Law and its subsidiary regulations and decisions issued for its application, the employer should do the following:~~

- He should refrain from employing the worker on unpaid labor and not seize his wage or part thereof without a judicial sanction. He should treat his workers with respect and not show, by word or deed, disrespect for their faith or injure their dignity.
- He should grant the workers necessary time to avail their rights as stated in this Law without cutting wages against this time. He can control the practice of this right so that it does not interfere with the continuation of work.
- He should assist the officials of concerned authorities in the application of the provisions of this Law.

In addition to the duties stipulated in this law, regulations, and resolutions issued in implementation thereof, the employer must do the following:

- 1. The employer must refrain from exploiting the worker for forced labor, must not withhold the worker's wages or any part thereof without judicial basis, must treat the workers with due respect, and must refrain from any statement or action that violates their dignity or religion.
- 2. The employer must provide workers with the necessary time to exercise their rights as stipulated in this Law, without deducting wages for this time. The employer may organize the exercise of this right in a manner that does not disrupt the workflow.
- 3. The employer must facilitate all tasks related to the implementation of the provisions of this Law for the employees of the relevant authorities.
- 4. The employer must refrain from doing anything that may invalidate or weaken the application of equal opportunities or treatment in employment and profession, whether through exclusion, differentiation, or preference among job applicants or employees based on

race, color, gender, age, disability, marital status, or any other form of discrimination.[5]

- 5. The employer must provide suitable housing for his employees, or he may substitute this by providing an appropriate cash allowance along with their salary.
- 6. The employer must provide suitable transportation for his employees from their residence to the workplace, or he may substitute this by providing an appropriate cash allowance along with their salary.

2025 Implementing Regulation Article (21) Subject to Article (61) of the Labor Law, the phrase "use the worker without pay" shall means: all works or services forced upon the worker and not included in the employment contract. Such works are ordered by threat of any punishment, and not performed by the workers without his own choice. This may neither include any work, service resulted by emergencies, or force majeure such as wartime, fires, floods, famines, earthquakes, epidemic diseases, plagues of animals, insects plant pests, etc.

Article 62-Wage owed when Employee Ready to Work

If the worker arrived on time to perform his work, or if proved that he is willing to perform his duties on time, and that only due to a reason concerning the employer he did not perform the work, he has the right to earn the wage of the period in which he has not performed the work.

Article 63-Contraband in the Workplace

The employer, his representative or any authorized person should

5. Some believe that this expansive language opens the door to eliminate discrimination against those who favor alternative lifestyles.

prevent the entry of any material legally prohibited, into the work place. Penalties stated in this Law will be applied to anyone who violates this Article, without prejudice to other legal penalties.

Article 64-Expiration of Employment Agreement

At the expiry of the work contract, the employer should: 1. Issue, upon the request of the worker, a service certificate at no charge to the employee showing date of hire, final day, *position* and final rate of pay.*The employer may not include anything that could harm the employee's reputation or minimize his job opportunities.*~~Reasons should be given if the certificate contains something that might degrade the reputation of the worker or lessens his future work opportunities.~~ [As amended.] 2. Return all certificates and documents belonging to the employee.

Second: Worker's Duties

Article 65-Obligations of Employee

In addition to the duties, regulations and decisions stated in this Law for its application, the worker should:

- Carry out the work in accordance with the rules of the profession and the instructions of the employer if these instructions do not contradict the contract, the Law or general rules of conduct, and carrying out of such work does not expose to hazards.
- Take full care of the machines, instruments, equipment and raw materials owned by the employer and put under the worker's management or custody and give back the non-consumed materials to the employer.
- Abide by the norms of good conduct and polite behavior during work.

- Offer all help and assistance without overtime wage in cases of disasters and dangers which threaten the safety of the work place or other persons working there.
- In accordance with the request of the employer, the worker must undergo medical examination required before joining the work or during his period of employment to make sure that he is free of the occupational or common diseases.
- Keep safe all technical, commercial and industrial secrets of the materials he produces or which directly or indirectly contribute to their production, and all occupational secrets related to the work or establishment the disclosure of which causes harm to the interest of the employer.

Third: Penalties

Article 66-Employee Sanctions

The penalties which the employer could impose on the laborer:

- Warning
- Fine
- Deprivation or delay in the grant of increments or additional allowances for a period not exceeding one year whenever decided by the employer.
- Delay of promotion for a period not exceeding one year whenever decided by the employer.
- Dismissal in the cases set by the Law.

Article 67-Prohibition on Irregular Sanctions

The employer has no right to impose any penalty not stated in this law or the implementing regulations.

Article 68–Repeat Violations

In case of a repeat violation, increased penalty should not be decided if a period of 180 days has passed after the previous violation took place. This period starts on the date on which the laborer was informed of the penalty for such violation.

Article 69–Limitations Period for Sanctions

The laborer should not be accused for a violation which was discovered more than 30 days back. No penalty should be decided after the end of investigation of the violation and its proof in favor of the worker for more than 30 days.

Article 70–Sanctions for Private Behavior Prohibited

A worker should not be punished for something he has committed out of the place of work unless it is related to work, or to the employer or manager in charge. Also he should not be punished for one violation with a fine exceeding five days wage and that more than one fine should not be levied for one violation. Not more than five days wage in a month should be deducted from his wage for the settlement of fines and the suspension period without pay should not exceed five days in a month.

Article 71–Sanction Notice Requirements

No penalty should be levied on the worker without notifying him in writing of his violation, realization of his response in his defense and proof of such violation in minutes placed in his personal file. Simple violations, the fine of which does not exceed warning or deduction of not more than one day's wage, could be verbally explained and such should be stated in the minutes.

Article 72-Employee Objection to Penalty

The worker should be notified in writing of the penalty and if he refuses to receive such or in case he is absent, the notification should be sent by a registered letter to his address stated in his personal file. The worker has the right to object to the penalty within 15 days, excepting any official holidays, from the date he is notified of the final decision levying the penalty. The objection should be submitted to the Labor and Settlement of Disputes Commission which should issue its decision within 30 days from the date of registration of objection.

Article 73-Fines

Fines levied on the workers should be written in a special register with the name of the worker, the amount of his wage, the amount of fine, the reason for such fine and the date. Fines should not be used other than for the welfare of the organization's employees. *Use of these penalties shall be determined by the organization's labor committee. If there is no committee, disposal of penalties shall be approved by the Ministry of Labor.* ~~and after obtaining the approval of the Ministry of Labor.~~ [As amended.]

Section 3 Expiry of the Work Contract

Article 74-Expiration of the Work Contract

Ed.note: 2024 revision

~~The employment agreement expires in any of the following cases~~

~~:~~

- ~~If the parties agree to terminate the employment agreement provide that the approval of the employee should be in writing.~~

- ~~If the period specified in the employment agreement expires, unless the agreement has expressly been renewed in accordance with the provisions of this law, it will continue to its expiry date.~~
- ~~For indefinite term employment contracts, where a party voluntarily seeks to terminate pursuant to Article (75) of this law.~~
- ~~When the employee reaches the age of retirement, sixty years for men and fifty-five years for women, unless the parties agree to continue work after this age. Retirement age may be reduced in case of early retirement provided for in the work rules. If the period of employment agreement is limited and its period extends beyond retirement age, the employment agreement expires at the end of its term.~~
- ~~Force Majeure.~~
- ~~Permanent cessation of business.~~
- ~~Termination of the activity in which the employee is working unless otherwise agreed.~~
- ~~In any other case provided for by law.~~

The employment contract shall terminate in any of the following cases:

- If both parties agree to terminate it, provided that the employee's consent is in writing.
- If the specified term of the contract expires, unless the contract has been explicitly renewed in accordance with the provisions of this Law; in which case, it shall continue until its term.
- Based on the will of one of the parties in contracts of indefinite duration, in accordance with Article (75) of this Law.
- Resignation.

- Upon the employee reaching the retirement age as stipulated by the Social Insurance Law, unless both parties agree to continue employment beyond this age.
- Force Majeure
- Permanent closure of the establishment.
- Cessation of the activity in which the employee is engaged unless otherwise agreed. item [*bis*] - Issuance of a final resolution or ruling by the competent court to terminate the employee's contract in any of the bankruptcy proceedings initiated under the Bankruptcy Law.
- Any other case stipulated by another law.

[6]

Article 75–Right to Terminate Unlimited Employment Contracts

Ed.note: 2024 revision ~~If the contract is unlimited, either of the two parties has the right to terminate based on a legal reason after giving written notice addressed to the other party before termination within~~

---

6. A previous version of Article 74 read as follows: The work contract expires in any of the following cases:

If the two parties agreed on its termination on condition that the worker's agreement should be in writing.

If the period stated in this contract has expired unless the contract was explicitly renewed in accordance with the rules of this law.

According to the intentions of one of the two parties for those contracts where the period is unlimited.

When the worker reaches the age of retirement which is 60 years, and 55 years for female workers unless the two parties agreed to the continuation of work after this age. The age of retirement may be decreased in the case of early retirement stated in the regulations. If the work contract is limited, and its period extends beyond the age of retirement, then the contract expires with the expiry of its period.

Force Majeure

[The fourth paragraph of this Article will apply two years following the effective date of this law.]

~~a period not less than *sixty*~~ thirty ~~days if the worker is paid on a monthly basis and not less than *thirty*~~ fifteen ~~days for others. [As amended]~~

- If the contract is of indefinite duration and the salary is paid monthly, either party may terminate it for a legitimate reason, as follows:
    - If the termination is initiated by the employee, they must provide written notice to the employer at least thirty (30) days prior to the termination date.
    - If the termination is initiated by the employer, they must provide written notice to the employee at least sixty (60) days prior to the termination date.
- If the contract is of indefinite duration and the salary is not paid monthly, the party terminating the contract based on a legitimate reason, whether the employee or the employer, must provide written notice to the other party at least thirty (30) days before the termination date.

Article 76–Financial Obligations upon Termination

If the party who terminated the contract does not observe the notice period mentioned in Article 75 of this Law, that party will be obliged to pay the other party compensation equivalent to the wage of the worker for the notice period or its remainder *unless the parties agree to a higher sum.* ~~The last wage of the worker would be considered as basis for the estimation of the compensation for workers who receive their wages according to time criterion.~~ As for the workers who receive their wages on a different basis, the provisions of Article 96 of this law will be used for the calculation.

Article 77–Unlawful Termination

Unless the contract includes specific compensation for the termination by either party for an invalid reason, the party affected by termination shall be entitled to compensation as follows:

- For indefinite term contracts: an amount equivalent to 15 days' wage for each year of the worker's employment.
- For fixed-term contracts: the wage for the remainder of the contract term.
- The compensation referred to in paragraphs (1) and (2) of this Article shall not be less than employee's wage for two months.

[7]

Article 78–Reinstatement

If notice is given by the employer, the employee is entitled to one full day of paid leave each week during the notice period or eight paid hours during the week in order to find new employment. The employee may choose the day or hours of absence provided the employer is given one day's notice. The employer may exempt the employee from work during the notice period whilst calculating his service as continuous until expiration of the notice period at which time the employer shall comply with those obligations imposed by law, particularly the obligation to pay the employee's wage for the entire notice period.
[8]

---

7. A previous version of Article 77 read: If the contract is terminated for an illegal reason, the party who is affected by loss due to this termination has the right to receive compensation estimated by the Labor and Settlement of Disputes Commission in which the corporeal and moral losses should be considered.

8. A previous version of Article 78 read: The workman who is dismissed without a

Article 79–Termination upon Death of Employee

The labor contract does not expire with the death of the employer unless his personality is considered in the making of the contract but it expires with the death of the worker or his inability to perform the work in accordance with a medical certificate approved by the authorized medical authorities or by the authorized doctor nominated by the employer.

*Article 79*bis *—Resignation Requests*

- The resignation request is considered accepted if thirty (30) days have passed since its submission without a response from the employer. The employer has the right to postpone the acceptance of the resignation request for a period not exceeding sixty (60) days if the interests of the work require it, and based on a written explanation provided to the employee. The postponement of acceptance must occur before the expiration of the thirty (30) days mentioned in this paragraph. The duration of the postponement of acceptance is calculated from the date the written explanation mentioned in the previous paragraph is provided to the employee.
- The employment contract ends upon the resignation being accepted by the employer, or after the thirty days mentioned in paragraph (1) of this article has passed without a response from the employer, or upon the expiration of the postponement period for acceptance as referred to in paragraph (1) of this Article.
- The employee has the right to withdraw the resignation

---

legal reason has the right to ask for reinstatement. This should be reviewed in accordance with this Law and the regulations before the Labor and Settlement of Disputes Commission.

request within a period not exceeding seven days from the date of its submission unless the employer accepts it before the withdrawal.

- A deferred date of resignation shall not be specified in the resignation request.
- The employment contract remains valid during the resignation request period, and both parties to the contract are obligated to fulfill all obligations arising therefrom during that period.
- An employee whose contract is terminated by resignation is entitled to all rights stipulated under this Law.

Article 80–Contract-Ending Acts

The employer may not terminate the employment agreement without employee being remunerated, notified or compensated, except in the following cases provided that he should be given a chance to express the reasons for objecting to the termination :

- If an employee assaults the employer, manager in charge, one of his superiors or subordinates during the work or in relation to the work.
- If an employee does not perform his material obligations as stated in the employment agreement or fails to obey legal orders or intentionally fails to observe posted work and safety rules after being notified in writing.
- If the employee is proven to have engaged in misconduct or committed an act showing a lack of honor or integrity.
- If an employee, intentionally or negligently commits any act meant to inflict material loss to the employer provided that the employer shall notify the concerned authorities of the incident within twenty-four hours from the time at which he learns of the incident.

- If it is proven that the employee has resorted to forgery to obtain the job.
- If an employee is terminated during the probationary period.
- If an employee is absent without a reasonable excuse for more than thirty days during one contractual year or more than fifteen successive days provided that the dismissal shall be preceded with a written notice from the employer to the employee after the employee is absent for twenty days in the first instance and after being absent for ten days in the second instance.
- If it is proved that an employee has exploited his position in an illegal manner to obtain personal benefit or profits.
- If it is proved that an employee has disclosed industrial or commercial secrets.

[9]

9. A previous version of Article 80 read: The employer has no right to cancel the contract without rewarding or notifying or compensating the worker but in the following cases and on condition that he grants him the opportunity to show his reasons behind his objection to the cancellation:

If the worker committed an aggressive act against the employer, the manager or one of his bosses during or because of work.

If the worker has not performed his main obligations in the labor contract, or has not obeyed the legal orders or has intentionally not observed the instructions concerning the safety of workers and labor announced in a visible place by the employer, although warned in writing.

If it was proved that he has misbehaved or done something which violates honor or honesty.

If the worker intentionally commits an act or failure which causes material loss to the employer on condition that the employer reports such to the concerned authorities within 24 hours as from the time he acknowledged the act or failure.

If it was proved that the worker has committed forgery to obtain his job.

If the worker is appointed on probation.

If the worker is absent without a legal reason for more than 20 days during one year or more than 10 successive days, dismissal should be preceded by a written warning from the employer after the absence of 10 days in the first case and his discontinuation for 5 days in the second case.

Article 81-Conditions for Resignation with Benefits

The workman has the right to leave work without notification while retaining all his statutory rights in any of the following cases:

- If the employer failed to fulfill his contractual or regular obligations towards the worker.
- If proved that the employer or his representative has committed cheating during the time of contracting in what relates to the provisions and conditions of the work.
- If the employer entrusted to the worker, without his consent, a job which substantially differs from the work agreed upon and what was stated in Article 60 of this Law.
- If the employer, one of his family members or the manager in charge has committed an aggressive act or misbehavior against the worker or one of his family members.
- If the worker is insulted by the employer or the manager in charge.
- If there is serious danger in the place of work which threatens the safety or health of the workers and acknowledged by the employer without doing anything about it.
- If the employer or his representative paid his dues and his reward and informed him about violation of the terms of the contract in order to make it appear as if the worker is terminating the contract.

If proved that he has illegally taken advantage of his professional status to obtain personal gains.

If proved that he has disclosed the industrial or commercial secrets related to the work he is practicing.

Article 82–Illness No Excuse

Illness is not an excuse to terminate the worker before the expiry of the period of leave for this purpose stated in this law. The worker has the right to extend sick leave through the use of unused annual leave.

Article 83–Trade Secrets

1. If the work assigned to the worker allows him to get acquainted with the employer's clients, the employer may, for the protection of his legitimate interests, require the worker not to compete with him upon termination of the contract. For this condition to be valid, it shall be in writing and specific in terms of time, place and type of work. The validity of such condition shall not exceed two years from the date of termination of the relationship between the two parties. 2. If the work assigned to the employee allows him to have access to the employer's business secrets, the employer may, for the protection of his legitimate interests, require the worker not to disclose such secrets upon termination of the contract. For this condition to be valid, it shall be in writing and specific, in terms of time, place and type of work. 3. As an exception to the provisions of this Law, the employer may file a suit within one year from the date of discovery of the worker's violation of any of his obligations pursuant to this Article. [10]

10. A previous version of Article 83 read as follows: If the work entrusted to the worker allows him to learn the identities of the clients of the employer or acquaint himself with the secrets of the work, the employer has the right to ask the worker not to compete with him or disclose his secrets after the expiry of the contract. This condition should be written and specific as for time, place and place of work, in a way that saves the legal interests of the employer. In all cases, the period of this agreement should not exceed two years from the expiry date of the relations of the two parties.

Section 4 End of Service Reward

Article 84–Obligation to Pay EOSB (Severance)

Upon expiration of the employment contract, the employer shall pay the worker an end of service reward for the period of his service calculated on the basis of a half month wage for each year of the first five years and a month wage for each of the successive years. The last wage is considered a basis of the calculation of the reward. The worker deserves a reward for the parts of the year in a percentage of the part he spent at work.

Article 85–EOSB and Resignation

If the expiry of the work relation was due to the resignation of the worker, in this case he deserves one-third of the reward for service not less than two successive years and not more than five years. He deserves two-thirds thereof if his service period exceeds five successive years and has not amounted to 10 years. He deserves full reward if his service period reached 10 years or more.

Article 86–EOSB and Commissions

With the exception of the provision of Article 8 of this Law, it is allowed to agree that all or some of the amounts of commissions, the percentages for the price of sales and the wage paid to the worker which are subject to be increased or decreased, must not be calculated in the wage on the basis of which the end of service reward is settled.

Article 87–EOSB and Force Majeure

With the exception of the provisions of Article 85 of this Law, the reward is fully vested in case the worker left work due to unavoidable *force majeure* circumstances. Additionally, a female employee is entitled to a full award if she resigns within six months from the date of her marriage or within three months after giving birth.

Article 88-Timeliness of EOSB

If the service of the worker has expired, the employer should pay his wage and settle his rights within seven days following the date of expiration of the work contract. If the contract was terminated by the worker himself, the employer should settle his rights fully within a period not more than two weeks. The employer has the right to deduct any of his due debts from the amounts due to the worker.

Chapter VI—Provisions and Conditions of Labor

Section 1 Wages

Article 89-Minimum Wage set by Regulation

The Council of Ministers shall, when necessary, have the right to determine a minimum wage according to the Minister's recommendation.

Article 90-Wage Payment Requirements

1. The wages of the worker and all due amounts must be paid by the currency of the country. Wages should be paid during the work hours and place of work in accordance with the following provisions:

- Wages of daily paid workers shall be paid at least once a week.
- Wages of monthly paid workers shall be paid once a month.

- If the work is performed by piece and it needs a period exceeding two weeks, a payment proportionate to the work completed by the workman must be made to him every week, and the full balance of his wages shall be paid within the week immediately following the delivery of the work.
- In cases other than those mentioned above, wages shall be paid to workers at least once a week.
- *Employers shall pay the wages to the employee' accounts through the banks approved in the Kingdom of Saudi Arabia provided that payment shall be made in accordance with the deadlines stated above. The Minister of Labor may exempt some employers from the requirements of this section.*

~~2. Wages can be paid at the banks approved in the Kingdom if the worker agreed to such condition but the date of payment should not exceed the above stated dates.~~[As amended.]

Article 91–Deductions for Damage to Property

1. If a workman causes the loss, damage or destruction of materials, machinery or products which belong to or are in the custody of the employer, where such loss, damage or destruction was the result of the worker's fault or due to contravention of the employer's instructions and not the result of a third party's fault or *force majeure,* the employer may withhold from the worker's wages the amount required for repair or for restoring things to their original condition, provided that the amount so withheld shall not exceed five days wages in each month. However, the employer may, if necessary, lodge a complaint to claim a higher amount if the worker has other property from which recovery can be made. The worker may also appeal the employer's assessment to the appropriate commission and if the latter rules that the employer had no claim

against the worker for the amount he withheld from the worker's pay or if the employer is awarded a smaller amount, the employer shall refund to the workman, within seven days from the date of issuance of the ruling, the amount unduly withheld. 2. The complaint of any of the parties will be within 15 working days otherwise the right will become null and void. For the employer, the beginning of complaint date will be from the date of the incident's discovery. As for the worker, the date of complaint begins from the date in which the employer has notified the worker of such.

Article 92-Garnishments

No amount may be deducted from the worker's wages in satisfaction of private rights, except in respect of the following:

- To recover the advances paid to him provided that no deduction, in this case, is made from the worker's wages in excess of 10% of his wages.
- Social insurance premiums and any other regular insurances due from the worker.
- The worker's contributions to the Savings Fund and the advances due to the Fund.
- Installments pertaining to any plan for the construction of houses for the purpose of transferring ownership thereof to the worker, or to any other services.
- Fines that are inflicted on the worker for offenses committed by him as well as any amount that is withheld from his pay for the damage he has caused.
- Any debt to be recovered in execution of a judiciary judgment provided that the monthly amount deducted in this respect shall not exceed one-fourth of the wages due to the worker unless the judgment included otherwise and provided that an alimony debt and debt for food,

clothing and lodging shall be satisfied before all other debts.

Article 93-Limitation on Deductions

In all cases, the percentage of the amounts deducted shall not exceed one-half of the wages due to the worker, unless the Commission finds that it is possible to increase the deduction beyond such percentage, or that the worker needs more than one-half of his salary. In this latter case, the worker shall under no condition be paid more than three-fourth of his salary.

Article 94-Procedure for Improper Deductions

1. If any amount is deducted from the worker's wages for reasons other than those specified herein, without the latter's consent, or if the employer delays, without justification, payment of the worker's wages when they fall due in accordance with the Law, the worker, his representative, or the head of the Labor Office may submit an application to the appropriate Commission so that it may order the employer to return to the workman any wrongfully deducted amounts or to pay him his outstanding wages. 2. If it is established to the said Commission that the employer has unjustifiably deducted the said amounts or delayed payment of the wages, the Commission may impose on the employer a fine that shall not exceed double the amount deducted from the worker's wages or double the outstanding wages.

Article 95-Determination of Wage when Employment Contract Unclear

1. If neither the labor contract nor the Labor Law nor the basic work rules stipulate the wages that the employer is obligated to pay, the wage determined for another work of the same kind, if it exists, shall

be adopted; otherwise, the wage shall be determined in accordance with the generally accepted practice of the trade and of the area in which the work is performed. If no such practice exists, the Settlement Commission for Labor Disputes shall determine the wage according to the requirements of justice. 2. The foregoing shall also be followed in determining the quality and scope of the service which the worker must render.

Article 96–EOSB and Commissions

1. If the worker's wage is fixed on a piecemeal basis or on production, the indemnity shall be determined on the basis of the average pay received by the worker for actual workdays during the last year of his service for the purpose of calculating any of his determined rights in accordance with this Law. 2. If the overall wage is the amounts of commissions or the percentage of the sales or the like which are by nature subject to increasing or decreasing, the average wage is determined on the basis of the average daily pay on the basis of what the workman received for the actual workdays, divided by them.

Article 97–Status of Wages upon Arrest of Employee

If the worker is stopped from work by the labor authorities, or is arrested by the relevant authorities, the employer must continue paying 50% of the wage to the worker until a decision is taken on condition that the period of arrest or suspension from work must not exceed 180 days, and if it exceeds such period, the employer will not be obliged to pay any part of the wage for the excess period. If the worker is proved to be innocent or that the investigation is kept due to the non-verification of the accusation or its invalidity, the employer has to give back the amount he has discounted from his wage. If the worker is found guilty, none of what he has paid should be recovered unless otherwise judged.

Section 2—Work Hours

Article 98—Work Week

A workman should not be employed for more than eight actual working hours in any one day, or 48 hours a week, with the exception of the month of Ramadan when actual working hours shall not exceed 6 hours a day or 36 hours a week.

Article 99—Work Hours

The number of working hours stated in Article 98 of this Law may be raised to nine hours a day in respect of certain categories of workers or in certain industries and operations where the worker does not work continuously. The number of daily working hours may be reduced to seven hours a day for certain categories of workers or in certain industries and operations of a hazardous or harmful nature. The categories of workers, industries and operations referred to in this Article shall be determined by a decision of the Minister of Labor.

Article 100—Work Hours in Special Circumstances

The employer shall have the right, with the approval of the Ministry, in those establishments where the nature of work requires the performance of intermittent work, to increase working hours to 8 hours a day or 48 hours per week on the condition that average working hours should not exceed 8 hours per day or 48 hours per week if calculated over a period of three weeks or less.

Section 3 Rest Intervals and Weekly Holidays

First: Rest Intervals

Article 101–Work Breaks

Working hours and periods of rest shall be scheduled so that no worker shall work more than five consecutive hours without an interval for rest, prayer and meals, which shall not be less than half an hour each time and that the worker shall not remain in the place of work for more than *twelve* ~~eleven~~ hours in any one day. [As amended.]

Article 102–Breaks not included in Work Hours Calculation

The rest, prayer and meals intervals will not be included in the actual working hours. During these intervals the worker shall not be under the authority of the employer. The employer shall have no right to compel the worker to remain in the place of work during these intervals.

Article 103–Scheduling of Breaks for Certain Positions

The Minister shall, by his decision, specify the conditions and operations where work should continue without rest interval for technical reasons or operation conditions. The employer, in these cases and operations, should allow an interval for prayer, meals and rest in a way scheduled by the management of the establishment during work.

Second: Weekly Holidays

Article 104–Friday the Day of Rest

1. Friday shall be a day of the weekly rest for all workers. The employer—after notifying the appropriate Labor Office—may replace this day for some of his workers by any other day of the week provided that the workers shall in all cases be enabled to perform their religious duties. The employer shall have no right to compensate for the weekly holiday with cash. 2. Full wage will be paid for the weekly holiday, which should not be less than 24 consecutive hours.

Article 105–Remote Sites

With the exception of the provision of Article 104 of this Law, and while working at a place far away from inhabited areas and in operations where continuous work is needed, the worker will have the right to accumulate his due weekly holiday hours for a period which does not exceed eight weeks if the employer and worker have agreed and the Ministry has approved this arrangement. The period of the accumulated weekly holiday should be considered from the arrival of the worker to the nearest town where means of transports are available and ends at returning to such town.

Article 106–Work Hours in Special Circumstances

The employer shall not be required to adhere to the provisions of Articles 98, 101 and Paragraph 1 of Article 104 of this law in the following cases:

- Annual stock-taking, preparation of the balance sheet, liquidation, closing of accounts, preparation for sales at reduced prices and preparation for festive seasons, provided that the number of days during which the workers remain on the job shall not exceed 30 days in any one year.

- Where the work is intended to prevent a dangerous accident, or to repair damage resulting from such accident, or to avoid the certain loss of perishable materials.
- Where the work is designed to cope with unusual work pressure.
- Holidays, festive seasons and other occasions and seasonal operations as may be determined by decision of the

In all the foregoing cases, the number of the actual working hours shall not exceed 10 hours a day or 60 hours a week. The maximum additional working hours allowed in a year will be determined by decision of the Minister of Labor.

2025 Implementing Regulation Article (22) Subject to Article (106) of the Labor Law, the overtime hours may not exceed 27 hours per year; however, they may be increased by the consent of the worker.

Article 107–Overtime

Ed.note: 2024 revision

~~1. The employer shall pay the worker for additional work hours an additional wage equivalent to the workman's normal wage plus fifty percent (50%) of his basic wage. 2. Where the work is performed on the weekly criterion for the work hours, the extra hours of this criterion are considered additional work hours. 3. All the work hours, which are performed on official holidays and feast days, are considered additional work hours.~~

- The employer shall pay the employee overtime compensation equivalent to the hourly wage plus 50

- If the establishment operates on a weekly standard of working hours, any hours exceeding the hours adopted for this standard shall be considered overtime hours.
- All working hours performed during holidays and official vacations shall be considered overtime hours.

Article 108–Exclusions from Overtime Eligibility

The provisions of Articles 98 and 101 of the Law shall not apply to the following cases:

- Persons of high positions with administrative and guidance responsibility if they enjoy the authority of the employer regarding the workers.
- Preparatory and supplementary operations which must be completed before or after the end of the work.
- Work which is necessarily intermittent.
- Workers assigned to perform guard duty and cleaning except civil security guard workers.

The Implementing Regulations shall determine the nature of work stated in paragraphs 2, 3 and 4 of this Article and the maximum work hours.

2025 Implementing Regulation Article (23) Subject to Article (108) of the Labor Law:

- 1. The preparatory works shall mean works to be completed before or after the work commencement. It shall also mean the works conducted by the worker in preparation for the work commencement, such as material and equipment processing, handling, and handing over from the officer assigned by the employer to maintain and store such materials.

- 2. Supplemental works shall mean the works performed by the worker at the end of work completion in order to restore the materials and equipment to the warehouses or the officer responsible for maintaining, storing, cleaning, greasing, and oiling the machines. They shall also include works used to hand over works by the worker to the one replacing him, if the work is performed on rotational basis.
- 3. Intermittent work shall mean the discontinued nature-based works, including working with intermitted periods in which workers do not perform any activity, are sustainably attentive, or only stay in their workplace for carrying out potential orders. Furthermore, it means works that require workers to intermittently come to work, such as technicians, mechanics, who are recruited for the purpose of repairing or operating machines, or the workers used for transporting, delivering, shipping, or unloading goods, as well as fuel workers, garage workers, drivers, redeployments in railways workers, stevedores, bellmen in airports and freight stations, etc.
- 4. Security Guards shall mean those assigned to secure places, objects, equipment, tools, or employer's property, whether in night or morning shifts, save they may not be assigned for other works outside the security works within the working hours. Such definition does not include those working in civil or industrial security missions.
- 5. Janitors shall mean those assigned to the cleaning tasks of the workplace or the relevant establishments during the work or within the cessation periods; provided that the working time may not exceed 6 hours successively.
- 6. The total time required for performing the preparatory or supplemental works by the worker may not exceed 30 minutes added to the working hours; provided that 15

minutes shall be allocated for preparatory works and 15 minutes for the supplemental works.

- 7. The actual working hours shall be determined for the intermittent works as 10 hours per day, which shall be reduced to 8 hours during Ramadan, so as the weekly working hours may neither exceed 48 hours in normal months, nor 36 hours during Ramadan for Muslim workers. In such case, any additional hours shall be calculated as overtime. The worker shall have a break of at least 10 hours per each 24 hours. The employer shall enable the workers to perform prayers on time.
- 8. The actual working hours for security guards and janitors shall be 12 hours per day, and reduced to 10 hours during Ramadan, so that the weekly working hours may neither exceed 48 hours in normal months, nor 36 hours during Ramadan for Muslim workers. In such case, any additional hours shall be calculated as overtime. The employer shall enable the workers to perform prayers on time.

Section 4—Vacations

Article 109-Annual Leave

1. The worker is entitled to an annual vacation not less than 21 days for each year. This vacation shall be increased to a period not less than 30 days when the worker completes five continuous years in the service of the employer. The vacation will be with salary payable in advance. 2. The worker shall have the right to enjoy his vacation in its due year and may not forego it, or collect cash against it during his service. The employer will have the right to choose the dates of these vacations according to work requirements, or to grant these vacations alternately to ensure the continuation of work. He should notify the

worker of the specific date of his vacation in ample time, which should not be less than 30 days.

Article 110–Deferral of Annual Leave

1. The worker may, with the employer's consent, defer his annual vacation or a number of days thereof to the next following year. 2. The employer will have the right to defer the worker's vacation after the end of its due year if the work requirements need such deferment for a period not exceeding 90 days. If the work requirements need the continuation of the deferment, the written consent of the worker should be obtained provided that such deferment must not exceed the end of the next year following the year in which the vacation became due.

Article 111–Unused Leave

If the worker leaves the work before using the days of his due vacation, he shall be entitled to receive pay for unused vacation days in respect of the period for which he has not taken his vacation. He shall be entitled to vacation pay for fractions of the year, in proportion to that part of the year, which he has spent at work.

Article 112–Paid Holidays

Each worker shall be entitled to days off with full pay on the festivals and holidays designated by the subsidiary regulations.

2025 Implementing Regulation Article (24) Subject to Article (112) of the Labor Law: I. Eids and ceremonies holidays shall be determined as follows:

- 1. Eid al-Fitr holiday shall be 4 days effective from the day following the 29th Ramadan, as per Umm al-Qura calendar.

- 2. Eid al-Adha holiday shall be 4 days effective from the day of Arafat.
- 3. Saudi National Day holiday shall be only one day on the first day of the Libra horoscope according to [the] Umm Al-Qura calendar.

II. In case the Eids and ceremonies leaves coincides with the following:

- 1. Weekend: The worker shall be compensated for the same exact number of days before or after those leaves.
- 2. Annual Leave: It shall be extended for the same exact number of Eid days.
- 3. Sick Leave: The worker shall be entitled to a full pay for the leaves days without considering the due wage for the sick leave.
- 4. If the Saudi National Day coincides with the leave days of Eids,the worker may not be compensated for such day.

Article 113–Life Event Leave

~~Subject to this law's provisions concerning female employee leave, an employee shall be entitled to five days leave with pay in case of the death of his wife, ascendants, descendants or due to his marriage and three days paid leave in case of childbirth. The employer may request supporting documentation in aforesaid cases.~~ Subject to the leave entitlements granted to female employees under this law, the employee shall be entitled to fully paid leave for (five) days upon marriage or in the event of the death of a spouse, an ascendant, or a descendant, and (three) days in the event of the death of a brother or sister, all of which shall be counted from the date of the incident. Additionally, the employee shall be entitled to (three) days of leave in the event of the birth of a child, to be taken within (seven) days from the date of birth. The employer shall have the right to request supporting documents for these cases. [11]

Article 114–Leave for Pilgrimage

The worker shall be entitled to a leave, with full pay not less than 10 days and not more than fifteen days including Eid Al Adha in order to perform Hajj once through the period of his service if he has not performed Hajj before. To be entitled to such vacation it is conditional that the worker should have spent at least two consecutive years in the service of the employer. The employer will have the right to determine the number of workers who will be entitled each year to such leave in accordance with work requirements.

Article 115–Educational Leave

1. If an employer approves of a worker's enrollment or continuance in an educational institution, he shall have the right to a leave with full pay to sit for an examination for an unrepeated year, the duration of which shall be based on the actual number of examination days. If the examination is for a repeat year, the worker shall have the right to a leave without pay based on the number of actual examination days. Without prejudice to the employer's right to disciplinary action, the worker shall be denied the wage if it is established that he did not sit for the examination. 2. If a worker does not obtain the employer's approval on his enrollment in an educational institution, the worker shall be entitled to a leave to sit for the examination based on the actual number of examination days which shall be considered part of his annual leave, if available. If this is not possible, the worker shall be

---

11. The antepenultimate version of Article 113 read as follows: The worker shall be entitled to one-day leave with full pay in the event a child is born to him and a three-day leave for his marriage, or in the event of the death of the worker's spouse or any of his ascendants or descendants. The employer shall have the right to require the worker to furnish documents in confirmation of the above cases.

entitled to a leave without pay for the actual number of examination days. 3. The worker shall apply for the leave at least 15 days in advance. 4. The employer may require the worker to submit documents supporting the leave application, as well as proof of having taken the examination. [12]

Article 116–Leave without Pay, Consent Required

With the consent of the employer, the worker shall be entitled to a leave without pay. The two parties agree to the period of such vacation. The work contract is considered suspended during the vacation period if it exceeds 20 days unless the two parties agree otherwise.

2025 Implementing Regulation Article (25) Subject to Article (116) of the Labor Law:

- 1. If the unpaid leave-agreed upon-exceeds 20 days and the employment contract has been suspended, all legal effects shall be suspended accordingly, unless otherwise agreed by the parties.
- 2. If the employment contract has a definite term, it shall be extended for the same suspension period of the contract, unless otherwise agreed by the parties.

---

12. The previous version of Article 115 read: The worker who is associated with an educational institution shall be entitled to a vacation with full pay in order to sit for examination for a non-repeated year the period of which is determined by the actual number of the examination days. If the examination is for a repeated year, the worker shall be entitled to a leave without pay to sit for the examination. The employer shall have the right to ask the worker to furnish documents in confirmation of his application for the vacation and his sitting for the examination. The worker has to submit his vacation application at least fifteen days before its date. If it is proved that the workman did not sit for the examination, he will be deprived of such vacation without prejudice to the disciplinary inquiry.

Article 117-Sick Leave

In case a worker's illness is confirmed, he shall be entitled to a sick leave with full pay for the first 30 days and with three-quarter pay for the next 60 days, and without pay for the next following 30 days in any one year, whether these vacations are continuous or intermittent. Any one year means the year starting from the date of the first sick leave.

2025 Implementing Regulation Article (26) Subject to Article (117) of the Labor Law, if the sick leave days coincides with the annual leave days, the annual leave days shall be suspended until the end of the sick leave days. Then, the remaining days shall be resumed after that. Meanwhile, if the weekend days coincides with the sick leave days, the worker may not be compensated for those days.

Article 118-Prohibition on Outside Employment During Leave Periods

The worker shall not, while enjoying any of his vacations stated in this section, work for another employer. Where the employer proves that the worker has violated this provision, he may deprive him of his wages for the vacation period or recovery of any vacation pay he may have paid to the worker.

Chapter VII—Part-time Work

Article 119-Status of Otherwise Full-Time Employees

Any full-time workers, who are affected by collective and temporary reduction of their working hours due to economical,technical or structural reasons, are not considered part-time workers.

Article 120–Part-time Employment Regulations

The Minister of Labor shall issue necessary rules and regulations to regulate part-time work in which he would determine the obligations attendant upon each of the part-time workers and the employer. The provisions of this Law will not be valid except within the limits determined by the Minister of Labor, with the exception of the protection granted to the full-time workers in regard to safety, occupational health and labor accidents.

2025 Implementing Regulation Article (27) Subject to Article (120) of the Labor Law: 1. The rules and controls of part-time work shall be as identified as follows:

- a. The part-time employment contract shall be in a written form and have a definite term. It shall include the working hours, so as it shall be reduced to half of the normal working days in the establishment, whether the work is performed on daily basis or throughout some days per week.
- b. The part time employment contract may be renewed for similar terms or a term agreed upon by the parties.
- c. If the part-time employment contract was terminated by either party for [an] illegal reason, the aggrieved party shall be entitled to claim for the remuneration of the remaining wage as a compensation, unless otherwise agreed by the parties.
- d. Part-timers shall be subject to the Labor law provisions in terms of leaves, weekends, official holidays and overtime.
- e. The Saudi worker working for an employer in one of the entities affiliated to part-time contract shall be included under the Saudization percentage according to the approved percentages stated under [the] Nitaqat program, provided that he shall be registered with the

General Organization for Social Insurance (GOSI) as a part-timer.

2. The Labor Courts shall have jurisdiction to consider the disputes arising out of the part- time employment contract.

Chapter VIII—Safety in the Workplace

Section 1 Protection Against Labor Hazards

Article 121-Occupational Health and Safety

The employer should keep the establishment clean and in a sanitary condition, supply drinking and washing water and other protection, safety and professional health measures, procedures and standards in accordance with the Minister's decision.

Article 122-Safety Precautions

Necessary precautions shall be taken to protect workers from hazards and diseases resulting from work and machines used and for protection and safety of work. He should also display, at a distinct place in the establishment, the safety instructions related to work and workers in the Arabic language and in any other language understood by the workers where necessary. The employer shall have no right to ask the workers to bear the burden of such protection or deduct any amounts from their wages in return of such protection.

Article 123-Notice of Hazards

The employer should inform the worker of hazards before he starts work and order him to follow and use the means of protection. He should also supply suitable equipment of personal safety for the workers and train them in the use of such equipment.

Article 124–Use of Safety Equipment Required

The worker shall use the safety equipment designated for each operation and shall preserve such equipment. He shall abide by the instructions laid down for the preservation of his health and for his protection from injuries and diseases. He should refrain from any act or negligence, which would result in failure to abide by the instructions or in misusing or impairing the equipment provided for the protection of the work site and the health and safety of his fellow workers.

Article 125–Fire Safety

The employer shall take necessary precautions against fire and shall provide the technical means of fire-fighting, including safety exits which he shall maintain in a serviceable condition at all times. Detailed instructions for the prevention of fire should be displayed at a distinct place in work places.

Articles 126–Business Invitee Safety

The employer shall be responsible for incidents which may cause injury to persons other than his workers, who enter the places of work in the pursuit of their official duties or with the consent of the employer or his agents, if such injury is due to his neglect, in taking technical precautions, which the nature of his work requires, and he shall compensate them for the damage they may suffer, in accordance with the general laws.

Section 2 Protection Against Major Industrial Accidents

Article 127–Application

The provisions of this section are applied to the establishments having major industrial accidents.

Article 128–Hazardous Materials Handling Included

1. The term "the Establishments having Major Accidents" means any establishment which permanently or temporarily produces one or more hazardous materials or parts thereof or prepares, removes, handles, uses or stores the same, in large quantities exceeding the permitted criteria. Such exceeding of limits leads to classifying the establishment among the establishments having major hazards. 2. The term "Hazardous Material" means any material or a mixture of material which creates hazard due to its chemical, physical or poisonous characteristics either by itself or in its combination with others. 3. The term "Major Accident" means any unexpected accident such as major leakage, fire or explosion inside an establishment having major hazards including one or more hazardous materials and which sooner or later results in a bigger danger to the workers, the public or the environment.

Article 129–Ministry to Classify Establishments

The Ministry is to set up rules to classify hazardous establishments due to type of work or the need to work with hazardous materials or both.

Article 130–Employer Requirements

The employers, in coordination with the Ministry, shall determine the status of their establishments on the basis of the rules mentioned in Article 129 of this Law.

Article 131-Ministry to Issue Regulations

The Minister of Labor shall issue the regulations and decisions, which include necessary measures to protect the establishment against major hazards, the duties of employers in this respect and the measures taken to protect the public and environment outside the location of every establishment having major hazards, the rights and duties of the workmen and also other necessary arrangements to prevent major accidents, to reduce their hazards and limit their effects. The following paragraph was added by Royal Decree No. M/5 dated 07/01/1442 H. (13/2/2021 G) "The Minister, by his/her decree, shall specify the professions and jobs which are deemed to be hazardous or may expose a worker to abnormal hazards or damage, and the categories which are – permanently or temporarily – prohibited to be employed therefor or may be employed therefor under special conditions, including the extent of the need for scheduling the working hours of such categories, according to the KSA's relevant obligations as stated in the international conventions and agreements."

Section 3 Workplace Accidents

Article 132-Employees Covered by GOSI Excluded

The provisions of this section shall not apply to establishments, which come within the purview of the occupational hazards in the social insurance law.

Article 133–Obligation of Employer to Provide Treatment

If the worker suffered a work accident or an occupational disease, the employer shall undertake to provide him medical treatment for the same and shall pay all necessary direct or indirect expenses including stay in hospital, examinations and medical diagnosis, x-rays, compensatory systems and the expenses of traveling to the centers of treatment.

Article 134–Workplace Injury Defined

An accident is considered a work accident according to what is stated in the social insurance law. Occupational diseases are to be considered work accidents and the date of the first medical examination for the disease is also to be considered the date of the accident.

Article 135–Injury Relapse

The relapse case or any complication resulting thereof is considered an injury and will be subject to help and treatment as an original injury.

Article 136–Classification of Occupational Diseases

The occupational diseases shall be determined in accordance with the table of the occupational diseases stated in the social insurance law, and the degrees of permanent complete or partial disability are determined in accordance with the manual table of the percentage of disability stated in the said law.

Article 137–Worker's Rights upon Injury

An injured employee, in case he is temporary unable to work due to work injury, is entitled to receive a subsidy equivalent to his full wage for sixty days and thereafter in an amount that equals (75%) of his wage throughout the period of his treatment. If his treatment period reaches one year or it is medically decided that his health condition would not enable him to work, the injury will be deemed a complete disability. Therefore, the employment agreement shall expire and the employee will be compensated for the injury. The employer shall have no right to refund what he paid to the injured employee during that year. [13]

Article 138-Permanent Disability

If the accident resulted in complete or permanent disability, or that the accident led to the death of the worker, the injured or his successors shall have the right to receive compensation equal to his wage for three years the minimum of which shall not be less than SR 54,000. If the accident resulted in a permanent partial disability, the injured will be entitled to compensation equals to the percentage of such estimated disability in accordance with the approved guide table of disability percentage multiplied by the value of compensation for permanent complete disability.

Article 139-Exclusions

The employer shall be excused from the provisions of Articles 133, 137 and 138 of this Law if any of the following is proved:

---

13. The previous version of Article 137 read: In case of a worker's disability resulting from a work accident, he shall be entitled to financial assistance in the amount of his full wage for the period of 30 days and 75% of his wage all through the period of his treatment. If the disability period is greater than one year or if it is medically reported that his recovery is doubtful and that his health condition will not allow him to work, the incident will be considered complete disability and the contract will be terminated and the worker would be compensated for his accident. In this case the employer shall have no right to recover the amounts he has paid to the injured worker during such year.

- If the worker intended to injure himself.
- If the accident was due to intentional bad conduct of the worker.
- If the worker refrained from seeing a doctor, or refrained from the treatment of the doctor who is appointed by the employer without any legal reason.

Article 140–Subsequent Employers

The responsibility of the previous employers with whom the injured worker with an occupational disease was employed shall be determined according to the medical report of the treating doctor. Those employers will be obliged to pay the worker compensation stated in Article 138 of this Law, each for percentage of the period spent by the injured in his service provided that the industries or occupations which they practice caused the disease suffered by the worker.

Article 141 Reporting of Workplace Injuries

The procedures of notifying work accidents are determined by a decision of the Minister of Labor.

2025 Implementing Regulation Article (28) Subject to Article (141) of the law, when the establishment is not subject to Occupational Hazards Branch included in the Social Insurance Law, the following procedures of reporting work injuries shall be taken:

- 1. The employer shall inform the competent labor office of the worker's injury within one week of his knowledge.
- 2. The labor office determines whether it is a work injury or not, as per the official reports.
- 3. In case of lack of any medical reports that determine the percentage of deficit resulted from the injury, or if either party appealed against the medical report, the labor office shall refer the injured person to any

governmental hospitals to get the necessary medical report.

- 4. The labor office shall determine the compensation due to the injured person as per the percentage of deficit indicated in the medical report.
- 5. If either party rejects the labor office's estimation, the subject shall be referred to the competent labor courts.

Chapter VIII—Health and Social Services

Article 142-First Aid Equipment Required

Every employer shall provide one or more storage cabinets for medical first aid as well as medicines etc. The implementing regulations shall determine the contents of this cabinet such as first aid instruments, their number, the quantity of medicines and the safety means for their storage and the conditions providing the standard of the person in charge of the first aid.

2025 Implementing Regulation Article (29) Subject to Article (142) of the law, the employer shall provide medical aid cabinet as follows:

- The first aid locker shall contain the following supplies:
- These types and quantities shall always be available.

Type
Quantity
Buns Gauze
(50) pieces
Sponge bandages
(10) pieces
Gauze pieces
(50) pieces
Sterile gauze pads 10 x 10

(50) pieces
Gauze pads 5 x 5
(50) pieces
Gauze ligaments
(10) ligaments
Tourniquet
(1)
Pressing ligaments (Various sizes)
(10) ligaments
Medical swabs
(100) pieces
Plaster rolls
(5) rolls
Sterile plaster pieces
(20) pieces
Sterile gloves
(20) pairs
Face masks
(10) muzzles
Eyewash solution
1 pack
Folding stretcher
(1)
Antiseptic solution for wounds
(1) pack
A set of positive airways
(1)
Thigh, leg and forearm splints
(1)
Solid sheet for spinal injuries
(1)
Cervical splint kit for neck injuries
(1)
Scissors, appropriate size

(2)
Large size blanket
(1)
Suitable size clamp
(2)

Article 143-Assignment of Physicians

Every employer shall assign one or more physicians to examine his workers who are likely be infected by one of the occupational diseases specified in the tables of such diseases included in the social insurance law. The medical examination should be all-inclusive at least once every year and the result of such examination should be stated in his records and the files of the workers.

Article 144-Preventative and Curative Care

The employer shall provide his workers with preventive and curative health care in accordance with the standards decided by the Minister with due consideration to what is stated in the cooperative health insurance law.]

Article 145-Establishment of Savings Fund

After obtaining the consent of the Minister, the employer shall have the right to establish a saving fund subject to the condition the contribution of the workers is optional. The operational rules of the fund must be declared.

Article 146-Employees in Remote Areas

With regard to workers who perform work in places far from inhabited areas, the employer shall be obliged to make arrangements for all or some of the following provisions in accordance with what is determined by the Minister of Labor:

- Provide shops, which sell food, clothes and other necessary goods at reasonable prices. This should be in areas where such shops are not available.
- Provide suitable means of recreation, education and sports playgrounds.
- Provide suitable comprehensive medical care for the workers and their families (wife, children, mother and father who reside with the worker).
- Provide schools for the education of the worker's children if no schools are available in the place of work.
- Provide mosques for workers to perform their prayers.
- Prepare programs for illiterate workmen.

Working places remote from inhabited areas shall be determined by the Implementing Regulations.

2025 Implementing Regulation Article (30) Subject to Article (146) of the law, the remote locations are determined as follows:

- 1. Workplaces that are far away from the urban growth boundaries determined by the secretariat and different municipalities by no more than 50 kilometers if the roads were paved, and 25 kilometers if the roads were not paved.
- 2. Residential areas where such facilities and services are unavailable.

Article 147–Obligation to House Remote Employees

With regard to workers who perform work in places far from inhabited areas, in mines, quarries and oil drilling centers, the employer is obliged to provide dwelling quarters, camps and meals to the workers.

The Minister of Labor shall determine the conditions of the dwelling quarters and camps, their specifications, the rent in return for such facilities, the number of meals, quantities and quality of meals and their prices and all that is necessary to keep the workers healthy.

Article 148–Obligation to Provide Transportation

Every employer shall provide his workers with the means of transport from the place of their residence or the center of their gathering to the places of work and back daily if such places are not reached by the regular means of transport on times which match with the working hours.

Chapter IX—Employment of Women

Update

Article 149 was deleted in accordance with Royal Decree No. M/5 dated 07/01/1442 H. (13/02/2021 G)

Article 149–Employment of Women Permitted

[14] [15]

14. The repealed version of Article 149 read: Women are prohibited from being hired in dangerous or harmful professions and works. The Minister of Labor shall, by his resolution, identify professions and works that are deemed dangerous or harmful that could expose women to specified risks or damages, thus they should be prohibited from work therein or their work shall be restricted with special terms.

15. The penultimate version of Article 149 read: Taking into account the provisions of Article 4 of this Law, women may work in any field that matches her nature. A woman may not be employed in hazardous operations or harmful industries. The Minister of Labor, by his decision, shall determine those hazardous jobs and operations which may cause specific hazard to female workers.

Article 150–Nighttime Employment of Women

Article 150 was deleted in accordance with Royal Decree No. M/5 dated 07/01/1442 H. (13/2/2021 G) [16]

Article 151–Maternity Leave

Ed.note: 2024 revision ~~1. A female employee is entitled to a full paid delivery vacation for ten weeks to be taken as she sees fit. Maternity leave begins no more than four weeks prior to the date of delivery. The probable date of delivery shall be determined in accordance with a medical certificate approved by a medical authority.~~

~~2. While on maternity leave, the employee is prohibited from being hired after delivery. At the expiration of the term of paid maternity leave, the employee may extend her leave for an additional month without pay.~~

~~3. A female employee, in the event of giving birth to a sick infant or a child with special needs and its health condition requires a continuous attendant, is entitled to a vacation of one full paid month starting after the expiry of the delivery vacation and she is entitled to extend that leave for an additional month without pay.~~

- A working woman shall be entitled to a fully paid maternity leave of (twelve) weeks, of which the six weeks following childbirth are mandatory, and she may distribute the remaining six weeks as she sees fit, commencing from four weeks before the expected date of childbirth. The expected date of childbirth shall be determined by a medical certificate certified by a health authority. If the remaining leave period is less than (six)

16. The repealed version of Article 150 read: Women may not be employed during the nighttime, which covers a period of at least eleven continuous hours, except in cases in which a decision is issued by the Minister of Justice.

weeks due to a delay in childbirth beyond the expected date, the remaining period shall be considered unpaid leave. In all cases, the female employee shall have the right to extend this unpaid leave for one month.

- A female employee, in the event of giving birth to a sick child or a child with special needs whose health condition requires continuous accompaniment, shall be entitled to a fully paid leave of one month commencing after the end of the maternity leave period, and she has the right to extend the leave for one month as unpaid leave.

17

Article 152-Reserved [See Art. 151, was Maternity Leave Pay]

Repealed.
18

17. The antepenultimate version of Article 151 read as follows: The female employee shall be entitled to take a maternity leave of four weeks immediately prior to the expected date of delivery and six weeks following that date. The probable date of delivery shall be determined by the physician of the establishment or by a medical certificate approved by a health authority. No employer may employ any woman during the six weeks immediately following her delivery.

18. The repealed version of Article 152 read: During her absence on maternity leave, the woman worker shall be entitled to half pay if she has been in the employer's service for one year or more and to full pay if she has been in the employer's service for three years or more, on the date of commencement of such leave. A woman worker shall not be paid any wages during her regular annual vacation if she had availed herself maternity leave with full pay in the same year, and she shall be paid half wages during the annual vacation, if she had availed herself a maternity leave with half pay in the same year.

Article 153-Maternity Health-Care]

An employer shall provide medical care for female workers during pregnancy and delivery.

Article 154-Nursing Breaks

When the woman worker returns to work following maternity leave, she shall be entitled to a period or periods of rest totaling not more than one hour daily for the purpose of feeding her newborn child, in addition to the rest periods granted to all workers. This period or periods are considered actual working hours and will not result in deduction from the wage.

2025 Implementing Regulation Article (31) Subject to Article (154) of the law:

- 1. The female worker is entitled to take a period or periods of rest with a full wage to breastfeeding her child not exceeding one hour per day and calculated from the actual working hours for 24 months from the delivery date, be it natural or other breastfeeding.
- 2. The period of rest taken for the purpose of breastfeeding is not included in the official periods of rests provided for the workers.
- 3. The period or periods of rest taken for the purpose of breastfeeding shall be determined upon the availability of the nursery within the establishment and according to the followings:
    - A. If the nursery was not available within the establishment, the female worker is entitled to take one hour for breastfeeding, at the beginning or the end of the working hours, as appropriate to the nature of work.

- B. If the nursery was available within the establishment; the female worker is entitled to choose period or periods of rest for a total of one hour for breastfeeding, as appropriate to the nature of work.
- 4. After coming back from the delivery leave, the female worker shall notify the employer in writing of the period or periods of rest as well as any change thereto.

Article 155-Prohibition on Termination during Maternity Leave

The employer shall not terminate the service of the woman worker or give notice of such termination to her, while she is on maternity leave.

Article 156-Prohibition on Termination due to Pregnancy-Related Illness

The employer shall not terminate the woman worker during her illness resulting from pregnancy or delivery, provided that such illness shall be confirmed by an authenticated medical certificate, and provided that the period of her absence shall not exceed 180 days. Nor shall her service be terminated, without any of the legitimate causes provided for in this Law, during the 180 days prior to the expected date of delivery.

Article 157-Forfeiture of Benefits

The woman worker shall forfeit her entitlements under the provision of this chapter if it is established that she has worked for another employer during the authorized leave. In such an event, the original employer may deprive her of pay for such leave or recover any wages he had paid to her.

Article 158–Facilities for Women

In all places and in all occupations where women are employed, they shall be provided with seats to ensure their comfort.

Article 159–Childcare

1. Every employer who employs 50 or more women workers will have to specify a suitable place where a sufficient number of nannies are available to take care of the women workers' children, who are under six years of age if the number of children amounted to 10 or more. 2. The Minister of Labor may oblige an employer who employs 100 women workers or more, in one town, to establish a nursery either by himself or jointly with other employers in the same town, or make a contract with an existing nursery to take care of the women worker's children, who are under six years of age during the work periods. In this event, the Minister determines the provisions and regulations governing this nursery, and also determines the percentage of the costs, which will be imposed on the women workers who make use of this service.

Article 160–Widow's Leave

1. A Muslim female employee whose husband dies is entitled to a full-paid waiting period leave for a period not less than four months and ten days from the date of her husband's death. She has a right to extend this vacation without pay if she is pregnant, during this period, until she gives birth to a child. She may not benefit from the rest of the waiting period vacation granted to her, in accordance with this law, after delivery. 2. A non-Muslim female employee whose husband dies is entitled to full paid leave for a period of fifteen days. During this period, the employee may not work for third parties. The

employer is entitled to request supporting documentation in the aforesaid cases. [19]

Chapter X—Employment of Juveniles

Article 161-Hazardous Positions

Minors may not be employed in hazardous jobs or harmful industries, or in occupations or jobs that may endanger their health, safety, or morals due to the nature or conditions of the same. The Minister shall specify such jobs, industries, and occupations pursuant to a decision issued by him.

[20] Ministerial Resolution No.2840 dated 09/09/1427AH determined: First: The following shall be considered among the professions and jobs that are likely to endanger the health, safety and morals of juveniles due to their nature or the circumstances in which they are performed:

- 1. Workinmines,quarriesandextractingmineralmaterials-fromunderground.
- 2. Industries with health risks.
- 3. Races with risks to life.
- 4. Any work whose location and circumstances may expose the juvenile to moral and psychological problems.

Second: Age of the juvenile in these works must not be less than

19. The previous version of Article 160 read: A woman worker, whose husband dies, shall be entitled to leave on full-pay for a period not less than fifteen days from the date of her husband's death.

20. The previous version of Article 152 read: Juveniles may not be employed in hazardous operations or harmful industries, or in occupations and operations which may expose their health, safety or behavior to hazards due to the nature of such occupations and operations or the conditions in which they are performed. The Minister of Labor shall, by his decision, designate such occupations and operations.

seventeen years. Third: [The] Undersecretary for Labor Affairs shall enforce this Resolution.

2025 Implementing Regulation Article (32) Subject to Article (161) of the Law, a minor who has completed fifteen years of age and not yet eighteen is prohibited from performing any works that may endanger his health, safety or morals due to the nature or conditions of the same, including but not limited to the following:

- 1. Work in mines, quarries, or extraction of mineral materials.
- 2. Industries with health risks.
- 3. Works that may expose the minor to physical hazards due to the usage of high-risk machinery and equipment, such as sharp cutting machines.
- 4. Any work that may expose the minor to moral, psychological, and physical problems.

Article 162–Prohibition on Child Labor

1. A juvenile who has not completed fifteen years of age shall not be employed, nor shall he be allowed to enter places of work. The Minister of Labor may, by his decision, raise this age limit in some industries, areas or for some categories of juveniles. 2. With the exception of clause 1 of this Article, the Minister of Labor may allow the employment or work in case of persons whose ages vary between 13-15 years in light operations subject to the following conditions:

- That such work should not be hazardous to their health or growth.
- That such work should not stop their attendance at school and their participation in the instruction or vocational training programs, and will not weaken their ability to benefit from their education.

2025 Implementing Regulation Article (33) Subject to Article (162) thereof, any person under the age of fifteen may not be employed under any circumstances whatsoever, except in the cases stipulated in the Minister's decision.

Article 163–Nighttime Work Hours for Juveniles

Juveniles shall not be employed for a period not less than twelve continuous hours during the night, except in cases determined by a decision of the Minister of Labor.

2025 Implementing Regulation Article (34) As exception to Article (163) of the Law, minors may be employed during the night in the following cases:

- 1. The establishment where work is limited to family members.
- 2. Work in vocational schools and training centers.
- 3. Work in bakeries, excluding the period from 9 PM to 4 AM.
- 4. Force majeure and emergency cases.

Article 164–Juvenile Work Hours

Juveniles shall not be actually employed for more than six hours in one day for all months of the year except during the month of Ramadan when their actual work hours must not exceed four hours. The working hours should be regulated so that the juvenile shall not work for more than four successive hours without a period for rest, food and prayers not less than half an hour once and so that the juvenile shall not stay in the place of work for more than seven hours. Also, juveniles shall not be employed in the weekly rest days, festivals, official vacations and annual leave. The exceptions stated in Article 106 of this Law will not apply to juveniles.

Article 165–Data Collection for Juvenile Workers

Before employing a juvenile, the employer shall secure from him the following documents and shall keep them in the juvenile's personal file:

- The national ID or an official certificate of his birth.
- A certificate of physical fitness for the required work issued by a competent physician and duly approved by a health authority.
- The consent of the juvenile's guardian.

Article 166–Notification to Labor Office

The employer shall, within the first week following the employment of every juvenile, notify the appropriate labor office of such employment and shall keep at the place of work a special register for juvenile workers in which he shall indicate the name of the juvenile, his age, the full name of his guardian, his place of residence and the date of his employment.]

Article 167–Provisions Inapplicable to Vocational or Training Schools

The provisions stated in this chapter shall not apply to the work performed by children and juveniles at schools for the purposes of the general, vocational or technical education and in the other training institutions. They also shall not apply to the work performed at establishment by persons who are at least fourteen years old if the work is executed in accordance with the conditions determined by the Minister of Labor and that the work forms a main part of the following:

- A teaching or training course whose main responsibility falls on a school or a training institution.
- A training program, the greater part of which or all of it, is executed in an institution if the concerned authority has determined it.
- A guidance or instructive program which aims at an easy choice of the profession or the kind of training.

2025 Implementing Regulation Article (35) Subject to Article (167) of the Law, the following conditions shall be met:

- 1. A direct supervision shall be conducted by the entity responsible for the activity.
- 2. Education and training shall be taken in a progressive manner, so that no difficulty could face the learner or the trainee.
- 3. Education and training may not hinder the academic achievement of the learner or the trainee.
- 4. Work may not be as hazardous as stipulated in Article (161) of the Labor Law.
- 5. The entity that desires to regulate educational or training programs shall have the approval of the Ministry as well as the entity licensing the activity.

Chapter XI—Marine Labor Contracts

Article 168-Definitions

Ed.note: 2024 revision ~~Wherever the following words and terms are mentioned, they mean the meanings shown before them unless otherwise stated.~~

- ~~Ship: Any floating vessel registered in the Kingdom of Saudi Arabia and whose load is not less than 500 tons.~~

- ~~Ship financier: Any natural person or any public or private organization on whose account the ship is fitted out.*This phrase is sometimes translated as 'shipowner.'*~~
- ~~Master: Any seaman who is qualified to the piloting of the ship and bearing its responsibility.~~
- ~~Seaman: Any person who works on board the ship under a Marine Labor Contract.~~
- ~~Marine Labor Contract: Any contract of employment for wage made between the owner or financier of a ship or between the representative of either and a seaman to perform work on board ship, is a marine labor contract to which the provisions of this Law shall apply when they are not inconsistent with the provisions of this chapter and the decision issued pursuant thereto.~~

The terms "ship," "shipowner," "master," "seafarer," and "maritime employment contract" as used in this Part shall have the meanings assigned to them under the Commercial Maritime Law.

Article 169–Authority of Vessel Master

All persons working on board ship shall be subject to the authority and orders of the master of the ship.

Article 170–Marine Labor Contracts

All labor contracts of all seamen working on a ship shall be entered in the ship's records or appended thereto. These contracts shall be written in a clear language. These contracts shall indicate whether they are made for a specified term or a voyage. If the contract is made for a specified term, the term is clearly specified. If it is made for one voyage, it must specify the town or seaport at which the voyage shall end, and at what stage of unloading or loading the ship at the said port the contract shall terminate.

Article 171–Marine Labor Contract Required Terms

The Marine Labor Contract shall indicate the date and place of its execution, the name of financier, the seaman's name, surname, age, nationality, domicile, the work he is bound to perform, the method of performing the work, the certificate permitting him to work in sea navigation and his marine identification card, his wages and the contract period. If the contract is for a single voyage, the date and seaport at which the voyage ends shall be indicated, and at what stage of unloading or loading the ship at the said port the work shall end, and the other details of the contract. The contract document must be made out in quadruplicate, one copy for the ship financier, the second for the ship master to be kept onboard the ship and a copy for the seaman.

Article 172–Marine Work Rules

The work rules and conditions onboard ship shall be posted in the ship and in the section reserved for the crew. These conditions and rules must specify:

- The seamen's obligations, duties, rules of work, service timetables and daily work hours onboard ship.
- The obligations of the ship's financier towards the seamen as regards their fixed wages, rewards and other forms of pay.
- The method of suspending the payment of wages, or of making deductions there from, as well as of payment of advances on wages.
- The place and time of settlements of wages and final payment of wages.
- The rules and principles governing the supply of food and sleeping accommodations onboard ship.
- The illness and injuries of seamen.

- The conduct of seamen and the conditions of their repatriation.
- The seamen's paid annual vacations.
- The end-of-service award and other indemnities payable in connection with the termination or expiration of the labor contract.

Article 173–Requirements for Seamen

A person who works as a seaman must satisfy the following requirements:

- He must have completed eighteen years of age.
- He must be in possession of a certificate permitting him to work in marine service.
- He must be medically fit.

Article 174–Payments to Seamen

All the seamen's entitlements shall be paid in the official currency, and they may be paid in foreign currency if they fall due while the ship is outside the territorial waters and the seamen so agree. The seaman may request that his employer to pay his wages in cash to whomever he shall designate.

Article 175–Unexpected Termination of Voyage

If the voyage is cut short, for whatever reasons, whether optional or unavoidable, and is limited to one marine voyage, the wage of a seaman who works under a marine work contract should not be decreased.

Article 176–Payment of Wages based on Voyage Profit

If the wage is specified as a part of the profits or as part of the ship's wage, the seaman will not be entitled to reimbursement in case of the voyage's cancellation, and will not be entitled to additional wages in case of delay or extension of the voyage. But if the delay or extension resulted from the shippers actions, the seaman will be entitled to reimbursement from the financier.

Article 177–Obligation to Pay Seaman where Voyage Frustrated

The seaman will be entitled to his wage if the ship is seized, sunk or becomes unsuitable for navigation up to the date of such accident.

Article 178–Maintenance of Seaman

textitEd.note: 2024 revision ~~The provision of food and lodging accommodation shall be at the expense of the shipowner. This matter shall be regulated by a resolution issued by the Minister.~~ Without prejudice to the provisions governing the seafarer employment contract under this Law, the Minister shall, in coordination with the General Transport Authority, issue regulations governing the seafarer employment contract. These regulations shall include provisions relating to the rights and obligations of both parties to the contract, living conditions, safety, food, accommodation, and recreational facilities on board the vessel, measures to be taken by the employer to prevent occupational injuries and diseases, healthcare, working hours, rest periods, leave entitlements, training and skill development of seafarers, repatriation of seafarers, issuance of a certificate of compliance with the provisions of this Law, inspection and monitoring mechanisms to ensure vessels' compliance, determination of violations and the penalties imposed for committing them, as well as provisions for the amicable settlement of complaints.

Article 179–Shipboard Work Hours

The work hours onboard ship, when it is on the high seas, must not exceed fourteen hours in a period of 24 hours, and 72 hours in a period of seven days.

subsubsectionArticle 180–Salvage Reward for Seaman Every seaman who participated in helping or saving another ship will collect a share in the reward entitled to the ship in which he works, whatever the kind of the wage or the work he performs.

Article 181–Death of Seaman

If a seaman died during the sea voyage, his successors shall have the right to receive his wage up to the day of his death of he collects his wage monthly. But if his wage is according to the voyage, his successors will have the right to receive his wage for the full voyage. And if the wage is a portion of the profits, his successors will be entitled to receive it completely. The due amounts of the dead or lost seaman or that who cannot receive his wage, should be deposited at the Labor Office in the port of arrival in the Kingdom.

Article 182–Cancellation of Marine Employment Contract

Ed.note: 2024 revision ~~The employer may cancel the contract without prior notice and without compensation in the following cases:~~

- ~~If the ship sinks, or is confiscated, lost or became unsuitable for use.~~
- ~~If the voyage was cancelled at its beginning or due to a *force majeure* event and that the wage is based on a single voyage unless otherwise stated in the contract.~~

The employer may also terminate the contract without prior

notice and compensation if the voyage is canceled before its commencement due to circumstances beyond the shipowner's control, provided that the wages are based on a per-voyage agreement unless otherwise stipulated in the contract.

Article 183–Obligations of Employer upon Expiration

The employer, in case of the expiry or cancellation of the contract, undertakes the following:

- To return the seaman back to the port from which he traveled at the beginning of the contract execution.
- To provide food and sleeping accommodation till he arrives at such port.

Article 184–Obligations of Vessel Owner

The financier undertakes to bring the seaman back home in the following cases:

- If the voyage is cancelled by the financier after the departure of the ship.
- If the voyage is cancelled after departure due to the prohibition of trading with the destination of the voyage.
- If the seaman has to leave the ship due to his illness, injury or handicap.
- If the ship is sold in a foreign country.
- If the seaman is excluded from service during the voyage without a legal reason.
- If the contract made with the seaman expires in a port other than the port stated in the contract.

Chapter XII—Mines and Quarries

Article 185-Definitions

Working in mines and quarries means the following:

- Special research operations or the discovery of mineral material including precious stones, their extraction or manufacturing in the place, for which the license is issued, whether these minerals are solid or liquid.
- The operations dealing with the extraction of the mineral deposits, on the surface of the earth or inside it, their collection and concentration or their production in the area of the license.
- The related building operations, installations and arrangements referred to in the two paragraphs 1 and 2.

Article 186-Prohibition on Employment of Minors

Any person who is under the age of 18, should not be employed in a mine or quarry. Also, no woman should be employed in any mine or quarry regardless of age. Royal Decree No. No. M/5 dated 07/01/1442 H. (13/2/2021 G) added the following sentence to this Article: "No person under the age of eighteen may be employed in a mine or quarry,"

Article 187-Medical Fitness

No person shall be allowed to work in the operations which are subject of this chapter except after a complete medical examination and the approval for the fitness of his health, for the required work. This medical examination should be periodical. The worker should not be burdened with costs pertaining to the necessary medical tests.

Conditions, situations and periods, which should be abided by, in this regard, are to be determined by the decision of the Minister of Labor.

Article 188-Work Hours

The actual hours spent by the worker, under the surface of the earth, should not exceed seven hours in one day. The worker must not be kept in the place of work, whether on or under the surface of the earth, for a period exceeding 10 hours in one day. If the work is under the surface of the earth, this period must cover the time taken by the workman to reach his place of work from the surface of the earth and the time he takes to come back to the surface of the earth.

Article 189-Unauthorized Entry Prohibited

Entry to the places of work and their annexes is not permitted for those who are not appointed and those who are not responsible for inspecting the mine or quarry. Only those who obtain a special permission from the concerned authority are allowed to enter such places.

Article 190-Daily Log Requirement

The employer must prepare a special record to write and determine the number of workers before their entry into the place of work and when they return from work to the surface of the earth.

Article 191-Safety Rules

The employer or the responsible manager must prepare a regulation of orders and instructions dealing with the general safety.

Article 192–Point of Rescue

The employer should establish a point of rescue near the place of work, equipped with necessary rescue implements and necessary first aid. There should be a suitable means of communication at this point to be used immediately. The employer must appoint a trained technical worker to supervise the rescue operation and first aid.

Article 193–First Aid Facilities On-Site

Without prejudice to the provision of Article 142 of this Law, in each mine or quarry where at least 50 workers are working, the employer should prepare a suitable place containing a room equipped with the means of rescue and first aid and another room for nursing in addition to one or more changing rooms. In mines and quarries where the number of workers is less than 50 and these are located in a 20-kilometer diameter circle, the employer may share in the construction of a place of rescue and help in a middle place, or construct such a place separately. The Minister of Labor shall have the right to determine the means of rescue and help and arrangements of protection in the mines and quarries, the responsibilities of the employers, and the rights and duties of the workers.

Chapter XIII—Labor Inspection

Article 194–Labor Inspectors

Work shall be inspected by the Ministry of Labor's staff or other Saudis determined by the Minister of Labor or his representative with powers and jurisdictions provided for in this law. [21]

---

21. The previous version of Article 194 read: The labor inspection shall be undertaken by competent inspectors to be designated by a decision of the Minister of Labor. They shall have the power and functions provided for in this Law.

Article 195–Labor Inspector Requirements

Ed.note: The 2024 revision deleted this Article. ~~When practicing his job, in addition to conforming to the general provisions for the appointment of employees, the labor inspector:~~

- ~~Should be completely neutral.~~
- ~~Should have no direct or indirect relation with the establishment which he inspects.~~
- ~~Should have passed a professional test after spending a training period not less than 90 days.~~

Article 196–Labor Inspector Duties

Ed.note: 2024 revision ~~Labor inspectors shall be responsible for:~~

- ~~Monitoring compliance with the provisions of this Law, its regulations, and the decisions issued in implementation thereof.~~
- ~~Providing employers and employees with technical information and guidance to help them adopt the best means of implementing the provisions of this Law.~~
- ~~Reporting deficiencies in the existing provisions that fail to address certain issues and proposing necessary amendments.~~
- ~~Recording violations of this Law, its regulations, and the decisions issued in implementation thereof.~~
- ~~Investigating violations detected by other competent government entities and referred to the Ministry.~~
- ~~Proposing appropriate fines in accordance with the schedule of violations and penalties.~~

Labor inspectors shall be responsible for:

- Monitoring compliance with the provisions of this Law, its regulations, and the decisions issued in implementation thereof.
- Providing employers and employees with technical information and guidance to help them adopt the best means of implementing the provisions of this Law.
- Notifying the competent authorities within the Ministry of deficiencies in the existing provisions that fail to address certain issues and proposing necessary amendments.
- Recording violations of this Law, its regulations, and the decisions issued in implementation thereof.
- Investigating violations detected by other competent government entities and referred to the Ministry.
- Proposing appropriate fines in accordance with the schedule of violations and penalties.

[22] to terminate footnote

2025 Implementing Regulation Article (36) Subject to Article (196/5) of the Law, if the labor inspector found any violations to the Labor Law, this Regulation, or the relevant decisions made by the competent governmental bodies, it shall prepare a record of the violations determined as per the provisions included in the Implementing

22. The antepenultimate version of Article 196 read as follows: Labor inspectors shall have the following functions:

He shall supervise the proper enforcement of the provisions, decisions and regulations of the Labor Law.

He shall provide the employers and workers with the information and technical guidance which enables them to adopt the best means for the enforcement of the provisions of the Law.

He shall inform the concerned authorities of the deficiencies, which the provisions in force fail to remedy, and suggest necessary action.

He shall record violations of the provisions of the Labor Law and of the decisions issued in application hereof.

Regulation for controlling and regulating inspection works and fulfilling the regulatory procedures.

Article 197-Oath of Office

Ed.note: The 2024 revision deleted this Article 197. [23] [24]

2025 Implementing Regulation Article (37) Subject to Article (197) of the Law, the labor inspector shall undertake before commencing the work to:

I, the labor inspector/..., having functional no. ( ), civil register no. ( ), undertakes before Allah and before my heads to perform my duties honestly and sincerely and not to disclose the secrets of any industrial invention or any other secrets, which may come to my knowledge by reason of my office, even after leaving such office. In case of violation, I will be deemed a violator and shall bear the legitimate and regulatory liability resulting therefrom. Issued on: [] /[] /[] Signature:

Article 198-Authority of Labor Inspectors

Ed.note: 2024 *revision* ~~Labor inspectors shall have the right to:~~

- ~~Enter an establishment subject to the provisions of the~~

---

23. Before deletion, Article 197 read as follows: Labor inspectors shall, before commencing their duties, sign an undertaking pursuant to the form prepared by the Ministry of Labor that includes their commitment to sincerely and honesty discharge their work and they would not disclose a secret of any industrial invention or other secrets of which they may become aware in the course of performing their duties. The labor inspector shall carry identification issued by the Ministry of Labor that proves his status.

24. The penultimate version of Article 197 read as follows: Before assuming their official duties, labor inspectors shall take the oath before the Minister of Labor to discharge their duties honestly and faithfully and not to disclose the secret of any industrial invention or any other secret which may come to their knowledge by reason of their jobs, even after they cease to have any connection with such jobs. Labor inspectors shall carry an identification card provided by the Ministry.

~~Labor Law at any time during day or night without prior notice.~~

- ~~Conduct any examination or investigation necessary to ascertain the proper enforcement of the law. They may particularly:~~
- ~~Question the employer, his representative or the workers separately or in the presence of witnesses concerning any matter relating to the enforcement of the provisions of the law.~~
- ~~Examine all books, records and other documents, required to be kept under the provisions of the Labor Law and of the decisions issued hereunder, and obtain any copies or extracts therefrom.~~
- ~~Take a sample or samples of the materials used or handled in the industrial and other operations that are subject to inspection, if such materials are believed to have harmful effects on the health or safety of the workers for the purpose of having such samples analyzed in government laboratories and determining the extent of such effects, also notifying the employer or his representative of such.~~

Labor inspectors shall have the right to:

- Enter any establishment subject to the provisions of the Labor Law at any time during its working hours without prior notice.
- Conduct any necessary inspection or investigation to ensure compliance with the law. In particular, they shall have the authority to:
    - Interview the employer, their representative, or employees—whether individually or in the presence of witnesses—regarding any matter related to the implementation of the law.

- Reviewing all books, records, and other documents required to be maintained under the provisions of this law and the decisions issued pursuant thereto, and obtaining copies or extracts thereof
- Collecting one or more samples of materials used or handled in industrial or other processes subject to inspection, if suspected of having harmful effects on workers' health or safety, for analysis in government laboratories to determine their impact, while notifying the employer or their representative accordingly.

Article 199–Cooperation with Labor Inspectors

Ed.note: 2024 revision ~~Employees and their agents shall extend to inspectors and the officials charged with labor inspection the necessary facilities to enable them to perform their duties, and shall furnish them with any information they may require, respond to any summons to appear before them and send a delegate to appear on their behalf if they are so required.~~

Employers, their representatives, and workplace officials shall provide labor inspectors and designated inspection officers with the necessary facilities to perform their duties. They must furnish any requested information related to the nature of their work, comply with summonses, and appoint a representative if required.

Article 200–Notification of Inspection

The persons performing the inspection shall notify the employer or his representative of his presence, unless he believes that the matter, for which he is making inspection, calls for a different course of action.

Article 201–Labor Inspector Orders

The inspector shall have the right to order employers to make modifications in the operating rules pertaining to the plant and equipment used in their establishments within the periods prescribed by the inspector in order to ensure the proper application of the provisions pertaining to the health and safety of the workers. Where there is an imminent danger threatening the workers' health and safety, the inspector may require immediate adaptation of whatever measures he may deem necessary to forestall such danger.

Article 202–Confidentiality

The labor inspector shall treat any complaints reaching him in respect of any deficiency in the plant or any violation of the provisions of the Law as strictly confidential and shall not disclose to the employer or his representative the existence of such complaints.

Article 203–Violations and Reports

Ed.note: the 2024 revision deleted Article 203. [25] [26]

25. Article 203 read: If a labor inspector, during inspection, finds a violation of the law, regulation or resolutions issued in implementing the law, he should make a written report documenting the discovery of the violation pursuant to the provisions set forth in the Implementing Regulations and file said report with the Minister so that he may make a decision with respect thereto.

26. The previous version of Article 203 read as follows: If, in the course of his inspection, the inspector finds that a contravention of the Labor Law or of any decisions issued hereunder has been committed, he may offer his advice and guidance to the employer as to how to avoid such contravention in a specific period of time, or he shall prepare a report according to the importance of the contravention and the other circumstances which will be assessed by the inspector.

Article 204-Experts and Consultants

Whenever necessary, doctors, engineers, chemists and specialists in safety and occupational health may participate in the inspection of labor. The director of the labor office and the inspectors, when necessary, ask the concerned executive authorities to offer help.

]

Article 205-Chief Regional Labor Inspector

Ed.note: the 2024 revision deleted Article 205. [27]

Article 206-Deputy Minister for Labor Affairs Report

Ed.note: the 2024 revision deleted Article 206. [28]

---

27. The previous version of Article 205 read as follows: [T]he chief of labor inspection in the area shall prepare a monthly report on the labor inspection activities, the aspects of inspection, the establishments inspected and the number and nature of the violations committed. He shall also prepare an annual report on inspection in the area and the results and effects thereof, in which he shall include his comments and suggestions. A copy of both the monthly and annual reports shall be sent to the Ministry of Labor

28. The previous version of Article 206 read as follows: [T]he Deputy Minister for Labor Affairs shall prepare an annual report on inspection in the Kingdom within a period not exceeding 180 days from the end of the year. Such report shall include all matters relating to the Ministry's control over the enforcement of the provisions of the Labor Law particularly the following matters:

A statement of the provisions covering inspection.

A list of the officials in charge of inspection.

Statistical data on the establishments that are subject to inspection and the number of workers therein.

Statistical data on the number of visits and inspection tours made by the inspectors.

Statistical data on the contraventions committed and the penalties to which the offenders were sentenced.

Statistical data on labor injuries.

Statistical data on occupational diseases.

Article 207–Forms

Ed.note: the 2024 revision deleted Article 207. [29]

Article 208–Training of Labor Inspectors

Ed.note: the 2024 revision deleted Article 208. [30]

Article 209–Issuance of Regulations

Ed.note: 2024 revision ~~The Council of Ministers shall issue executive regulations to control the activities of inspection and its organization as laid down in this Chapter.~~ ~~The Minister shall issue the Executive Regulations for the oversight and organization of inspection activities.~~

29. The previous version of Article 207 read as follows: [T]he Ministry shall prepare forms for contravention reports, inspection records, notices and warnings, and shall lay down the necessary rules for the safekeeping and use of such forms and for distribution in the labor offices.

30. The previous version of Article 208 read as follows: [T]he training of labor inspectors shall be conducted in training courses, specially covering the following matters:

Principles of organizing inspection visits and of contacts with employers and workers.

Principles of auditing books and records, computer, organizing and preparing inspection minutes and explanation of persons.

Principles of counseling the employers in the requirements of the statutory provisions and the benefits to be derived from their application, and assisting the employers in such application.

Fundamental principles of industrial technology and means of protection against work injuries and occupational diseases.

Fundamental principles of productivity and its relation to the extent of providing favorable conditions for the performance of the work.

Chapter XIV—Labor Disputes Committee

Article 210-Identification

Repealed. [31]

Article 211-Appointment of Commissioners

Repealed. [32]

Article 212-Composition of Committees

Repealed. [33]

Article 213-Venue Where No Commission Established

Repealed. [34]

---

31. The previous version of Article 210 read: The Labor Disputes Settlement Commissions are:

  Primary Committee for Settlement of Disputes.

  The Supreme Committee for Settlement of Disputes.

32. The previous version of Article 211 read: The members of the Primary Commissions for Settlement of Disputes are to be named, from persons holding Shari'a and Rights licenses, by the Minister's decision after the consent of the Prime [stet] Minister. *Saudi Arabia has no prime minister, "the Minister" is probably what was meant originally.*

33. The previous version of Article 212 read: The Primary Committees shall be constituted by a decision of the Minister of Labor, at every labor office, to be determined by the Minister. A Primary Committee shall be composed of one or more members to decide resolutions of disputes. If the Commission is composed of more than one member, the Minister appoints a president from among the members to take over — in addition to his job — the distribution of cases among members of the Commission, and arrangement of the administrative and clerical tasks.

34. The previous version of Article 213 read: [I]f a Primary Commission is not constituted in one of the labor offices, the Minister of Labor will, when necessary, assign the constituted commission in the nearest labor office the duties and functions of the commission which was not constituted.

Article 214–Jurisdiction

Repealed. [35]

Article 215–Supreme Commission for Settlement of (Labor) Disputes

Repealed. [36]

Article 216–Jurisdiction of Sub-Commissions

Repealed. [37]

---

35. The previous version of Article 214 read: [T]he Primary Commission shall have exclusive jurisdiction to:

Render final decisions on:

Labor disputes, of whatever kind they are, the value of which does not exceed SR 10,000.

Complaints about the fine imposed by the employer on a worker.

Imposition of fines, as stated in this Law, for a violation, the value of which does not exceed SR 5,000, and for violations the total value of which does not exceed SR 5,000.

Initial decision in respect of the following:

Labor disputes the value of which exceeds SR 10,000.

Disputes pertaining to labor injuries whatever the amount involved may be.

Disputes pertaining to termination of service.

Imposition of fine, as stated in this Law, for a violation, the amount of which exceeds SR 5,000, and violations the total amount of which exceeds SR 5,000.

Violations relating to the imposition of fines and subsidiary fine.

36. The previous version of Article 215 read: [T]he Supreme Commission for Settlement of Disputes is composed of a number of sub-commissions where a single sub-commission will not be composed of less than three members. The Council of Ministers shall issue a decision according to the nomination of the Minister's to designate the chairman and members of the Supreme Commission who are licensed in Shari'a and Rights and are experienced in labor disputes. The number of the sub-commissions of the Supreme Commission and the areas of their work is determined by the Minister's decision according to the proposal of the Commission's chairman. The heads of sub-commissions, the distribution of work and the supervision of all matters related to their administrative functions shall be determined by the chairman of the Commission.

37. The previous version of Article 216 read: [E]very sub-commission under the

Article 217–Appeal Period

Repealed. [38]

Article 218–Effect of Failure to Timely Appeal

Repealed. [39]

Article 219–Conduct of Investigation and Proceedings

Repealed. [40]

Article 220–Commencement of Action

Repealed. [41]

Supreme Commission shall finally judge all the decisions of the Primary Commissions which are submitted for appeal.

38. The previous version of Article 217 read: [T]he period of appeal is 30 days from the date of hearing by and decision of the Primary Commissions and from the date of notification.

39. The previous version of Article 218 read: [I]f the decision of the Primary Commissions is not appealed within the period specified in the previous article, the decision will be considered final and enforceable. The decisions of the Supreme Commission are considered enforceable as from the date of its issue.

40. The previous version of Article 219 read: [E]ach of these commissions alone shall have the right to examine all disputes related to this Law and the disputes arising from the labor contracts, and may summon any person for interrogation or assign one of its members to conduct such interrogation. It may also require the presentation of documents and evidence and adopt any other measures it may deem fit. The Commission shall also have the right of access to any premises occupied by the establishment for the purpose of conducting the required investigation and examine all the books, records and documents that the Commission deems necessary.

41. The previous version of Article 220 read: [S]uits shall be filed through the competent labor office before the Primary Commissions in the locality of the place of work before transferring the dispute to the commission to follow the necessary legal procedures in order to settle the dispute amicably. The Minister of Labor shall issue rules for the processing of complaints.

Article 221–Prompt Adjudication

Repealed. [42]

Article 222–Limitations

Repealed. [43]

Article 223–Governing Law

Repealed. [44]

Article 224–Private Dispute Resolution

Repealed. [45]

---

42. The previous version of Article 221 read: [L]awsuits resulting from the provision of this Law should be examined promptly.

43. The previous version of Article 222 read:

The commissions stated in this Law shall not accept any lawsuit in relation to claims for any of the rights mentioned in this Law or resulting from the labor contract after the expiry of twelve months from the date of ending of the work relationship.

Any lawsuit related to the claim of one of the rights stated in the previous labor law shall not be accepted after the expiry of twelve months from the date of application of this Law.

Any complaint for violations taking place against the provisions of this Law, regulations and decisions thereof shall not be accepted after the expiry of twelve months from the date of the violation.

44. The previous version of Article 223 read: [N]one of the commissions provided for in this chapter may abstain from rendering a decision on the pretext that there are no applicable provisions in this Law. In such a case, the commissions shall be guided by the principles of the Islamic shari'a, established judicial precedents, local rules and principles of justice.

45. The previous version of Article 224 read: [E]ither party may include a provision in the labor contract deciding the settlement of disputes by jurisdiction. They may also agree to this after the beginning of the dispute. In all cases, the provisions of the effective judicial law in the Kingdom and its executive regulations shall apply.

Article 225–Estoppel

Repealed. [46]

Article 226–Retaliation Prohibited

Repealed. [47]

Article 227–Award of Costs

Repealed. [48]

Article 228–Rules of Procedure

Repealed. [49]

Chapter XV—Penalties

Article 229–Application

[*Note: Extensive revisions were made to Articles 229–end. The old versions of these articles have been deleted.*] 1. Without prejudice to a more severe penalty provided for by other law, anyone who breaches

---

46. The previous version of Article 225 read: [N]either party to a dispute may raise again the issue in respect of which a definitive decision has been rendered by one of the commissions provided for in this chapter before such commission or the other judicial authorities.
47. The previous version of Article 226 read: [I]n the course of conciliation or arbitration proceedings before any of the commissions provided for in this chapter, the employer may not change the operational conditions, which were in force before the commencement of such proceedings, so as to cause prejudice to the workman.
48. The previous version of Article 227 read: [T]he commission may by its decision, decide that the party who lost the lawsuit should pay to the other party all or some of the costs he has incurred.
49. The previous version of Article 218 read: [T]he Council of Ministers shall issue procedural rules for the Labor Commissions for the Settlement of Disputes.

any provision of the law provisions, regulation, resolutions issued in implementing the law shall be penalized with one or more of the following penalties:

- A financial penalty not exceeding hundred thousand Saudi riyal.
- Closing down the organization for a period not exceeding thirty days.
- Closing down the organization for good .

2. The penalty, inflicted on a violator, may be doubled in case of repletion of committing the violation. 3. Penalties shall be multiplied where multiple individuals have committed the violation.

*Article 229*bis*—Article 30 Violations*

Ed.note: 2024 revision Whoever violates the provisions of Paragraph (1) of Article (30) of this law shall be punished with a fine of no less than (SR. 200,000) two hundred thousand riyals and no more than five hundred thousand riyals, without prejudice to the provisions of Article (Two Hundred Twenty-Nine Bis) thereof.

Article 230–Saudization Violations

Ed.note: 2024 revision ~~1. The Ministry may, pursuant to a decision by the Minister or his designee, impose both or either of the two penalties provided for in subparagraphs (a) and (b) of paragraph (1) of Article 229 of this Law, provided that half of the maximum limit set for each of them is not exceeded. The penalty decision may be appealed before the competent administrative court. 2. Pursuant to a decision by the Minister, a table shall be issued listing violations and the corresponding penalties that do not exceed half of the maximum limit of the two penalties provided for in subparagraphs (a) and (b) of paragraph (1) of Article 229 of this Law, taking into account that the~~

~~fine shall be commensurate with the gravity of the violation. 3. Pursuant to a decision by the Minister, a table shall be issued listing violations whose penalties exceed half of the maximum limit of the two penalties provided for in subparagraphs (a) and (b) of paragraph (1) of Article 229 of this Law. Such table shall also list violations whose penalties are provided for in subparagraph (c) of paragraph (1) of Article 229. 4. If the violation warrants a penalty that exceeds half of the prescribed maximum limit, or if it warrants the permanent closure of the firm, in accordance with the table provided for in paragraph (3) of this Article, the Ministry shall file a suit before the competent court to review the case and impose the appropriate penalty provided for in Article 229 of this Law. 5. The Ministry and the violator may agree to settle the violation by means of paying the fine issued by the Ministry provided that a decision to this effect is issued by the Minister.~~

- The Ministry, by a decision of the Minister or whomever he delegates, may impose either or both of the penalties stipulated in subparagraphs (A) and (B) of Paragraph (1) of Article Two Hundred Twenty-Nine Bis of this law, provided that neither exceeds half of the maximum prescribed limit for either. The decision imposing the penalty may be appealed before the competent administrative court.
- The Minister shall issue a schedule specifying the violations and their corresponding penalties, which shall not exceed half of the maximum limit for the penalties mentioned in subparagraphs (A) and (B) of Paragraph (1) of Article Two Hundred Twenty-Nine Bis of this law. The schedule shall take into account the principle of gradual escalation in determining penalty amounts and their proportionality to the severity of the violation.
- The Minister shall issue a schedule specifying the violations for which penalties exceed half of the

maximum limit for the penalties mentioned in subparagraphs (A) and (B) of Paragraph (1) of Article Two Hundred Twenty-Nine Bis of this law. This schedule shall also define the violations subject to the penalty provided in subparagraph (C) of Paragraph (1) of the same Article.

- If a violation requires a penalty exceeding half of the prescribed maximum limit or falls under violations warranting the permanent closure of the establishment, as per the schedule referred to in Paragraph (3) of this article, the Ministry shall file a lawsuit before the competent court to consider the case and impose the appropriate penalty as stipulated in Article Two Hundred Twenty- Nine Bis of this law.
- A settlement may be reached between the Ministry and the violator by agreeing to pay a fine amount determined by the Ministry, provided that a decision approving the settlement is issued by the Minister.

2025 Implementing Regulation Article (38) Subject to paragraphs (1/4/5) of Article (230) of the Law: I. The penalties of the list indicated in Clause (First) of Paragraph (1) of the Minster's decision, regarding the violations and penalties to be applied to the violators, shall be imposed by the administrative unit concerned with penalty applications approved by the Minister. II. Deputy Minister for Inspection and Development of Work Environment shall establish, under the Minister's approval, a unit or center for receiving the record of work violation control from the labor inspector. Such unit is to review how far the violation is recorded according to law, classifying and verifying it, issuing the decisions of proposed penalties or filing the record and taking any of the following procedures:

- 1. Issuing an administrative decision for penalty application to the violator if the penalties to be imposed are included in the penalty list of Clause (First), Paragraph (1) of the above decision.

- 2. Guiding those specialized in filing cases against violators before the competent court (labor courts) if the penalties to be imposed are included in the penalty list of Clause (First), Paragraph (2) of the above decision.
- 3. Directing to file the record if the violation has not been established.

III. upon drafting any control record for any violation to the Labor Law, this Regulation, or the relevant decision requiring the imposition of the penalties stipulated in the schedule of violations and penalties, the labor inspector shall submit it to the competent department or to the workers concerned with penalty application as indicated in Clause (Second) of this Article. IV. Deputy Minister for Inspection and Development of Work Environment shall establish, under the Minister's approval, a unit or center to undertake the following:

- 1. Considering the appeals submitted by the violators against the administrative decisions issued for imposing work violation penalties;
- 2. Considering violation settlement requests submitted by the violators; As follows:
  - • As for the appeals submitted against the administrative decisions issued for imposing work violation penalties, the unit or center shall issue its decisions as per Clause (Fifth & Sixth) stipulated in Article (38) of this Regulation.
  - • As for settlement,unit or center shall submit its recommendations to the Minister for approval.

V: the administrative decision of imposing work violation penalties shall be appealed within (30) days from notifying the violator with the administrative decision. Such appeal may not suspend the implementation of the relevant penalty. VI: If the appeal against the administrative decision has been accepted and another decision has been issued for its termination, the amounts collected shall be returned to the appellant as per the procedures followed by HRDF. VII: the following procedures are required to submit requests for work violation settlement:

- 1. An administrative decision shall have been issued to impose any of the penalties stipulated in the schedule of violations and penalties indicated in Clause (First), Paragraph (1) of the above decision. A final judgment shall have been issued by the competent court to impose any of the penalties stipulated in the schedule of violations and penalties indicated in Clause (First), Paragraph (2) of the above decision.
- 2. The settlement may not be made to a violation occurring for the third time over two years from imposing the penalty or to a violation that has been settled previously.

VIII: the following procedures shall be taken upon work violation settlement:

- 1. The violator shall submit the settlement request within (90) days after being notified with the administrative decision, provided that the competent department shall decide on the settlement request within no later than (70) days from its submission. In this case, it may suspend the implementation of the penalty until the request is decided.
- 2. The violator shall eliminate all violations, subject of settlement, and provide the documentary evidences.

- 3. The competent department may summon the violator and ask him about the settlement and its items, paying the due regard to the circumstances surrounding.
- 4. The competent department shall submit the settlement agreement, attached with the recommendation, to the Minister for issuing settlement decision in case of approval.
- 5. The violator shall implement the settlement decision within (60) days from notification, otherwise the settlement is deemed cancelled.
- 6. The Minister authorizes the Deputy Minister of Labor and Social Development to develop the detailed condition of violation settlement.

Article 231-Correction of and Continuing Violations

The violator is required to rectify the violation within a period specified by the Regulations. Otherwise, it shall be considered a new violation.

2025 Implementing Regulation Article (39) Subject to Article (231) of the Law, the violator shall eliminate the violation within (10) days from the date of penalty application. If such violation was not eliminated within the time limit specified, it is deemed a repetition for the violation and the penalty shall be doubled.

Article 232-Dispostion of Fines

Fines prescribed under this Law shall be collected in accordance with the procedures for collecting public funds. Collected amounts shall be deposited with the Human Resources Development Fund.

2025 Implementing Regulation Article (40) Subject to Article (232) of the Law and without prejudice to the procedures followed for collecting the public funds, the violator shall pay the imposed fines within (60) days from being notified of the administrative decision or the final judgment. Failure to do so, the Ministry's services shall be suspended until the payment of the fines. The implementation by the decision may not be suspended by any grievance before the competent administrative court against any administrative decision of imposing the penalty of the list included in Clause (First), Paragraph (1) of the Minster's decision that is relevant to the violations and penalties, expect upon the court's decision.

Article 233-Payment of Reward

The Minister may grant a financial reward of not more than 25

Article 234-Limitations

[A.] Labor courts may not hear any claim arising from this Law or from an employment contract upon the lapse of 12 months from the date of termination of the employment relation unless the claimant provides justification acceptable to the court or the defendant admits the right subject of the claim.

[B.] Labor suits shall be expeditiously heard.

Article 235-Status Quo

An employer may not, during the hearing of a suit before a labor court, alter employment conditions existing prior ot the initiation of proceedings in a manner that undermines the interest of the worker in the suit.

Article 235-Repealed

Repealed.

Article 236-Repealed

Repealed.

Article 237-Repealed

Repealed.

Article 238-Repealed

Repealed.

Article 239-Repealed

Repealed.

Article 240-Repealed

Repealed.

Article 241-Repealed

Repealed.

Article 242-Repealed

Repealed.

Chapter XVI—Concluding Provisions

Article 243-Issuance of Implementing Regulations

The Minister shall issue, within 180 days from this Law's entry into force, the decisions and regulations necessary for implementing the provisions thereof. The Implementing Regulations shall be published in the Official Gazette.

Article 244–Prior Law Repealed

This Law shall replace the Labor and Workers Law promulgated by Royal Decree No. M/21 dated 6/9/1389H and shall repeal all the provisions that are inconsistent therewith. Regulations and decisions issued prior to the effective date of this Law shall remain in effect until they are amended.

Article 245–Effective Date

This Law shall be published in the Official Gazette and shall enter into force 180 days after the date of its publication.

CHAPTER 4
IMPLEMENTING REGULATIONS

Article (1)

SUBJECT TO ARTICLE (6) of Labor Law:

1. If both parties to the temporal or incidental employment contract continue the contract enforcement for a period exceeding (90) ninety days, the temporal or incidental employment contract shall be deemed as a permanent employment contract subject to all provisions of the Labor Law. Neither the job title indicated in the work permit submitted by the worker- if expatriate , nor the residence period granted thereunder is considered.

2. The Labor Courts shall have the jurisdiction to consider the disputes arising between the parties over the incidental, seasonal and temporal employment contract.

Article (2)

Subject to the provisions of sub-paragraph (d) of paragraph (1) of Article (7) of the Law: The agricultural workers, shepherds and the like shall mean agricultural workers, shepherds and the like who work in individual's houses, farms, livestock farms, setting aside those working in establishments.

Article (3)

Subject to the provisions of paragraph (1) of Article (12) of the Law, the unified form of the work regulations shall be approved as per the form attached hereto (Annex No. 1).

Article (4)

Subject to the provisions of paragraph (2) of Article (12) and paragraph (2) of Article (13) of the Law, the establishment's work regulations shall be approved according to one of the following procedures:

- 1. The establishment may select the online unified form of the work regulations, in order to regulate the establishment's work without any amendments or additions, through the Ministry's e-services portal, and to follow-up the required steps pending the final approval, by issuing relevant e-certificate.
- 2. If the establishment desires to prepare a special work regulation rather than selecting the unified form regulations, such regulations shall be audited and approved by the law firms certified by the Ministry of Labor and Social Development. Relatedly, the law firm shall ensure that no contradiction with the provisions of Labor Law, its Implementing Regulations or enforcement decisions is established. Consequently, such regulations shall be referred to the competent authority determined by the Ministry in order to be approved as per the applicable procedures.

Article 5

Subject to Article (17) of the Law, the employer shall incorporate under the statements, records and files maintained in the workplace- whether in hard or soft copies- the following details:

- 1. Workers' Name Statement: including names, occupations, ages, nationalities, and identifications numbers of workers, and numbers and dates of work permits in case of non- Saudis.
- 2. Workers' Wage Payroll: including wages of workers, dates of receipt, deducted amounts and deduction reason.
- 3. Fine Record: including the name and wage of worker, and the amount, reason and [the] effective date of fine.
- 4. Attendance Record: including the attendance and departure to/from the workplace as well as any other statements specified by the employer.
- 5. Saudi Training Record: including the training program's title, category, duration, year, enrolled workers and their percentage out of total workers.
- 6. The medical examination record for the establishment's workers who are likely to be infected with occupational disease: including the workers names who were examined as well as the date and result of examination.
- 7. Work file for workers: including data, address, copy of the employment contract and any certificates or documents submitted to the employer.

Article (6)

Subject to Article (20) of Labor Law: The employer may not withhold the passport, residence or medical insurance card of non-Saudis.

Article (7)

Subject to the provisions of Article (22, 23, 24 and 25) of Labor Law, there shall be mutually coordinated between the Ministry and Human Resources Development Fund (HRDF) in order to activate and support the employment units affiliated to HRDF to employ, qualify, train the national workers to replace the expats.

Article (8)

Subject to the provisions of paragraph (2) of Article (26) of Labor Law, the obligatory Saudization rates for establishments shall be determined through programs set out by the Ministry. Through such programs, the Saudization rates for each activity of the private sector shall be followed-up. Furthermore, all or part of the Ministry's services provided for establishments failing to achieve the specified Saudization percentage shall be ceased, such as the Program for Incentivizing Establishments to Saudize Jobs (Nitaqat); provided that the Ministry periodically updates these programs whenever necessary.

Article (9)

Subject to Article (28) of Labor Law,

- 1. A person with disability means every person proven under a medical report issued by the Ministry of Health or Hospitals of other governmental sectors or under one of the identification cards issued by the Ministry of Labor and Social Development (MLSD) that he has one or more permanent disability as in the following forms: Visual, hearing, mental, physical, and motor impairment, learning disability, speech disorder, behavioral and emotional disorders, autism, or any other disability requires one form of the facilitating measures and services.

- 2. The facilitating measures and services:mean the engineering modifications and provision of appropriate work conditions and environment according to the standards stated under Chapter (2) of architectural requirements folder, under Saudi Building Code and any of the arrangements indicated under the guiding list attached hereto (Annex No. 2) that might be required to enable the person with disability to perform the assigned tasks.
- 3. The ability to work means that the person with disability has fulfilled the vacancy requirements, or the work applied for, including the science, vocation, skill and/or other requirements that help him perform his work.
- 4. In order to consider the person with several disabilities according to [the] (Nitaqat) program, the following requirements shall be applicable:
    - a. The person with disability shall obtain the identification card from MLSD indicating the type and degree of disability.
    - b. The functions and employment nature held by the worker as well as the type and degree of disability.
- 5. Each and every worker shall benefit from the necessary facilitations and measures in order to perform his work if proven according to a medical report issued by the authorities stipulated under clause (1) of this Article that he suffers from an illness or disability that does not require a leave for a period exceeding 120 days after the date of disability.
- 6. Workers with disability shall have all rights and benefits provided for others, specified under the Labor

Law, these Regulations or the establishment's work regulations.

- 7. The disability may not be regarded as a main reason to reject the person-with-disability employment, promotion, or the provision of professional trainings if the ability to work is fulfilled under the definition included in clause (3) of this Article.
- 8. There may be no wage discrimination among workers based on disability, which shall be deemed as a misconduct.
- 9. The establishment shall keep the data, work nature, wages, and types of measures and facilitations of the workers with disability. Such data shall be disclosed to the work inspectors upon request.
- 10. The job applications submitted by persons with disability shall be in accordance with the forms and controls applicable by HRDF.
- 11.The establishment recruiting persons with disability shall maintain the place-based requirements and explanatory services stipulated under the guide attached hereto (Annex No. 2).
- 12. The work inspectors shall, upon paying an inspection visits for establishments, examine the persons-with-disability number, work nature, arrangement types and explanatory services.

Article (10)

Subject to Article (30) of Labor Law, the licensing requirements of Saudization activity, recruitment activity, renewal and termination of licenses, and Saudis' tasks, as well as their implications shall be determined through the following:

- 1. Controls and rules of Saudization as per the format attached hereto,which shall be deemed an integral part hereof (Annex No. 3).
- 2. Controls and rules of practicing the outsourcing activity for recruitment and provision of the labor services as per the form attached hereto which shall be deemed an integral part hereof (Annex No. 4).

Article (11)

Subject to Article (36) of the Labor Law: I: The non-Saudis may not be recruited for any of the following occupations:

- 1. Senior HR Manager.
- 2. Director of Personnel Department.
- 3. Director of Labor Affairs
- 4. Director of Personnel Relations Department
- 5. Personnel Specialist
- 6. Personnel Affairs Clerk
- 7. Recruitment Clerk
- 8. Staff Affairs Clerk
- 9. Attendance Clerk
- 10. General Reception Clerk
- 11. Hotel Reception Clerk
- 12. Patient Reception Clerk
- 13. Complaint Clerk
- 14. Treasurer
- 15. Private Security Guard
- 16. Expediter (Government Relations Officer)
- 17. Key Smith
- 18. Customs Broker.

Furthermore, any of the functions included under the above-mentioned occupations and employments may not be assigned to a non-Saudi worker - directly or indirectly - under any other job title.

II: Working in any activity, occupation or jobs may be reserved for Saudis as determined by the Ministry.

Article (12)

Subject to Article (37) of the Labor Law, the non-Saudi employment contract shall have a definite term regardless of any extended terms. In any event, the contract may not be amended to have an unspecified term even if agreed to by the parties.

Article (13)

Subject to Article (39) of the Labor Law, the non-Saudi part-time employees shall be subject to its provisions; except those excluded by the Ministry and included under the *Ajeer* Program.

Article (14)

Subject to Article (41) of the Labor Law, there shall be determined:

I. Requirements, controls and procedures of recruitment as follows:

- 1. The recruitment process shall not lead to a competition among Saudis or excluding from an occupation, or a number of occupations, crafts, or activities.
- 2. The employer failure to recruit Saudis may not be deemed as a reason for recruiting non-Saudis.
- 3. The establishment wishing to carry out the recruitment shall achieve the Saudization percentage in order to carry out the recruitment process established under (Nitaqat) Program.

- 4. Any recruitment visas granted to the non-Saudi applicants that may decrease the Saudization percentage below the standards of the Ministry may not be issued.
- 5. The workers recruited for the establishments shall be determined according to [the] Nitaqat program.
- 6. Codes and titles of occupations shall be strictly adhered to as per Saudi vocational Classification Guide upon request for recruitment visas.
- 7. The non-Saudis recruitment and employment shall be limited to the activities indicated under [the] Nitaqat program.
- 8. No workers may be recruited for occupations reserved for Saudis.
- 9. Workers under the age of 18 or above the age of (60) may not be recruited for work. Meanwhile, the experts, physicians and others determined by the Minister shall be exempted from the maximum limit for working age.
- 10. The recruitment applications shall be submitted through the e-services website of the Ministry as per the Nitaqat program.
- 11. An approval letter sent by a governmental or private agency, supporting the need of the establishment to a number of workers, may not be deemed as an approval by the Ministry to recruit those workers. Such approval shall subject to the standards stated under the Nitaqat program or to the decisions of the Ministry.
- 12. The Ministry may reject the recruitment application in the following cases:
    - a. If there is a collective delay of wages, a commercial concealment is established or there has been proven that the employer allows all or part of his workers to illegally work for third parties or work for their own account.

  - b. If the establishment fails to achieve the minimum limit of the required Saudization percentage.
  - c. If the establishment submits or has submitted to the Ministry or the Labor Office, incorrect data, information or confirmations. Consequently, all procedures related to the recruitment shall be suspended for a period of at most five years. In addition, the visas issued for the establishment shall be canceled. Nonetheless, no work permits may be issued for the establishment based on such recruitment visas. The statutory procedures shall be enforced for the implementation of Anti-Forgery Law and other relevant laws stated under [the] Nitaqat program.
  - d. If the establishment was proven to have sold the obtained work permits. Consequently, all relevant procedures for recruitment shall be suspended for five years.
  - e. If the establishment failed to renew the work permits or residence of its workers.
  - f. Any other cases stated under the Nitaqat program.
- 13. Whosoever is granted one or more visas may request termination. In such case, he may not be granted an alternative visa. Any request for an alternative visa shall be deemed as a recruitment request that shall be subject to the requirements of approving the visas stated under [the] Nitaqat program.
- 14. An alternative visa replacing the terminated one may be issued if it has a governmental accreditation, with no need for a new governmental endorsement, provided that the alternative visas application shall be conducted within (6) six months after the date of previous visa's termination. In addition, the remaining term of the

governmental contract may not be less than (6) six months.

- 15. In case of expiration or termination of visas, paid application fees shall be refunded.

II. Terms, controls and procedures for employing expats for others as follows:

- 1. No specific term for the expats working for a specific employer is required to be realized in order to be employed to another employer; unless the controls stated under (Nitaqat) program otherwise stated.
- 2. Transferring the employment of a worker to another establishment shall be rejected if the establishment, to which the transfer occurs, has an expatriate worker holding an expired work permit or residence that were not renewed, or if such expatriate had entered [the Kingdom of Saudi Arabia] [and remained for] (3) three months ago without obtaining [a] work permit or residence. The following expats shall be excluded: the one reported as absent from work for a period exceeding (15) fifteen days; the one who has an employment transfer application under review by the Ministry and the one who obtained [a] final exit visa.
- 3. The services of workers, of nationalities that prohibit their services transfer, may not be transferred according to laws.
- 4. The services may not be transferred to an employer who was reported for a collective delay of wages or proven to have committed a commercial concealment or to allow all or part of his workers to illegally work for third parties or work for their own account.
- 5. The services of the new expat for whom no work permit was issued may be transferred without the

consent of his employer according to the controls stated under [the] Nitaqat program.

- 6. The expat services may be transferred if his authorized contract, work permit or residence was expired without the consent of the current employer according to the controls stated under [the] Nitaqat program.
- 7. The Minister or his deputy may approve transfer of the expat's services to another employer without the consent of the worker's current employer in the following cases:
    - a. If there is a claim between the worker and the employer considered before a court, while the employer caused the extension of the case consideration. This shall be established by any of the following cases: • If the employer or his representative do not appear before the court in two hearings of the same judicial degree without legal justification accepted by the judiciary. • If the court establishes that the employer or his representative cause the extension of the case in a way differs from the above-mentioned case. The above two cases require the worker to never causes or contribute to extension of the claim consideration.
    - b. Based on a recommendation by the court during the proceedings in order to avoid any damages that might affect the worker.
    - c. If the establishment do not pay the worker's wages for three successive months or delays the remuneration beyond the maturity date on the third month, provided that the worker may not have caused such actions based on a request submitted by the worker within the Hijri year effective from the maturity date on the third month.
    - d. If the employer is absent due to travel, imprisonment, death or any other reason which leads

to the establishment's inability to fulfill its obligations towards its workers for 3 months without appointing an official to be responsible for the establishment and personnel affairs.

- e. Some categories or nationalities of workers who have special instructions regulating their conditions, if the employment contract is expired or terminated by the employer.
- f. The expat whose services are transferred to work for any establishment after the expiry of the work relation as per the controls and arrangements set out by the Ministry.
- g. Family reunification: • If one of the spouses entered into a valid contract inside KSA, provided that the employment contract is expired or terminated by the employer. • If one of the spouses was a Saudi national.
- h. If the worker reported a commercial concealment against the employer while providing the supporting proof, provided that the worker may not be involved in such case.
- i. Any other cases required for the public interest and determined by the Minister or his authorized representative.

- 8. The services of the expat residing in KSA may be transferred under the statutory measures to the establishment that fulfills the recruitment terms stipulated under Article (14) herein. In order to transfer the service, the following conditions shall be fulfilled:
    - a. The expat shall be (18) years old or above.
    - b. The services transfer requirements indicated in this Article shall be fulfilled.
    - c. The occupation requirements stated under

paragraph(2) of clause(III) herein shall be fulfilled except [for]the paragraphs (a, c and d).

- 9. The establishment requiring the services to be transferred shall achieve the Saudization percentage for the activity or entity according to [the] Nitaqat program.
- 10. The services transfer requests shall be submitted for the purpose of online working through the e-services website of the Ministry.
- 11. The Ministry may coordinate with HRDF in order to ensure that there is no Saudis available to the occupations for which the services required to be transferred.
- 12. The Ministry may ensure the coordination between the activity and occupations for which the services required to be transferred.
- 13. The previous and current employers shall maintain a written consent of the worker, for transferring his services to the new employer before conducting the relevant procedures.
- 14. An e-consent by the employer for the request of transferring the worker's services or a hard copy for the unconditional waiver for the worker's services by his employer addressed to the applicant of service transfer, endorsed by an official authority. Such e- consent or hard copy waiver shall exempt the followings:
    - a. Cases of transferring services without the employer's consent stated under such regulations and [the] Nitaqat program.
    - b. Cases of transferring the workers' services for the new contractor in the ongoing Management, Operation and Maintenance contracts (OMM) concluded with the governmental agencies; if they were recruited or their services transferred in order to execute such contracts.

- 15. If no consent is obtained for the worker's services' transfer after the e-consent or the hard copy waiver is endorsed by the previous employer had been issued, for whatsoever reason, the worker shall remain in service of the principal employer.
- 16. Prior to conducting the transfer procedures, no contradicting decision or final judgment may have been issued.
- 17. If no consent was obtained for transferring the worker's services for any of the cases stated in paragraph (7) of this clause, the Minister or his authorized representative shall authorize the worker to work for another employer. The authorization terms shall be determined as part-time work for (six months). It shall be regularly renewed until the full achievement of the authorization's purpose.
- 18. The following cases may not be deemed as services transfer cases, rather, job retitled cases:
    - a. Desire by one or some of the heirs to continue the activity of their decedent, as long as an authorization from the heirs to the appointed heir who would continue the business is obtained, the business status changed to be a company managed by all or part of inheritors, or an approval by the Ministry of Commerce and Investment obtained.
    - b. Change of the establishment's name, purposes, all or part of the partners, business status while maintaining the commercial register, obtaining an approval by the Ministry of Commerce and Investment (MOCI).
    - c. Merger of two or more establishments whether by changing the legal status or not, save the change status shall be specified in the Articles of Association

and an approval by the Ministry of Commerce and Investment issued.

- d. Separation and independence of one or more partners with their individual shares; provided that such procedure shall be specified in the company's amendment contract or company's splitting up contract and an approval by the Ministry of Commerce and Investment shall be obtained.
- e. Transformation of the sole proprietorship to a partnership through one or more partners.
- f. Transfer of establishment ownership to another owner while maintaining the same workers and commercial register and obtaining an approval by the Ministry of Commerce and Investment.
- 19. The following cases may not be deemed as service transfer cases, rather, workers' registration transfer ones:
  - a. Transferring the expats' registration among branches in the same entity for more than once with no restrictions according to the provisions of [the] Nitaqat program.
  - b. Transferring the expats' registration among entities of the same establishment according to the provisions of [the] Nitaqat program.

III. Terms, controls and procedures for occupation change as follows:

- 1. The occupation change means the authorization of the non-Saudi worker to work in another occupation other than the one he was authorized for.
- 2. In order to change the occupation, the following conditions shall be fulfilled:
  - a. The employer of the worker shall have a valid business license or valid commercial register

registered with the Labor Office and the business shall be existing.

- b. The occupation required to be changed shall be specified as per the Saudi vocational Classification Guide.
- c. The worker shall have the supporting academic qualifications and experience required for the occupation. Such academic certificates shall be certified by the competent authorities in the worker's home country and the Saudi Embassy, if it was issued outside KSA. Such condition may not include the following cases:
  - • If the occupation change was resulted from a gradual promotion achieved by the worker.
  - • If the occupation change does not require academic qualification, training or experience.
- d. The establishment shall achieve the required Saudization percentage according to [the] Nitaqat program.

- 3. The occupation change may not be applied to occupations reserved for Saudis.
- 4. The occupation change may not be applied to occupation prohibited under regulatory instructions.
- 5. The occupation change request shall be applied via the e-services website of the Ministry.
- 6. If change of specific occupation requires obtaining prior work permit, consent or work permit certificate in accordance with laws or the instructions of other official authorities, the approval of the relevant authorities, that is, Saudi Council of Engineers and Saudi Commission for Health Specialties, shall be obtained in order to change the occupation category to engineering or medical field occupation, etc.

Article (15)

Subject to Article (42) of the Labor Law, each and every employer, in order to replace non-Saudis with Saudis, shall observe the following terms and rules:

- 1. Preparation of job description for the tasks and functions of the employment according to the adopted Saudi vocational Classification Guide, and, accordingly, determination of the relevant job requirements.
- 2. Identification of the relevant career paths of employments for the workers.
- 3. Provision of the required training and qualifying programs for jobs, according to paragraph(1) of this Article. Employer shall also seek to be updated of the new techniques, within his tasks and functions and to enable the Saudis to receive the relevant training and qualifying programs.
- 4. Generation of timelines as per the vocational categories and classifications for all posts held by non-Saudi workers; through which the employer shall provide the appropriate means for qualifying and training the Saudis replacing the non-Saudis.
- 5. Provision of the opportunities for Saudis to occupy the vacancies of non-Saudis enabling them to acquire experience and on-the-job-training so as to observe paragraphs (2) and (3) of this Article.
- 6. Preparation of a report for the Saudis replacing the non-Saudis.

Article (16)

Subject to Article (44) of the Labor Law: I: The establishment requiring training shall observe the following standards and rules:

- 1. Various training programs shall be prepared for all occupations required by the establishment, since such programs boost the worker's efficiency and skills that are required for the employer's objectives.
- 2. The establishment shall direct the training programs to focus on the most needed occupations, crafts and works needed, especially those occupied by non-Saudis, in order to gradually replace the non-Saudis by Saudis.
- 3. Whenever professional standards or aptitude tests in any sector is adopted by the competent governmental agencies such as Saudi Commission for Health Specialties or other, the training standards set forth by the establishment shall be compatible with the very standards and tests.
- 4. The training program duration may not be less than 16 hours.
- 5. The employer shall determine the worker's employment term after the completion of training, provided that such duration may not exceed the duration of the training program for which the worker has undergone. Furthermore, he shall determine the employment term if the employment contract term is undetermined or if the remaining employment term in undetermined contract is less than the period required for the training program.
- 6. The programs shall include theoretical and practical training with single or multi-levels scaled according to the skills and productivity of the worker, so as to increase the worker's skills and efficiency.
- 7. The training programs shall have direct or indirect relation with the trainee's work.
- 8. In case the trainee passes the course's examination, the establishment shall provide the Ministry with a the course completion certificate, including the trainee's

name, title, type, duration and year of the program via the Ministry's e-portal.

- 9. The training fees shall be on the employer's account. The establishment shall conduct the training in the workplace if it was certified by the Technical and Vocational Training Corporation (TVTC) or it may assign the training to any training centers or institutes certified by the competent authority or e-training platforms. The training may be conducted inside or outside KSA.
- 10. The establishment shall notify each Saudi worker of the training data including the title, type and duration of training, the entity conducting the training, training mechanism and method and the examination result in case the trainee passes the examination within one month of the training date.

II. The employer may charge the training and qualifying fees to the worker in the following cases:

- a. If the worker decides to terminate the training or qualifying program before the due date without an acceptable justification.
- b. If the employment contract is terminated according to the cases specified under Article (80) of the Labor Law, except for paragraph (6) therein, during the training and qualifying term or within the period determined by the employer after the completion of the training or qualifying program term in proportion with the remaining period.
- c. If the worker resigned or abandon the job for reasons other than those specified under Article (81) of the Labor Law during the training and qualifying program term or within the period specified by the employer after the

completion of the training or qualifying program term in proportion with the remaining period.

III: Meeting the determined training percentage is not a requirement for the establishments recruiting more than 50 workers, while their Saudization percentage determined in [the] Nitaqat program required is less than (12 %) of their total workers. In such case, it is only required to train all Saudis annually.

Article (17)

Subject to Article (49) of Labor Law, the Labor Courts shall have jurisdiction to consider disputes arising out of the training and qualification Contracts.

Article (18)

Subject to paragraph (1) of Article (52) of the Labor Law, the employment contract shall be approved as per the attached form hereto as a unified form for the employment contract (Annex No. 5). The employer shall conclude an employment contract with the worker, provided that the employment contract shall at least include the obligatory clauses stated under the unified form. Other clauses may be added to the contract, without prejudice to the provisions of this Law, Regulations and decisions issued for its implementation.

Article (19)

Subject to Article (53) of the Labor Law, if both parties agree to extend the probationary period, such period shall be extended after the commencement of the employment contract, within the valid probationary period. Such extension may carry out once or more times; provided that it shall be conducted based on a prior written agreement per each time. In any event, the original probationary period along with the extension periods may not exceed 180 days.

Article (20)

Subject to Article (58) of Labor Law, if the employment contract included a condition specifying the workplace of the worker within KSA or allowing the employer to transfer the worker from his original workplace to another one which requires the worker to change its residence per work requirements, this condition, then, shall be deemed as a written consent by the worker to be transferred to another place requiring the residence change per the above-mentioned Article.

Article (21)

Subject to Article (61) of the Labor Law, the phrase "use the worker without pay" shall means: all works or services forced upon the worker and not included in the employment contract. Such works are ordered by threat of any punishment, and not performed by the workers without his own choice. This may neither include any work, service resulted by emergencies, or force majeure such as wartime, fires, floods, famines, earthquakes, epidemic diseases, plagues of animals, insects plant pests, etc.

Article (22)

Subject to Article (106) of the Labor Law, the overtime hours may not exceed 27 hours per year; however, they may be increased by the consent of the worker.

Article (23)

Subject to Article (108) of the Labor Law:

- 1. The preparatory works shall mean works to be completed before or after the work commencement. It shall also mean the works conducted by the worker in preparation for the work commencement, such as material and equipment processing, handling, and handing over from the officer assigned by the employer to maintain and store such materials.
- 2. Supplemental works shall mean the works performed by the worker at the end of work completion in order to restore the materials and equipment to the warehouses or the officer responsible for maintaining, storing, cleaning, greasing, and oiling the machines. They shall also include works used to hand over works by the worker to the one replacing him, if the work is performed on rotational basis.
- 3. Intermittent work shall mean the discontinued nature-based works, including working with intermitted periods in which workers do not perform any activity, are sustainably attentive, or only stay in their workplace for carrying out potential orders. Furthermore, it means works that require workers to intermittently come to work, such as technicians, mechanics, who are recruited for the purpose of repairing or operating machines, or the workers used for transporting, delivering, shipping, or unloading goods, as well as fuel workers, garage workers, drivers, redeployments in railways workers, stevedores, bellmen in airports and freight stations, etc.
- 4. Security Guards shall mean those assigned to secure places, objects, equipment, tools, or employer's property, whether in night or morning shifts, save they may not be assigned for other works outside the security works within the working hours. Such definition does not include those working in civil or industrial security missions.

- 5. Janitors shall mean those assigned to the cleaning tasks of the workplace or the relevant establishments during the work or within the cessation periods; provided that the working time may not exceed 6 hours successively.
- 6. The total time required for performing the preparatory or supplemental works by the worker may not exceed 30 minutes added to the working hours; provided that 15 minutes shall be allocated for preparatory works and 15 minutes for the supplemental works.
- 7. The actual working hours shall be determined for the intermittent works as 10 hours per day, which shall be reduced to 8 hours during Ramadan, so as the weekly working hours may neither exceed 48 hours in normal months, nor 36 hours during Ramadan for Muslim workers. In such case, any additional hours shall be calculated as overtime. The worker shall have a break of at least 10 hours per each 24 hours. The employer shall enable the workers to perform prayers on time.
- 8. The actual working hours for security guards and janitors shall be 12 hours per day, and reduced to 10 hours during Ramadan, so that the weekly working hours may neither exceed 48 hours in normal months, nor 36 hours during Ramadan for Muslim workers. In such case, any additional hours shall be calculated as overtime. The employer shall enable the workers to perform prayers on time.

Article (24)

Subject to Article (112) of the Labor Law: I. Eids and ceremonies holidays shall be determined as follows:

- 1. Eid al-Fitr holiday shall be 4 days effective from the day following the 29th Ramadan, as per Umm al-Qura calendar.

- 2. Eid al-Adha holiday shall be 4 days effective from the day of Arafat.
- 3. Saudi National Day holiday shall be only one day on the first day of the Libra horoscope according to [the] Umm Al-Qura calendar.

II. In case the Eids and ceremonies leaves coincides with the following:

- 1. Weekend: The worker shall be compensated for the same exact number of days before or after those leaves.
- 2. Annual Leave: It shall be extended for the same exact number of Eid days.
- 3. Sick Leave: The worker shall be entitled to a full pay for the leaves days without considering the due wage for the sick leave.
- 4. If the Saudi National Day coincides with the leave days of Eids,the worker may not be compensated for such day.

Article (25)

Subject to Article (116) of the Labor Law:

- 1. If the unpaid leave-agreed upon-exceeds 20 days and the employment contract has been suspended, all legal effects shall be suspended accordingly, unless otherwise agreed by the parties.
- 2. If the employment contract has a definite term, it shall be extended for the same suspension period of the contract, unless otherwise agreed by the parties.

Article (26)

Subject to Article (117) of the Labor Law, if the sick leave days coincides with the annual leave days, the annual leave days shall be suspended until the end of the sick leave days. Then, the remaining days shall be resumed after that. Meanwhile, if the weekend days coincides with the sick leave days, the worker may not be compensated for those days.

Article (27)

Subject to Article (120) of the Labor Law: 1. The rules and controls of part-time work shall be as identified as follows:

- a. The part-time employment contract shall be in a written form and have a definite term. It shall include the working hours, so as it shall be reduced to half of the normal working days in the establishment, whether the work is performed on daily basis or throughout some days per week.
- b. The part time employment contract may be renewed for similar terms or a term agreed upon by the parties.
- c. If the part-time employment contract was terminated by either party for [an] illegal reason, the aggrieved party shall be entitled to claim for the remuneration of the remaining wage as a compensation, unless otherwise agreed by the parties.
- d. Part-timers shall be subject to the Labor law provisions in terms of leaves, weekends, official holidays and overtime.
- e. The Saudi worker working for an employer in one of the entities affiliated to part-time contract shall be included under the Saudization percentage according to the approved percentages stated under [the] Nitaqat

program, provided that he shall be registered with the General Organization for Social Insurance (GOSI) as a part-timer.

2. The Labor Courts shall have jurisdiction to consider the disputes arising out of the part- time employment contract.

Article (28)

Subject to Article (141) of the law, when the establishment is not subject to Occupational Hazards Branch included in the Social Insurance Law, the following procedures of reporting work injuries shall be taken:

- 1. The employer shall inform the competent labor office of the worker's injury within one week of his knowledge.
- 2. The labor office determines whether it is a work injury or not, as per the official reports.
- 3. In case of lack of any medical reports that determine the percentage of deficit resulted from the injury, or if either party appealed against the medical report, the labor office shall refer the injured person to any governmental hospitals to get the necessary medical report.
- 4. The labor office shall determine the compensation due to the injured person as per the percentage of deficit indicated in the medical report.
- 5. If either party rejects the labor office's estimation, the subject shall be referred to the competent labor courts.

Article 29

Subject to Article (142) of the law, the employer shall provide medical aid cabinet as follows:

- The first aid locker shall contain the following supplies:
- These types and quantities shall always be available.

Type
Quantity
Buns Gauze
(50) pieces
Sponge bandages
(10) pieces
Gauze pieces
(50) pieces
Sterile gauze pads 10 x 10
(50) pieces
Gauze pads 5 x 5
(50) pieces
Gauze ligaments
(10) ligaments
Tourniquet
(1)
Pressing ligaments (Various sizes)

(10) ligaments
Medical swabs
(100) pieces
Plaster rolls
(5) rolls
Sterile plaster pieces
(20) pieces
Sterile gloves
(20) pairs
Face masks
(10) muzzles
Eyewash solution
1 pack
Folding stretcher
(1)
Antiseptic solution for wounds
(1) pack
A set of positive airways
(1)
Thigh, leg and forearm splints
(1)
Solid sheet for spinal injuries
(1)
Cervical splint kit for neck injuries
(1)
Scissors, appropriate size
(2)
Large size blanket
(1)
Suitable size clamp
(2)

Article (30)

Subject to Article (146) of the law, the remote locations are determined as follows:

- 1. Workplaces that are far away from the urban growth boundaries determined by the secretariat and different municipalities by no more than 50 kilometers if the roads were paved, and 25 kilometers if the roads were not paved.
- 2. Residential areas where such facilities and services are unavailable.

Article (31)

- 1. The female worker is entitled to take a period or periods of rest with a full wage to breastfeeding her child not exceeding one hour per day and calculated from the actual working hours for 24 months from the delivery date, be it natural or other breastfeeding.
- 2. The period of rest taken for the purpose of breastfeeding is not included in the official periods of rests provided for the workers.
- 3. The period or periods of rest taken for the purpose of breastfeeding shall be determined upon the availability of the nursery within the establishment and according to the followings:
    - A. If the nursery was not available within the establishment, the female worker is entitled to take one hour for breastfeeding, at the beginning or the end of the working hours, as appropriate to the nature of work.

- B. If the nursery was available within the establishment; the female worker is entitled to choose period or periods of rest for a total of one hour for breastfeeding, as appropriate to the nature of work.
- 4. After coming back from the delivery leave, the female worker shall notify the employer in writing of the period or periods of rest as well as any change thereto.

Article (32)

Subject to Article (161) of the Law, a minor who has completed fifteen years of age and not yet eighteen is prohibited from performing any works that may endanger his health, safety or morals due to the nature or conditions of the same, including but not limited to the following:

- 1. Work in mines, quarries, or extraction of mineral materials.
- 2. Industries with health risks.
- 3. Works that may expose the minor to physical hazards due to the usage of high-risk machinery and equipment, such as sharp cutting machines.
- 4. Any work that may expose the minor to moral, psychological, and physical problems.

Article (33)

Subject to Article (162) thereof, any person under the age of fifteen may not be employed under any circumstances whatsoever, except in the cases stipulated in the Minister's decision.

Article (34)

As exception to Article (163) of the Law, minors may be employed during the night in the following cases:

- 1. The establishment where work is limited to family members.
- 2. Work in vocational schools and training centers.
- 3. Work in bakeries, excluding the period from 9 PM to 4 AM.
- 4. Force majeure and emergency cases.

Article (35)

Subject to Article (167) of the Law, the following conditions shall be met:

- 1. A direct supervision shall be conducted by the entity responsible for the activity.
- 2. Education and training shall be taken in a progressive manner, so that no difficulty could face the learner or the trainee.
- 3. Education and training may not hinder the academic achievement of the learner or the trainee. 4. Work may not be as hazardous as stipulated in Article (161) of the Labor Law.
- 5. The entity that desires to regulate educational or training programs shall have the approval of the Ministry as well as the entity licensing the activity.

Article (36)

Subject to Article (196/5) of the Law, if the labor inspector found any violations to the Labor Law, this Regulation, or the relevant decisions made by the competent governmental bodies, it shall prepare a record of the violations determined as per the provisions included in the Implementing Regulation for controlling and regulating inspection works and fulfilling the regulatory procedures.

Article (37)

Subject to Article (197) of the Law, the labor inspector shall undertake before commencing the work to:

I, the labor inspector/..., having functional no. ( ), civil register no. ( ), undertakes before Allah and before my heads to perform my duties honestly and sincerely and not to disclose the secrets of any industrial invention or any other secrets, which may come to my knowledge by reason of my office, even after leaving such office. In case of violation, I will be deemed a violator and shall bear the legitimate and regulatory liability resulting therefrom. Issued on: / / Signature:

Article (38)

Subject to paragraphs (1/4/5) of Article (230) of the Law: I. The penalties of the list indicated in Clause (First) of Paragraph (1) of the Minster's decision, regarding the violations and penalties to be applied to the violators, shall be imposed by the administrative unit concerned with penalty applications approved by the Minister. II. Deputy Minister for Inspection and Development of Work Environment shall establish, under the Minister's approval, a unit or center for receiving the record of work violation control from the labor inspector. Such unit is to review how far the violation is recorded according to law, classifying and verifying it, issuing the decisions of proposed penalties or filing the record and taking any of the following procedures:

- 1. Issuing an administrative decision for penalty application to the violator if the penalties to be imposed are included in the penalty list of Clause (First), Paragraph (1) of the above decision.
- 2. Guiding those specialized in filing cases against violators before the competent court (labor courts) if the penalties to be imposed are included in the penalty list of Clause (First), Paragraph (2) of the above decision.
- 3. Directing to file the record if the violation has not been established.

III. upon drafting any control record for any violation to the Labor Law, this Regulation, or the relevant decision requiring the imposition of the penalties stipulated in the schedule of violations and penalties, the labor inspector shall submit it to the competent department or to the workers concerned with penalty application as indicated in Clause (Second) of this Article. IV. Deputy Minister for Inspection and Development of Work Environment shall establish, under the Minister's approval, a unit or center to undertake the following:

- 1. Considering the appeals submitted by the violators against the administrative decisions issued for imposing work violation penalties;
- 2. Considering violation settlement requests submitted by the violators; As follows:
    - • As for the appeals submitted against the administrative decisions issued for imposing work violation penalties, the unit or center shall issue its decisions as per Clause (Fifth & Sixth) stipulated in Article (38) of this Regulation.
    - • As for settlement,unit or center shall submit its recommendations to the Minister for approval.

V: the administrative decision of imposing work violation penalties shall be appealed within (30) days from notifying the violator with the administrative decision. Such appeal may not suspend the implementation of the relevant penalty. VI: If the appeal against the administrative decision has been accepted and another decision has been issued for its termination, the amounts collected shall be returned to the appellant as per the procedures followed by HRDF. VII: the following procedures are required to submit requests for work violation settlement:

- 1. An administrative decision shall have been issued to impose any of the penalties stipulated in the schedule of violations and penalties indicated in Clause (First), Paragraph (1) of the above decision. A final judgment shall have been issued by the competent court to impose any of the penalties stipulated in the schedule of violations and penalties indicated in Clause (First), Paragraph (2) of the above decision.
- 2. The settlement may not be made to a violation occurring for the third time over two years from imposing the penalty or to a violation that has been settled previously.

VIII: the following procedures shall be taken upon work violation settlement:

- 1. The violator shall submit the settlement request within (90) days after being notified with the administrative decision, provided that the competent department shall decide on the settlement request within no later than (~~70~~ 90) days from its submission. Such authority may recommend suspending penalty enforcement while considering the claim. ~~In this case, it may suspend the~~

~~implementation of the penalty until the request is decided.~~ (*Amended by Ministerial Decision No.54908 dated 16/03/1441*)

- 2. The violator shall eliminate all violations, subject of settlement, and provide the documentary evidences.
- 3. The competent department may summon the violator and ask him about the settlement and its items, paying the due regard to the circumstances surrounding.
- 4. The competent department shall submit the settlement agreement, attached with the recommendation, to the Minister for issuing settlement decision in case of approval.
- 5. The violator shall implement the settlement decision within (60) days from notification, otherwise the settlement is deemed cancelled.
- 6. The Minister authorizes the Deputy Minister of Labor and Social Development to develop the detailed condition of violation settlement.

Article (39)

Subject to Article (231) of the Law, the violator shall eliminate the violation within (10) days from the date of penalty application. If such violation was not eliminated within the time limit specified, it is deemed a repetition for the violation and the penalty shall be doubled.

Article (40)

Subject to Article (232) of the Law and without prejudice to the procedures followed for collecting the public funds, the violator shall pay the imposed fines within (60) days from being notified of the administrative decision or the final judgment. Failure to do so, the Ministry's services shall be suspended until the payment of the fines.

The implementation by the decision may not be suspended by any grievance before the competent administrative court against any administrative decision of imposing the penalty of the list included in Clause (First), Paragraph (1) of the Minster's decision that is relevant to the violations and penalties, expect upon the court's decision.

CHAPTER 5
ANNEX 1 MODEL WORK RULES

ARTICLE (12) of the Labor Law promulgated by Royal Decree No. (51/) dated 23/08/ 1426H, amended by Royal Decree No. (24/) dated 12/05/1434H and Royal Decree No. (46/) dated 5/6/1436H and each employer shall prepare work rules to organize the work in his company according to this form.

Data of Organization

Name of Organization: ....

Head Office: ....

Number of Employees: ....

Employees Activity: ....

Address: ....

P O Box: (.......................) Area Code: (......................)

Wassel Mail No: ....

Phone: ....

Fax: ....

Email: ....

CR No: ....

Date of Issue of CR: ..../.../......Hijri **Article (1)**

The term "Organization" shall mean as defined in these Regulations: ....

The term "Employee" shall mean as defined in these Regulations: Any natural person who works for the benefit of this organization and under its management or supervision for a wage even if it is far from its sight.

Article (2)

The applicable calendar in the organization is: .... Calendar.

Article (3)

- The provisions of these Regulations shall apply to all employees of the Organization and its subsidiaries.
- The provisions of these Regulations shall not prejudice the rights acquired by employees and shall be deemed to be complementary to the employment contracts in a manner that does not contradict with these rights.
- The Organization shall be aware of these regulations at the time of signing the contract and shall provide for such in the employment contract.

Article (4)

- The Organization may issue its own resolutions and policies giving employees better rights than those contained in these Regulations.
- The Organization shall have the right to include additional conditions and provisions in this Regulation provided not to detract employees' rights acquired under the Labor Law, its implementing regulations and the decisions issued in its implementation. Such additions or amendments shall not be effective until the Ministry of Labor has approved them.
- Any text, which is inconsistent with the provisions of the Labor Law, its executive regulations and the decisions issued in implementation thereof added to these regulations shall be deemed null and void.

Article (5)

Employees are employed on jobs with specific titles and specifications. The following shall be taken into account in the recruitment:

- Job applicant shall be Saudi national
- He shall have educational qualification and the experience required by the organization for the position.
- He shall pass the tests established by the organization or pass interviews required by the position.
- He shall be medically fit in accordance with medical certificate issued by an authority determined by the organization.
- Non-Saudi may be employed pursuant to terms and conditions provided for in Articles (26, 32 and 33) of the Labor Law.

Article (6)

Employee shall be hired in accordance with an employment contract written in two copies in Arabic language pursuant to the standard form designed by the Ministry of Labor. One copy shall be delivered to the employee and the other one shall deposited to the employee's service file kept by the organization. The employment contract shall include the name of employer, employee's name, nationality, original address, selected address, type, place of work, agreed basic salary and any other agreed benefits, and whether the contract is a limited-period contract or unlimited period contract, for performance of certain work, probation period if agreed to, date of starting the work and any necessary data. The employment contract may be written in another language beside the Arabic language provide the Arabic version shall always prevail.

Article (7)

Subject to the date fixed in the employment contract for starting the work, the organization may cancel the contract of an employee who does not start his work without legal excuse within seven days from the date on which the employment contract has been signed by the parties if the contract was signed in the Kingdom or from the date of employee' arrival in the Kingdom if the contract was signed outside the Kingdom of Saudi Arabia.

Article (8)

Compliance with the expenses of travel of the employee or his family members shall be determined pursuant to the following controls:

- At the beginning of contract as per agreed in the employment contract.
- When an employee takes his annual vacation as per agreed to in the employment contract.
- When an employee's service expires pursuant to Article (40), paragraph (1) of the Labor Law.
- The organization shall not bear expenses of employee's return back to his country in case he is not fit for the job during the probation period or if he wishes to return to his country without legal cause or if he commits a violation lead to his deportation in accordance with an administrative decision or judicial ruling.

Article (9)

Subject to Article (58) of the Labor Law, an employee who has been relocated from his original workplace to another place requiring change of his residence place shall be entitled to receive the expenses of his relocation along with the expenses of his dependents who live with him on the date of relocation including expenses of travel plus transport cost of their luggage unless the relocation is done upon the employee's wish. **Article (10)**

The organization, in case it rehabilitate or train Saudi employee, shall incur all costs. If the place of rehabilitation or training is outside of the organization, the organization shall provide two-way-tickets on a class identified by the organization. The organization shall also secure accommodation such as food, housing and internal transport during the training period or the organization shall give the employee an allowance instead. The organization shall continue to pay the employee's salary throughout the period of rehabilitation and training.

Article (11)

- The organization may terminate the rehabilitation or training contract of non-employees if the reports issued by the authority that undertakes the training or rehabilitation proved the incapability or inability to complete the training program beneficially.
- Trainee or the person who is subject to rehabilitation program, his guardian or trustee shall have the right to terminate the training or rehabilitation if the reports issued by the training or rehabilitation authority proved his incapability or inability to complete the training program beneficially.
- In both previous cases, the party that wishes to terminate the contract shall notify the other party of such termination at least one week prior to the date of stopping from the training and rehabilitation.
- The organization shall oblige the trainee or the person who is subject to the rehabilitation program, after completion of the period of training or rehabilitation, to work with the organization for a period similar to the period of training and rehabilitation.
- The organization shall oblige the trainee or the person who is subject to the rehabilitation program to pay the costs of training or rehabilitation it incurred or oblige him with the remaining period proportion in case he refuses to work for the similar period or part of it.

Article (12)

First: the organization may require the person who is subject to the training or rehabilitation program after completion of training and rehabilitation period to work with it for a period no exceeding the period that is similar to the period of the training and rehabilitation program if the employment contract period is unlimited or the remaining period of contract in fixed-period contracts if the remaining period of the employment contract is less than the period that is similar to the period of the training program.

Second: the organization may terminate rehabilitation or training of employee and oblige him to pay the training costs incurred by the organization or to pay part of the costs in the following cases:

- If the employee decides to terminate the training or rehabilitation before the fixed date without legal excuse.
- If the employee's employment contract is terminated pursuant to one of the cases set forth in Article (80) of he Labor Law except paragraph (6) during the period of training or rehabilitation.
- If the employee resigns or leaves work for cases other than those set forth in Article (81) of the Labor Law during the period of training or rehabilitation.

Third: the organization may oblige the employee to pay the training or rehabilitation costs incurred by the organization or oblige him to pay part of the costs if he resigns from work or left the work for cases other than those set forth in Article (81) of the Labor Law prior to expiration of the employment period stipulated by the organization after expiry of training or rehabilitation. **Article (13)**

Subject to any procedures or arrangements provided for in the Wage Protection Program, the wages of employees shall be paid in the official currency of the country when the wages fall due and deposited to the employees' account at certified banks in the Kingdom of Saudi Arabia.

Article (14)

Overtime hour's wages payable to the employee shall be paid at the end of the month in which the commissioning has been made.

Article (15)

In the event the day of paying the salary coincides with the weekend or an official holiday, the payment shall be made on the prior working day. **Article (16)**

The organization shall periodically prepare reports on the performance of all employees at least once every year pursuant to the forms established thereto. The reports include the following factors:

- Ability to work and the degree of perfection (competency).
- Employee's behavior, how far he is cooperative with his superiors, colleagues and the organization's clients.
- Perseverance and assiduity.

Article (17)

Employee's performance in the report shall be assessed by the estimations identified by the organization. A measurement of five grades shall be followed in such assessment.

Article (18)

The report shall be prepared with the knowledge of employee's direct boss provided that the report should be approved by the authorized person. The employee shall be provided with a copy of the report as soon it has been approved. The employee is entitled to appeal the report pursuant to the Complaint Rules provided for in these regulations.

Article (19)

- The organization may grant the employees annual bonuses whose rates are determined based on the light of the organization's financial position.
- The employee shall be qualified to receive the bonus whenever he obtains, in his periodical report, an

intermediate level at least in the Form established by the organization after passage of one full year from the date of joining the work or from the date of obtaining the prior bonus.

- The organization management may grant the employee an exceptional bonus pursuant to the controls established by the organization in this regard.

Article (20)

The organization establishes a functional ladder for its own positions in which the organization determines the number and titles of jobs pursuant to Saudi Vocational Rating & Description Guide, degree of each position, terms of taking position and beginning of its wage. The employee shall be qualified to higher position when the following terms are met:

- Availability of higher vacancy.
- Availability of qualifications for taking the position for which employee is nominated to upgrade.
- If employee obtains a level above intermediate at least in the last periodic report.
- Authorized person's approval.
- The organization management may grant the employee exceptional upgrade pursuant to the controls established by the organization in this respect.

Article (21)

If more than one employee meets the upgrade conditions for a higher position, the preference for upgrade shall be as follows:

- Nomination of authorized person.
- An employee who obtains higher estimation. [1]

---

1. Probably means the employee who has higher work evaluations.

- An employee who obtains higher educational certificates or more training courses.
- An employee who has more experience in the field of the organization business.
- Seniority in work at the organization.

Article (22)

If an employer is delegated to perform work outside his workplace, the organization shall:

- Secure for the employee the necessary means of transport unless he receives transport allowance upon his consent.
- The employee shall receive indemnity for the costs he incurs for accommodation, food etc. unless the organization secures the same for him.
- Value of daily allowance for delegation according to the employee's grade.

Such obligations shall be identified in the delegation resolution according to the categories and controls established by the organization in this regard. These expenses shall be calculated from the time of employee's departure to his workplace to the time of his return according to the period fixed to him by the organization. **Article (23)**

The organization secures to its employees appropriate housing as well as means of transport if provided for in the employment contract. The employment contract may provide for that the organization shall pay the employee a housing allowance and cash transport allowance. **Article (24)**

- The number of working days are ... Days per week. (...) day shall be the full paid weekend rest for all employees. The organization, after notifying the competent labor office, may replace this day, for some of its employees, with any other day of the week and shall enable them to perform their religious duties. The weekend may not be compensated for cash consideration.

- Working hours shall be (eight) working hours per day and may be reduced to (six) hours per day during holy month of Ramadan for Muslim employees.

Article (25)

- In the event an employee is commissioned to work overtime, this shall be done in accordance with a written or electronic commissioning directed to him issued by the authority in charge in the organization. In such written commissioning, the number of overtime hours which are assigned to the employee and the number of required days shall be defined pursuant to Article (106) of the Labor Law.
- The organization shall pay the employee for the overtime hours an additional wage equal to hour wage plus (50%) of his basic salary.

Article (26)

Employees shall enter and exit from their workplace through designated points. All employees shall be subject to inspection (administrative inspection) whenever requested to do so.

Article (27)

The organization may oblige the employee to prove his attendance and departure by one of the means designed for this purpose.

Article (28)

The employee, for every year of service, is entitled to enjoy a full paid annual vacation not less than 21 days that may be increased to a period not less than thirty days if his service reached five successive years. The employee, after organization's approval, shall obtain part of his annual leave at rate of period of year he spent in the work. It may be agreed in the employment contract that the annual leave period could be more than that.

Article (29)

The employee is entitled to a full paid leave at Eid holidays and occasions pursuant to the following:

- Four days for Eid al Fitr, commencing from the day following the 29th days of holy month of Ramadan according to the Umm al Qura Calendar.
- Four days for Eid al Adha beginning from the day of standing at Arafa.
- One day for the Kingdom National Day (first of Libra).

If the days of these holidays coincided with the weekend, the employee would be compensated with the equivalent prior to or after the days of these holidays. If the holidays of one Eid coincide with the National Day, the employee shall not be compensated.

Article (30)

The employee is entitled to take full paid leave in the following cases:

- Five days when the employee gets married.
- Three days when a new baby is borne for him.
- Five days in case employee's wife, one of origin or branch is dead.
- Four months and ten days in the event a Muslim employee's husband died. She has a right to extend such leave without pay if she is pregnant until she gives birth to a baby. She may not benefit from the rest of the waiting period leave granted to her after she has given birth to a child.

- Fifteen days in case of death of a non-Muslim employee's husband.

The organization is entitled to request the documents supporting the previously mentioned cases.

Article (31)

The employee, who proves his sickness by a medical certificate issued by the organization's doctor or by an approved medical reference, is entitled to a sick leave during a year commencing from the date of first sick leave whether such leaves successive or intermittent; as follows:

- The first thirty days with full pay.
- The next sixty days with three fourth pay
- The next thirty days without pay.

The employee is entitled to link his annual leave with his sick leave. **Article (32)**

The organization shall secure medical insurance for its employees according to the Cooperative Medical Insurance Law and implementing regulations. The organization shall subscribe for all employees at the Vocational Risk Branch at the General Organization for Social Insurances pursuant to GOSI Law.

Article (33)

The organization shall designate, at all places in which women work, places and seats for female employees rest plus toilettes far away from men.

Article (34)

Female employee is entitled to take a full paid maternity leave for ten weeks distributed, as she likes. Such leave starts at maximum with four weeks prior to the probable date of delivery. This date shall be determined by medical authority approved by the organization or by a medical certificate certified by a medical authority. A female employee may not work during the six weeks that follow her delivery.

In the event of giving birth to a sick child or a child with special needs, the employee is entitled to take a full paid leave for one month after elapse of maternity leave. She may extend the maternity leave for one month without pay.

Article (35)

A female employee, when she returns to practice her work after maternity leave, is entitled to take a period or periods of rest in order to breast breeding her child no exceeding one hour per day in addition to the periods of rest given to all employees. This period/ periods shall be calculated from actual working hours for twenty-four months form the date of delivery. This may not result in reducing the wage. The female employee, when she returns from her maternity leave, shall notify the employer in writing of the time of period/ periods of that rest and amendment to that time. Breast breeding period/ periods shall be determined in light thereof according to the implementing regulations of the Labor Law. **Article (36)**

The organization shall provide the following social services:

- Prepare a place for performance of prayers.
- Prepare a place for eating food.
- Organization shall provide the necessary requirements, services and facilitation utilities for employees with disability to enable them to perform their works according to the requirements provided for in the implementing regulations of the Labor Law.

Article (37)

- The organization may oblige all or some of the employees to wear a uniform. In all cases, men's clothes shall be suitable to the public sense. For women, they shall wear good, decent, wide and nontransparent clothes.

- All employees of the organization should comply with the requirements of the Islamic Sharia Laws and social practice applicable in dealing with others.
- All employees are prohibited from being a lone with female employees. The organization shall take all precautions to prevent employees from sitting privately with female employees in the organization.
- All employees shall refrain from doing, in any way, any kind of insult, physical, utterance abuse, abuse by allusion, taking any attitude that touches decency, dignity, reputation, liberty, meant to seduce any person to illegitimate relationship even if by way of joking and kidding upon direct communication or by any other means of communication. The organization shall take all arrangements, necessary action to notify all employees thereof.

Article (38)

- All practices of positive, negative abuse, all forms of exploitation, blackmailing, seduction, temptation, threat whether physical, psychological or sexual threat that happen at workplace by the employer against the employee, by employee against the employer, by employee against another employee or against any person available at the worksite are deemed an abuse. Assistance and covering this crime shall be considered as an abuse.
- It shall be deemed an intentional abuse provided for in the foregoing paragraph, everything that happened by using any means of communication whether by utterance, writing, signal, allusion, drawing, using a phone, other electronic means or by any form of behavior that indicate thereto.

Article (39)

- Without prejudice to the right of the victim of abuse at workplace to resort to the competent government authorities, he/ she is entitled to file his/her complaint to the organization within maximum five days from occurrence of abuse. Everyone who saw or knew the incident of abuse may report to the organization thereof. If the abuse is made by the employer or by higher authority in the organization, the complaint shall be filed to the competent government authorities.
- The organization, upon filing the complaint, shall, with a resolution issued by the competent official, form a committee whose task is to investigate the cases of abuse, view the evidence and recommend imposition of appropriate disciplinary penalty on the person who has been condemned during five working days form receiving the complaint or notification.

Article (40)

- Subject to confidentiality principle the Committee shall listen to all parties and witnesses and shall record everything in minutes signed by the parties and witnesses then to be signed by the Committee members at the end of each page.
- The Committee is entitled to summon any employee whom it thinks it is necessary to interrogate and listen to his words. Any person to be summoned shall appear before the Committee otherwise he/she shall be under liability.
- The Committee may file a recommendation to the organization management to differentiate between the

complainant and the defendant during the period of investigation.

- If abuse incident is proved by any method of good methods of proof, the Committee shall recommend by majority to enforce the appropriate disciplinary penalty on the offender.
- If the assault constitutes a criminal offense, the Committee shall file the complaint to the general manager to notify the competent government authorities.
- In case the abuse is not proved, the Committee shall recommend enforcement of disciplinary penalty on the informer if it has been proved that the complaint or notification was vicious.
- The disciplinary penalty enforced by the organization on the offender shall not impede the complainant's right to resort to competent government authorities.
- Enforcement of other legal penalty on the offender shall not prevent the organization from enforcing a disciplinary penalty on the offender.

Article (41)

Violation is every act committed by an employee and requires any of the following penalties:

- Written notice: is a letter directed by the organization to the employee explaining the type of violation committed by the employee while drawing his attention to possibility of being exposed to a harder punishment if he continues to commit the violation or redo like it in the future.
- Financial penalty: is to deduct rate from the wage (part of daily wage) or deduct from wage ranging between a day wage and five days per months as maximum.

- Stop from work without pay: is to prevent the employee from practicing his work during a certain period plus depriving him from his wage during that period. The stopping period shall not exceed five days per month.
- Deprivation from upgrade, periodical bonus for maximum period of one year form the due date.
- Dismissal from work with remuneration: is dismissal of an employee based on legal cause due to committing the violation, without prejudice to his right to the End of Service Bonus.
- Dismissal from work without remuneration: is a termination of the employee's employment contract without remuneration, notice or compensation as he commits any of the cases provided for in Article (80) of the Labor Law.

The penalty imposed on the employee shall be commensurate with the type and size of violation committed by him.

Article (42)

Every employee who commits any of the violations set forth in the Table of Violations and Penalties, attached to these resolutions, shall be punished by the penalty defined for the violation committed.

Article (43)

The organization (authorized person) is empowered to enforce the penalties set forth in these regulations or shall be enforced by his representative. He may replace the penalty established for any violation with a lighter penalty.

Article (44)

If an employee commits the same violation after passage of one hundred eighty (180) days, he shall not be deemed a repeater, but it shall be deemed as if it has been committed for the first time.

Article (45)

In the event of multiple offenses arising out of a single act, enforcement of the most severe penalty established in these Regulations shall be enough.

Article (46)

No more than one penalty may be imposed on an employee in case of a single offense. It is not permissible to enforce a fine in excess of five days' wages on an employee for one offense. It is not permissible to deduct from the employee's wage more than five days in a month, in fulfillment of the fines imposed on him.

Article (47)

The Organization shall not enforce any sanctions exceeding the penalty of one day's fine only after the employee has been informed in writing of the violations attributed to him, hearing his statements and realizing his defense, in accordance with a minutes filed in his own file.

Article (48)

The Organization may not enforce any penalty on the employee for an issue committed outside the workplace unless it has a direct relationship with the nature of his work, the organization or its responsible director, without prejudice to the provisions of article 80 of the Labor Law.

Article (49)

An employee may not be held liable for a violation that has been detected for more than thirty days from the date of the organization's knowledge of its perpetrator, without being subject to any investigation procedure.

Article (50)

The Organization may not enforce any penalty on the employee if more than thirty days passed since the violation date has been proved.

Article (51)

The organization is obliged to inform the employee in writing of the penalties imposed, the type, the amount and the penalty that will be incurred in case of repeated violation. If the employee refrains from receiving the notification, refuses to sign the acknowledgment of receipt or if he is absent, the notification shall be sent to him by registered mail at his fixed address identified in his service file, by personal email fixed in the employment contract or approved by the organization. Notification by any of these means shall result in all legal effects.

Article (52)

A penalty sheet shall be allocated for each employee in which the type of violation committed by employee, date of occurrence and the penalty imposed on him shall be recorded. This penalty sheet shall be kept in the employee's service file.

Article (53)

The fines imposed on the employees shall be recorded in a special register in accordance with the provisions of Article (73) of the Labor Law. Disposal of fines by the Labor Committee shall be for the benefit of employees. In the absence of a labor committee, the Ministry of Labor shall approve the disposal of fines.

Article (54)

Without prejudice to the employee's right to resort to the competent administrative, judicial authorities or bodies, an employee may appeal to the management of the organization against any act, action or penalty taken against him by the management of the organization. The employee may lodge a complaint with the management of the organization within three working days from the date of knowledge of the act or action against which he complained. The employee shall not be harmed by the submission of his grievance. The employee shall be notified of the outcome of the decision on his grievance within a period not exceeding five working days from the date of filing the grievance. **Article (55)**

The provisions of these Regulations shall be implemented on the Organization as from the date of notification of their adoption and shall apply to the employees from the day following the declaration.

Penalties

qqq

Presence without justification, during work hours in an unauthorized place

1st: 10%;2nd: 25%;3rd: 50%;4th: 1 day.

Receiving non-work related guests

1st: Written Warning;2nd: 10%;3rd: 15%;4th: 25%.

Personal use of company material

1st: Written Warning;2nd: 10%;3rd: 25%;4th: 50%.

Interference with work of others

1st: 50%;2nd: 1 day;3rd: 2 days;4th: 3 days.

Entry/Exit through unauthorized doors

1st: Written Warning;2nd: 10%;3rd: 15%;4th: 25%.

Negligence in cleaning or maintenance

1st: 50%;2nd: —;3rd: 2 days;4th: 3 days.

Failure to return equipment to assigned location as instructed

1st: Written Warning;2nd: 25%;3rd: 50%;4th: 1 day.

Remove posted notices

1st: 2 days;2nd: 3 days;3rd: 5 days;4th: Dismissal.

Failure to care for company equipment

1st: 2 days;2nd: 3 days;3rd: 5 days;4th: Dismissal.

Eating in unauthorized places

1st: Written Warning;2nd: 10%;3rd: 15%;4th: 25%.

Sleeping

1st: Written Warning;2nd: 10%;3rd: 25%;4th: 50%.

Sleeping when vigilance required

1st: 50%;2nd: 1 day;3rd: 2 days;4th: 3 days.

Wandering about workplace

1st: 10%;2nd: 25%;3rd: 50%;4th: 1 day.

Falsifying arrival or departure times

1st: 1 day;2nd: 2 days;3rd: Elimination of bonus/upgrades;4th: Dismissal.

Failure to comply with oral or written work orders

1st: 25%;2nd: 50%;3rd: 1 day;4th: 2 days.

Encourage others to ignore work orders

1st: 2 days;2nd: 3 days;3rd: 5 days;4th: Dismissal.

Smoking in prohibited areas

1st: 2 days;2nd: 3 days;3rd: 5 days;4th: Dismissal.

Harmful negligence

1st: 2 days;2nd: 3 days;3rd: 5 days;4th: Dismissal.

CHAPTER 6

ANNEX NO. 2—PASSPORT REQUEST LETTER

CONFIRMATION OF PASSPORT **Delivery**

I am the employee:.........

of ....Nationality,

holding Passport number:.........

Issuer: ....

Expiration date: ... /. ./ .....

Resident Identity number: ....

That I agree, in my full capacity and my choice, to hand over the attached passport to the company / establishment

....

to keep it on my behalf as I fear it would be stolen, lost or damaged. My passport shall remain in its possession during my work with it provided that the company/ establishment shall return the passport back to me upon my request.

This is my acknowledgment:

Acknowledged by:

Name of employee: ....

Signature:..................

. . .

Received by:

Name:..........................

Capacity:.......................

Signature:....................

Date:..........................

Stamp:........................

CHAPTER 7
ANNEX NO. 3—DISABLED EMPLOYEES

Wheelchair Users

OFFICE POSITIONS, Researcher, Policies, Laws or Plans Analyzer, Planning Consultant, Legal Advisor, Data Entry, Article Writer, Human Resources / Personnel Affairs, Administrative, Secretarial / Receptionist

Ramps, toilets with handles, suitable height for the toilet, basin and sink under the basin, power buttons with appropriate height, empty bottom tables that allow wheelchair access under it, suitable height for shelves and safe exit in the state of emergency.

Technical and training positions

Checking beds with a suitable height for the wheelchair. Placing racks for pharmacists at appropriate heights, providing aids, training tools, and arranging the hall so that the trainers can train and move easily.

Teaching in schools and universities

The transfer of rooms and lecture halls, regardless of the difference from year to year, to the ground floor unless there is an equipped lift. Placing the board inside the classroom or lecture hall at a low height appropriate for the person, taking into account the spaces between the drawers, allowing reasonable movement of the teacher or lecturer.

Manual and muscular functions Driver, Carpenter, Commissar, Tailor, Textile worker, Packaging Workers, Auto Mechanic, Heating and Cooling worker, Satellite TV Installation Technician (Satellite). etc. Equipped motor vehicles, tools, woodworking machines, blacksmithing machines, mantle, dismantle machines, lifting and other machines, with suitable handles and position separating machines from the person's thigh or wheelchair edge. A simple mechanical or manual lift to lift the wheelchair to reach a machine or hanged machine, tables with heights suitable for the placement of machines, attachments, counters and telephones at heights suitable for the person sitting on the wheelchair.

Upper Limb Physical Disability

Office positions A computer with a modified keyboard that can be adjusted according to the nature of the disability in the hands or in one of them or a finger. Text-to-speech converter software to replace manual printing and a table and chair that can be raised, lowered and flexed in various directions to enable a person to use his feet to pick up objects and possibly print and write. Also, put telephones and electric buttons at low altitude to control them by either elbow, foot or mouth as appropriate to the person's request. Technical Positions Computers that can controlled by touch by mouth, lip or foot. Hand-held handles with a reasonable space for office equipment of any kind to enable the person to capture and use it with any part of his body such as mouth, arms or feet. Having a personal companion where necessary. Teaching at schools or universities Provision of type of chalk, pens if the teacher or lecturer wants to use his mouth to write. Provision of personal companion where necessary upon the person's request. Putting handles for the doors at lower height that the teacher or lecturer can control with his shoulder, elbow or knee. Manual labor Equipped car that could be driven with one hand. Tools, amended, flexible machines with handles and reasonable space that could be controlled by feet, upper arms, chest, mouth etc. Speech converter to commands in telephones.

Height-related Disabilities

2 All positions and previous jobs Taking into account the appropriate height for equipment, tools, machines, door handles, buttons, furniture, elevator buttons, etc. Provision of pallets, escalators and supports that enable the short person to ride on them when he deems it necessary. In addition to equipping the vehicles to be used effectively and safely. All positions and all movement disabilities Modifying the behavior and attitudes of employees

Visual Impairments

2 Office positions A computer with a screen reader in Arabic and English such as "Goz, Hull, Ebsar ..." The electronic line that converts the text on the computer screen to Braille, a screen magnifier for visually impaired people, a phone with a talking program such as a TALKS or an iPhone Originally a voice-over-talk program. Braille printing machine, a manual machine called a board or a library ... and a scanner program, usually a screen reader, a Braille printer for personal use if the nature of the work requires the person to print hard copies of Braille, Sound alarm and safe way out in the state of emergency. Technical Positions A portable speaker screen saved on CD-ROM or a memory card that can be operated on any computer easily for computer maintenance and technicians, calculators, cash counting machines for accountants, professional accounting software for use of screen reader, personal companion wherever necessary and pharmacological information in the Braille method for pharmacists. Teaching positions Provide the school building or lectures at the university with ground and wall signals that allow the person to move inside the building easily, provide curricula, materials for teachers or

lecturers in Braille or in electronic format. Designate personal accompaniment if necessary at the request of the person and his desire to provide the curriculum, information and materials in large print For people who are visually impaired. Manual labor Modifying the behavior and attitudes of employees.

Hearing Impairment

2 Office positions Sign language interpreter or training of sign language personnel, light alarms in the state of emergency, telephone with video call feature, concussion feature and reference dictionary if available. Technical Positions Surveillance monitors for clinic, pharmacy or labs reveal to the deaf person - with light signals - every movement within the place where he works whether it is a private clinic or pharmacy, secretary / female secretary who speaks sign language. Teaching positions Assign a companion to facilitate communication between the teacher or the lecturer and the students and arrange the classroom or lecture hall, allowing the translator to stand in a rear place outside the focus of the vision of students to focus with the teacher or lecturer. Provide curricula and materials in sign language and provide specialized reference dictionaries whenever available. Manual labor Machines and equipment with light warning signals indicating the rotation, stopping and disabling of machine, etc., telephones with signal to speech converter and vice versa, and equipped with glass and light instead of bell. All positions for hearing impaired employees A loudspeaker, a headset selected by the person, and training of a number of people reading the lips of the phones equipped with the amplification. Modifying the behavior and attitudes of employees.

Psychological Disabilities

2 Office positions Color of rooms paint shall be comfortable to eyesight and not neurotic. Develop a flexible schedule of work and

rest times and introduce this into computerized system. Technical positions As per the previously mentioned arrangements for this disability. Teaching positions Taking into account the color of the rooms and modification and flexibility in the lessons time required by the teacher. Lectures should be on ground floors if a person has phobia of high or crowded areas. Manual labor Taking into account breadth, ventilation of the place and lack of height for those who have phobia of closed, crowded, narrow or high areas. All positions Modifying the behavior and attitudes of employees.

Mental Disabilities

2 Office positions Transfer all necessary documents and materials into simple language. Presence of an educational expert to facilitate communication if necessary or training a staff member / female employees. Training on how to use equipment relevant to functions of the post and flexibility in the timing of completion of the functions as required.

Technical positions Provide tools with maximum security and safety. Train the employee on tools requirements. Personal companion wherever necessary. Teaching positions Provision of a teacher or "shadow" lecturer and any assistant to the person upon request. Manual labor All the above, taking into account the specialized training according to each profession or craft will be done by the employee. All positions Modifying the behavior and attitudes of employees.

Temporary Disabilities; Chronic of Temporary Disease

2 Office positions Providing private space for rest and lying, equipped with a bed and mattress / medical mattress for employees who need to rest a few minutes from time to time, as is the case for patients of disc, spine and rheumatism.

Provision of comfortable seats, back and foot supports for

employees who suffer from Disc, spine and vascular diseases as appropriate. Technical positions, Manual labor Provision of tools, machines, equipment and devices with high security and safety to reduce instances of injury or scratches to employees who are patient of diabetes, blood thinness or those who use blood clotting drugs. All positions Calculation of days during which the worker is absent for physiotherapy, occupational, dialysis, chemotherapy or radiotherapy sessions and paid leave.

If work is divided into shifts, the requirements of employees who suffer from night blindness and employees who attend morning treatment sessions should be observed so that their work will always be during morning shift. Office positions Allow employees to wander and move their body from time to time as per the nature of their condition as the case of disc, vascular disease etc.

All positions, Including field positions Provision of an equipped vehicle if the employee uses a wheelchair temporarily and provision of personal companion as required. All positions (Dietary Needs) If an organization provides meal to employees, sugar-free meals should be provided to diabetic patients. Salt-free meals should be provided to blood pressure patients. All positions (Epilepsy) Removal of employees who are patients of epilepsy from the high places and remove edges, sharp machines or any object that would harm them in the event of epilepsy and fall to the ground from the surrounding where they are sitting. All positions (General) Provision of all arrangements and services to the employees with temporary disabilities or a disease that would create effect on any of the body's sensual, nervous, visual, psychological or mental functions as appropriate throughout the period of temporary disability or effect of disease. All positions (Attitudes) Modifying behavior and attitudes.

CHAPTER 8

ANNEX NO. 4—SAUDI EMPLOYMENT AGENCIES

RULES AND REGULATIONS **for Saudi Employment Agencies—for Saudi Nationals Seeking Employment**

Part 1: Introductory Provisions

Article (1)

The following terms and phrases, wherever they appear in such controls, shall have the meanings given to them unless the context otherwise requires:

Controls: controls and rules of practicing the activity of brokering the employment of Saudis.

Licensee: A Saudi recruitment office or company licensed by the Ministry of Labor to provide regulated activity in these regulations.

Job Applicant: Every Saudi citizen applying for employment in accordance with the provisions of these regulations.

Employer: Any natural or legal person requesting a Saudi employee or more Saudis in accordance with the provisions of these regulations.

Mediation in employment: Employment of male and

female Saudis for the benefit of the employer in the Kingdom of Saudi Arabia.

Office: A Saudi employment office licensed by the Ministry of Labor to engage in the activity of mediating in the employment of Saudis.

Company: A Saudi employment company licensed to practice activity of mediation in the employment of Saudis in accordance with the provisions of these regulations.

***License*:** A license granted by the Ministry of Labor to the applicant after fulfilling the conditions and requirements stipulated in these regulations and relevant laws, authorizes him to exercise the activity to which he has been licensed in accordance with these regulations.

Applicant: A person who submits an application to the Ministry of Labor applying for a license to establish an office or company for employment of Saudis in accordance with these regulations.

License applicant: Is the holder of initial approval to apply for a license to engage in mediation activity in employment of Saudis, whether office or company license.

Article (2)

The activity contained in these controls may be exercised only through offices or companies established for this purpose after obtaining a license from the Ministry of Labor in accordance with the conditions and procedures stipulated in these regulations. In case of violation, the Ministry of Labor shall be entitled to apply the penalties stipulated in the two schedules of violations and corresponding penalties issued by the Minister of Labor Decree No. 4786 on 28/12/1436H and any amendments that may take place thereto.

Part 2: License Requirements

Article (3)

- To obtain a license of (office) to engage in mediation activity in the employment of Saudis, the following shall be required:
- The office owner must be a Saudi national.
- The office owner must be at least 25 years old.
- The holder of the office must have a university qualification or equivalent or have a high school diploma with at least three years of experience in the field of employment.
- The owner of the office should not have ever been convicted of an offense that touched honor and honesty or of combating trafficking in persons unless he has been rehabilitated.
- The office owner shall manage his own office by himself and he may appoint a deputy who meets the previous conditions.

2. To obtain a license of (company) to engage in mediation activity in the employment of Saudis, the following shall be required:

- Shall be a company with an independent Commercial Registration in accordance with the Companies Law.
- Capital of company shall be fully owned by natural or legal Saudi persons.
- Company's capital registered in the Commercial Registration shall not be less than five hundred thousand (SR 500,000).

3. The natural person who engages in incorporating the company or joined the company after incorporation shall:

- Be a Saudi citizen.
- He should not have ever been convicted of an offense

that touched honor and honesty or of combating trafficking in persons unless he has been rehabilitated.

- He should not have ever obtained a license of an office of mediating in the employment of the Saudis, he was a partner in a company engaged in mediating the employment of Saudis or he was a partner in a company, which was a partner in a company of mediation in the employment of Saudis and the license was canceled in virtue of a decision issued as a penalty.
- The legal person, who participates in the establishment of a company or joins it after incorporation, shall have achieved the minimum rate of Saudization.
- A person who meets the conditions met by the owner of the office shall be appointed a manager of the company provided that the company shall maintain the these conditions in the company manager throughout the term of the license.

Article (4)

A license must be obtained for the activity of mediating in the employment of Saudis. Initial approval shall be issued by the Ministry of Labor to establish an office or a Saudi recruitment company in accordance with the following procedures and controls:

First: The license applicant or his representative shall apply for the initial approval to grant an office or company license to carry out the recruitment activity of the Saudis. Such application shall include the name and identity number of the owner of the office or a list of the names and national identification numbers of each of the applicants for the establishment of the company and the percentage of ownership therein along with an undertaking of non-change of this list. The following shall be attached to the application:

- Company's articles of association if the license is for a company.

- Office or company's work plan during the required period of the license.

Second: the Ministry of Labor, after studying the application, shall take one of the following decisions:

- Granting the initial approval and a stamped and signed document shall be issued authorizing him to start establishing a company to mediate in the recruitment of Saudis.
- Rejection of application provided the decision in this case shall be the reason.

Article (5)

If the Ministry of Labor decides to reject the application, withdraw or cancel the initial approval after it has been issued, the person who obtains such approval may not apply for another license before passage of one year from the date on which he was notified of the application rejection, withdrawal and cancelation of approval decision.

Article (6)

To obtain a license of office or company to exercise activity of mediating in employment of Saudis the following procedures shall be taken:

First : License applicant or his representative shall submit a request to the Ministry of Labor accompanied with the following documents:

- Copy of office or company's Commercial Registration (+ original for matching).
- Copy of title deed or lease contract of the office or company premises (+ original for matching).
- Bank guarantee of (SR 100,000) for an office license. For company license (SR 300,000). The bank guarantee

issued by a local bank shall be irrevocable guarantee pursuant to the Form approved by the Ministry of Labor.

Second: After study the request, the Ministry of Labor shall take one of the following decisions:

- Grant the license and a document thereof shall be issued by the Deputy Minister of Labor to the Customer Service and Labor Relations.
- Rejection of license request provided the decision should be the reason.

Article (7)

A licensee shall exercise his activity within a maximum period of six months from the date of obtaining the license. During this period, an interactive website shall be set up according to the requirements determined by the Ministry provided that it should include the following electronic records:

- Electronic record in which the contracts signed with the employers are recorded in particular the date of agreement between the licensee and the employer.
- An electronic record in which the applications submitted by the applicants, the name of the establishments to which they were joined, their activity and any other data that is necessary are recorded.

Article (8)

The period of license shall be two renewable Hijri years pursuant to the following procedures:

First: The licensee or his representative shall submit to the Ministry of Labor a request for renewal of the license in accordance with the prepared Forms, sixty days prior to the expiry of the license to which the following shall be attached:

- Office or company's business report during the prior period.
- Renewal of bank guarantee to include the term of renewal.
- Any other document required by the Ministry of Labor.

Second: After studying the request, the Ministry of Labor shall take one of the following decisions:

Renewal of the license: The Deputy Minister shall for Customer Service and Labor Relations shall issue the license for the new period.

Rejection of license renewal: for one of the following reasons:

- If it is proved that the licensee has ceased to exercise his activity for six consecutive months unless the interruption is for a reason accepted by the Ministry of Labor.
- If the licensee violates one or more of the license conditions.

In this case, the Ministry of Labor shall notify relevant authorities. The licensee shall cease to exercise his work after expiry of the license. The licensee shall settle all his obligations towards his employees, job applicants and employers dealing with him. The licensee or partners shall remain subject to the Ministry's authority and shall be liable to it for any irregularities or actions resulted rights for third parties.

Article (9)

Licensee may dispose of the license by assign his ownership to third parties provided that the assignee shall have the same conditions stipulated to the license applicant in accordance with the provisions of these controls in the same applicable procedures of granting initial approval and granting the license stipulated in these controls. In the event the Ministry of Labor agrees to transfer ownership, the

Deputy Minister for Customer Services and Labor Relations shall provide the assignee with a new license containing the remaining period of the original license.

Article (10)

Saudi employment agencies should operate according to the following procedures:

- Obtain accurate information from employers about vacancies, in particular, the name of profession or job title, place of work, remuneration, benefits, qualifications, experience and other conditions required and the period specified for employment.
- Receiving the applications of Saudi citizens wishing to work according to the form prepared for this, and receiving the copies of the documents submitted by them and recording them in a special register and giving the applicant a registration card that contain name of applicant and application number in the register and the fixed date for follow-up.
- Interviewing job applicants for employment in jobs that suit their abilities, qualifications, experience and specialties and provide advice and guidance for those who require training or retraining for suitable jobs.

Article (11)

Without prejudice to the statutory rights of the employer arising from the contract of employment, the licensee shall be responsible for the Saudi employee for whom he mediated in his employment during the probation period specified in the employment contract. The limits of that liability are the refund of the fees paid by the employer during the agreed probation period in the following cases:

- Employees' refusal to work or leave the work for reasons not attributable to the employer.

- Non-compliance of employee to carry out his duties in accordance with the employment contract concluded with him.

Article (12)

The employee whose employment is mediated by the licensee shall be deemed an employee of the employer; consequently, a direct contractual relationship exists between the employer and the Saudi employee so that the employer is responsible for paying all the financial rights of the employee arising from that relationship.

Article (13)

The Ministry of Labor is competent to apply the provisions of these controls, supervise and monitor execution of the provisions. The Ministry of Labor shall issue resolutions and controls that it thinks necessary to improve the performance of the licensee.

Article (14)

The licensee shall comply with the following:

- Practice activity in a separate place according to the spatial terms established by the Ministry of Labor.
- All works at office or company of employment of Saudis shall be limited to Saudis only except cleaning and hospitality services.
- The licensee shall write his name and license number in all of its printing materials and stamps.
- He shall use the Saudi Vocational Description and Rating Guide in his works.
- He shall obtain his fees for provision of his services from the employer. No financial amounts shall be taken from job applicant for mediation in recruiting him.

Article (15)

The Ministry of Labor may oblige the licensee to be electronically connected with the Ministry and the relevant authorities.

Article (16)
The licensee shall refrain from the following:

- Mediation in hiring non-Saudis whether from inside the Kingdom or from abroad.
- Opening a branch in the same city or in other cities without the Ministry of Labor's approval.
- Perform any practice that constitute trafficking in persons or assistance in such act according to the Anti-Trafficking in persons Act and the international treaties approved by the Kingdom of Saudi Arabia.
- Carry on any practice that constitutes infringement against employees or help in such action.
- Refrain from medication in hiring children and juveniles contradicting the Labor Law including the cases in which the licensee knows that the age of said child in the document presented to prove its legibility to work is different from the real age of child.
- Dealing with any employer practices any work that constitutes, contributes, and facilitates trafficking in persons, infringement against employees or hiring children.
- Perform any works help in false employment with employers.

Article (17)
The Ministry of Labor may stop the services provided to the licensee and relevant authorities or withdraw any amount of money from the bank guarantee to pay his liabilities or both after giving him a grace period of fifteen days from the date of notification to fulfil these liabilities if the following cases are proved correct:

- Licensee's inability and refrain from paying Saudi and non-Saudi employees' entitlement or pay the expenses of their return back home and resulting fines and penalties.

- Licensee's inability or refrain to payback the amounts he obtained from employers for performance of his licensed activity which he did not do.
- In implementation of a final judicial ruling or decision issued against the licensee.
- Penalties imposed by the Ministry of Labor on the licensee in accordance with the Labor Law.
- Any other amount that the Ministry of Labor thinks it could be taken from the bank guarantee arising from applying the provisions of these controls.

The licensee must complete the bank guarantee at the volume reduced from it during one month from the date on which he is notified of withdrawal.

Article (18)

The Ministry may cancel the license in the following cases:

- If it is proved that the licensee did not start the activity within maximum period of six months from the date he received the license unless the stopping is due to a reason acceptable to the Ministry of Labor.
- If the licensee lost one necessary condition or more conditions.
- If the documents submitted the licensee, on which he was granted the license are proved to have been forged.
- If the data provided by the licensee proved to be incorrect.
- If it is proven that, the licensee is mediating in the employment of non-Saudis or assisting them in doing so.
- If the licensee does not complete the bank guarantee insofar as the withdrawal has been made after the expiry of the specified time limit.

- If the licensee requests to revoke the license.

Article (19)

In the case of a decision to impose the penalty of the final closure of the licensee or revocation of the license in the manner specified in the previous article, he must liquidate his work within two months from the date of notifying him. He may not be granted a new license before the expiration of three years from the date of closure or cancellation.

Article (20)

The licensee may not, directly or indirectly, lease the license or give third parties the right to utilize it by any means whatsoever even if without financial consideration.

CHAPTER 9

ANNEX NO. 5—RULES FOR MANPOWER SUPPLY OFFICES

CONTROLS AND RULES **for the Practice of Recruitment Activity and Provision of Labor Services**

The following terms and expressions - wherever they appear in these controls - shall mean the meanings given to them unless the context otherwise requires:

Ministry: Ministry of Labor.

Minister: Minister of Labor.

Labor Law: the Labor Law issued by Royal Decree No (51/م) dated 23/08/1426H amended by Royal Decree No (24/م) dated 12/5/1434H amended by Royal Decree No (46/م) on 05/06/1436H and amendments thereto.

Controls: Controls and rules for the practice of recruitment and provision of labor service.

Licensee: Recruitment company or recruitment office after obtaining a license from the Ministry to provide the activities provided for in these controls.

Expatriate employee: Non-Saudi employee who works in public sector or private sector.

House labor: laborers of house service and the alike.

Mediation in recruitment: male and female expatriate

employees recruitment service for the benefit of employers in the Kingdom of Saudi Arabia.

Labor service provision: The licensee to recruit employees affiliated to him in order to perform work in certain professions at his clients' premises within a specified period in return for the benefit of the licensee. This does not include any contract between the Licensee and the Customer for the performance of specific works.

Employer: Any natural or legal person contracting with the licensee to mediate the recruitment of one or more employees to employ them for a certain period for consideration.

Client: Any natural or legal person contracting with the licensee to provide labor services for a certain period for financial consideration from the licensee.

Company: Recruitment Company licensed to practice activity of mediation in recruitment and provide labor services in accordance with the provisions of these controls.

Office: Recruitment office licensed to practice activity of mediation in recruitment or any other associated activity permitted by the Ministry.

Applicant: The person who submits to the Ministry a request for preliminary approval or a license to establish a recruitment company or a recruitment office in accordance with the provisions of these regulations.

Initial Approval: An approval given by the Ministry of Labor to the applicant authorizing him to start establishing a recruitment company or recruitment office in accordance with the provisions of these controls and relevant laws.

License: A license granted by the Ministry of Labor to the applicant after he meets the terms and requirements set forth in these controls and relevant laws authorizing him to practice the activities licensed to him in accordance with these controls.

Month: Thirty days in the provisions of these controls.

Article (2)

It is not permissible to practice any of the activities mentioned in these regulations except through companies or offices established for this purpose after obtaining a license from the Ministry in accordance with the conditions and procedures contained in these regulations. In case of violation, the Ministry of Labor is entitled to apply the penalties stipulated in the two schedules of the violations and corresponding penalties Minister of Labor No. (4786) and dated 28/12 / 1436H.

Article (3)

The recruitment company practices is business by a license for any of the following activities:

- The activity of mediation in the recruitment of labor in addition to the provision of public labor services and domestic employment (men and women).
- The activity of mediation in the recruitment of labor in addition to the provision of house labor services only (men and women).

Article (4)

By a decision of the Minister, in accordance with conditions and procedures established by the Ministry, all or some of the recruitment companies may be empowered to mediate in the transfer of labor services.

Article (5)

To obtain the license of the recruitment company to practice any of the two activities stipulated in these regulations, the following shall be required:

- To be a closed joint stock company consisting of at least five Saudi partners.
- A natural partner may should not have ever been convicted of a crime involves honor or trust or any of the offenses related to the provisions of the Convention on

the Protection of Children or the Combating Trafficking in Persons unless he has been rehabilitated.

- The natural partner should not have ever obtained a license of an office of recruitment, he was a partner in a company to carry out any of the activities contained in these controls, he was a partner in a partner company - in its legal capacity - in a recruitment company, and such license was canceled by judicial award or decision as a sanction based on these controls or any Another system within five years of the penalty.
- The company's capital shall be fully owned by Saudi persons. In the event of the participation of a legal person in the company, its capital shall be wholly owned by natural persons of Saudi nationality and the legal person shall have achieved a minimum of Saudization.
- The paid company's capital shall not be less than:

a. One hundred million Saudi riyals in the event of license to practice the activity of mediation in recruitment of labor in addition to provision of public labor services and house labor (men and women).

b. Twenty million Saudi riyals in case of license to practice activity of mediation in recruitment of labor in addition to provision of house labor services only (men and women).

Article (6)

Initial approval shall be obtained from the Ministry of Labor to establish a recruitment company in accordance with the following procedures and controls:

First: The applicant or his representative shall apply for the preliminary approval, including a list of the names and national identification numbers of each applicant for the establishment of the company and the percentage of their ownership therein. This list shall not be changed except with the approval of the Ministry of Labor. The list will be accompanied by the following documents:

- Draft Company Articles of Association.
- A feasibility study for the company prepared by a licensed consultant office that includes the number of branches of the company to be opened in less than two branches in each administrative region of the Kingdom according to the conditions and specifications set by the Ministry of Labor.
- The company's first five-year business plan.
- The company's plan for housing the workers that are brought to provide their labor services in each administrative area.
- Plan of the recruitment, rehabilitation and training of Saudis to work in the company.
- Provide an irrevocable bank guarantee from a local bank in the name of the applicant as one of the partners with the equivalent of (2%) of the company's capital according to the Form approved by the Ministry of Labor, valid for a period determined by the Ministry of Labor and renewable automatically.

Second: After studying the application, the Ministry of Labor may take one of the following decisions:

- Grant initial approval. A stamped document shall be issued which authorizes him to immediately establish the recruitment company. The Ministry of Labor shall retain the initial guarantee provided by him until he applies for the license and submit a final bank guarantee from the company.
- To request the applicant to complete any documents or documents or to request his presence or the presence of his representative to the Ministry to answer any inquiry or to clarify any matter related to the request for approval within a maximum of thirty working days from the date

of notification thereof. Otherwise, it may reject the application.

- The Ministry may reject the application that the decision in this case shall be the reason. The applicant may get back the initial bank guarantee that he submitted. The applicant may not submit new application before one year from the date of notifying him of the refusal decision.

Article (7)

The company shall appoint a manger after approval from the Ministry of Labor. He shall have the following conditions:

- He shall be a Saudi citizen.
- He should not have ever been convicted of crime of honor, trust, any violations related to the provisions organizing the protection of children or anti-trafficking of persons unless his honor has been restored.

Article (8)

To obtain a recruitment company license, the following procedures shall be taken:

First: a company's representative shall submit a request to the Ministry to obtain the license to which the following documents are attached:

- A copy of the company's articles of association (+ origin for matching)
- A copy of the company's commercial registration (+ original CR for matching)
- A copy of title deed or leas contract of company's head office (+ original for matching)
- Title deed or lease contract of employees' housing + original documents for matching or a written undertaking

from the company's representative to secure housing for employees recruited to the company. This should be done during one month from the date of obtaining the visas of employees' recruitment.

- A chronic plan for the opening of the branches of the company and their places mentioned in the economic feasibility study submitted in accordance with the provisions of paragraph (First/2) of Article (6) of these controls.
- A written commitment of the company's compliance with the conditions and specifications set by the Ministry of Labor for the branches of the company, employees' housing and adherence to the necessary legal controls, including the availability of security and safety conditions.
- A written undertaking from the company that it would execute the Saudis employment plan presented in accordance with paragraph (First/5) of Article (6) within hundred and twenty business days from the date of obtaining the license.
- A final irrevocable bank guarantee issued by a local bank for the company equal to (10%) of the company's capital in accordance with the Form approved by the Ministry of Labor.

Second: The Ministry of Labor shall study the request of obtaining the license and it may take any of the following procedures:

- Preview the company's headquarters and see the equipment and procedures taken to start the activity.
- Requesting the completion of the missing documents or information or providing them with any additional information deemed necessary for the decision of the

application within a period not exceeding thirty days from the date of notification.
- Conduct any survey related to the license application or the company.
- Ensure that the company has obtained the license and necessary approvals from relevant authorities.

Third: After studying the license application, the Ministry of Labor may take one of the following decisions:

- Grant initial approval. A document thereof shall be issued signed by the Minister or his representative and stamped with the seal of the Ministry of Labor. Such document authorizes the company to start practicing the licensed activity.
- Rejection of the license request as the decision would the reason. In this case, the initial approval decision shall be deemed void. The applicant shall get back the presented bank guarantee. He may not submit a new request before one year from the date of notification of the rejection decision.

Fourth: the Ministry of Labor shall consider the request within thirty working days from the date of completion and notify the applicant of license thereof.

Article (9)

The company shall practice its licensed activity during maximum twelve days from the date of obtaining the license provide the following procedures shall be taken:

- Creation of an interactive website in accordance with the regulations set by the Ministry within a maximum period of one hundred and twenty days from the date of issuance of the license.

- Automatic linking with the Ministry and relevant authorities within a maximum of one hundred and twenty days from the date of issuance of the license through the adoption of an electronic system, mechanism and a database containing the electronic records requested by the Ministry.
- Allocation or establishment of a communication center and channels to receive complaints from employees, employers or customers according to the criteria determined by the Ministry.
- Opening branches in accordance with the chronic plan in paragraph (First/5) of Article (8) of these controls.
- Secure housing for employees in accordance with the plan in paragraph (Fist/4) of Article (6) of these controls during one month form the date of obtaining employees' recruitment visas taking into account the suitability of the absorptive capacity of the housing with the number of employees of each sex, provided that the percentage of the absorptive capacity shall not be less than (10%) of the number of visas granted to the company in accordance with the regulations adopted by the Ministry of Labor.

Article (10)

The license period for the recruitment company shall be ten Hijri years renewable in accordance with the following procedures:

First: the company shall submit to the Ministry of Labor the license renewal request hundred and eighty days prior to expiry of period to which the following document are attached:

- A report on the company's business within the previous period.
- Company's business plan for the renewal period.
- Renewal of bank guarantee to include the period of renewal.

- Any other document required by the Ministry of Labor.

Second: After studying the license application and review the assessments and violations detected on the company, the Ministry of Labor may take one of the following decisions:

- Approval of license renewal request. The company shall be provided with a document of the new period signed by the Minister or his representative and stamped by the seal of the Ministry of Labor.
- Reject the license renewal request provided the decision should be the reason. In this case the Ministry of Labor notifies relevant authorities thereof. The company should stop practicing its activity after expiration of the license, liquidate all its liabilities towards its employees, workers, clients and employer dealt with it. The partners shall remain subject to the Ministry's authority and liable for any violations that may appear or action resulting in rights for third parties. The Ministry shall maintain the bank guarantee for two years from the date of license expiration.

Article (11)

The company may request change of its license from the activity it exercises to another activity provided for in Article (3) of these controls, not contradicting with the provisions at any time during validity of license period. This shall be according to the following procedures:

First: the company shall submit to the Ministry a license amendment request to which the following are attached:

- Proposing the amendment that the company wishes to make, the reasons that led to the amendment and its impact on its work.

- The company undertakes to fulfill all the obligations arising from the license to be amended and to comply with all the licensing requirements stipulated in Article 5 of these controls. The undertaking shall include a declaration from the company representative that if the company is late in fulfilling these obligations, the Ministry is entitled to deduct the corresponding value of these liabilities from the bank guarantee without objection.
- A statement of how the company is dealing with the obligations and the rights resulting from such obligations under the proposed amendment.
- A statement of the workers brought by the company for the provision of labor services and the impact of this amendment on their rights.
- A statement of the visas obtained by the company and the required employees have not been recruited.
- A statement of the number of employees of the company and determining the impact of the amendment on its financial obligations towards them.
- A statement of necessary period to conduct the amendment.

Second: After studying the license application and review the assessments and violations detected on the company, the Ministry of Labor may take one of the following decisions:

- Initial approval of the license renewal request. A document stamped by the Ministry of Labor shall be issued thereof, authorizing the company to complete the procedures and the requirements provided for in Articles (8) and (9) of these controls. The company's capital and the bank guarantee shall be amended according to the amendment required to obtain the new activity license.

- Rejection of request provided that the rejection decision shall be the reason.

Article (12)

The company may request cancellation of the license at least hundred and eighty days prior to the date fixed for license cancelation in accordance with the following procedures:

First: the company shall submit to the Ministry a license cancelation request to which the following are attached:

- The company's undertaking of fulfilling all obligations arising from the license to be canceled. The undertaking shall include a declaration from the company's representative that in case the company is late in complying with these obligations, the Ministry is entitled to deduct the corresponding value of these obligations from the bank guarantee to fulfill it without objection.
- A statement of how the company deals with the obligations and the rights resulting under the cancelation.
- A statement of employees brought by the company to perform labor services and how far the cancelation affect their rights and how their status could be remedied.
- A statement of the contracts concluded by the company to mediate in the recruitment and visas obtained by the company and the recruitment of the required labor has not been provided.
- A statement of the number of company's employees and determine how far the cancelation affect its financial liabilities toward them.
- A statement of necessary period for cancelation and liquidation of the company.

Second: The company shall cease practicing its activity on the date it determined. The company shall conduct liquidation procedures and fulfil its obligations. The Ministry of Labor shall notify relevant authorities of the cancelation decision and oblige the company to take any precautions it thinks necessary to protect the rights of third parties. The partners shall remain subject to the Ministry's authority and responsible for violations that might occur or actions resulting in rights for third parties. The Ministry shall maintain the bank guarantee for two years from the date of license cancelation.

Article (13)

The company shall receive and lodge the employees that would be recruited until delivered to the employers in accordance with the procedures established by the Ministry of Labor by coordination with the relevant authorities.

Article (14)

The company, after the Ministry's approval, may reduce its capital to not less than the minimum provided for in these controls according to the type of its license in accordance with the provisions of these controls.

Article (15)

The recruitment office exercises its business under a license for one of the two following activities:

- Activity of medication in recruitment of public employees and house workers (men and women).
- Activity of medication in recruitment of house employees only (men and women).

Article (16)

By a Minister's resolution in accordance with terms and procedures established by the Ministry, all or some of the recruitment offices may be empowered to provide house workers services to third parties commensurate with the value of the bank guarantee provided by the Office.

Article (17)

By a Minister's resolution, the number of visas, which the office can mediate in its recruitment, may be determined. The office may increase these numbers to be more than the fixed number by raising the value of the bank guarantee according to the rates and controls established by the Ministry of Labor.

Article (18)

The office owner (applicant) shall be:

- Saudi national.
- His age shall not be less than twenty-five years old.
- He shall have a university degree or secondary school certificate plus practical service not less than three years. The periods to obtain any qualification after secondary school shall be calculated from the years of working service.
- He should not have received a valid license of another recruitment office.
- It shall not have been proven that he had practiced any activity of these controls without a license.
- He shall not have been convicted of a crime against honor, trust or any violation related to the provisions that organize protection of children or combating traffic in persons unless his honor has been restored.
- He should not have ever received a license independently, he was a partner in a company to practice any of the activities provided for in these controls or he was a partner in a company participating in its legal capacity in a recruitment company and such license had been canceled by a decision or judicial award as penalty based on these controls or any other law, during five years of enforcement of penalty.

Article (19)

The owner of the recruitment office must manage his office by himself. He may appoint a deputy who has the terms provided for in the prior article.

Article (20)

An initial approval shall be obtained from the Ministry of Labor to establish a recruitment office in accordance with the following procedures:

First: A request shall be submitted to the Ministry to obtain an initial approval along with the office business plan during the period of license.

Second: After studying the application, the Ministry of Labor may take one of the following resolutions:

- Grant initial approval. A document thereof shall be issued signed by the Ministry of Labor authorizing him to start establishing the recruitment office.
- Request attendance of applicant or his representative to the Ministry of Labor to answer any inquiry or to explain any issue related to the approval request during maximum period of thirty working days from the date of notification, otherwise the request would be rejected.
- Rejection of request provided the decision is the reason in this case. The applicant shall retrieve the initial bank guarantee and he many not submit new request before one year from the date of notification of the rejection resolution.

Third: the Ministry of Labor shall decide the request within thirty working days from the date of completion and notify the applicant thereof.

Article (21)

The person who receives initial approval shall submit the final bank guarantee during maximum period of thirty days from the date of receiving the initial approval.

Article (22)

To obtain a recruitment office license the following procedures shall be taken:

First: the office owner shall submit to the Ministry a request to obtain the license along with the following documents:

- A copy of the office commercial registration (+ original CR for matching)
- A copy of a title deed or a lease contract of the office premises (original deed for matching)
- A written undertaking of the office's compliance with the terms and conditions established by the Ministry.
- Provision of an irrevocable bank guarantee from a local bank in accordance with the Form adopted by the Ministry of Labor where its value shall be as follows:

A bank guarantee its value not less than SR 750,000 if the activity to be licensed is mediation in recruitment of general labor and house labor (mend and women).

A bank guarantee its value is not less than SR 450,000 if the activity to be licensed is mediation in recruitment of house labor only (men and women)

Second: the Ministry shall study the license request and it may take any of the following procedures:

- Preview the office premises and see equipment and procedures taken to start the activity.
- Requesting the completion of missing documents or information or providing them with any additional information deemed necessary for the decision of the application within a period not exceeding thirty working days from the date of notification.
- Conduct any survey related to the license application or office.

- Ensure that the office owner obtains the necessary approvals and approvals from the relevant authorities؛

Third: After studying the application, the Ministry of Labor may take one of the following resolutions:

- Grant the license. A document stamped by the Ministry shall be issued signed by the minister or his representative authorizing the office to start practicing the licensed activity.
- Rejection of license request provided the decision is the reason. In this case the initial approval resolution shall be deemed void. The applicant shall retrieve the bank guarantee and he may not submit a new request before one year from the date of notification of the rejection decision.

Fourth: the Ministry shall decide the request within thirty working days from the date of completion and notify the applicant thereof.

Article (23)

The office shall exercise its activity within maximum six months from the date of obtaining the license. The following procedures shall be taken:

- Electronic link with the Ministry of Labor and relevant authorities within maximum sixty days from the date of issue of license by adopting a system, electronic mechanism and data base that include electronic records required by the Ministry of Labor.
- Registration on the Ministry's electronic portal designed

for recruitment offices and compliance with all the terms and procedures of the electronic portal.

- Designate or create communication center and channels to receive the complaints of employees, employers or clients according to the criteria determined by the Ministry of Labor.

Article (24)

The value of bank guarantee may be increased by the Minister's resolution according to the type of license issued to the office, number of visas to be recruited and any other powers may be granted to the office by the Ministry of Labor.

Article (25)

The period of license for a recruitment office shall be two Hijri years, renewable for similar period/ periods based on the criteria as determined by the Ministry of Labor.

Article (26)

The license of the recruitment office shall be renewed in accordance with the following procedures:

First: the office owner shall submit a request of license renewal to the Ministry of Labor ninety days before expiry of the license period along with the following documents:

- Report on office business during the previous period.
- Renewal of the bank guarantee to include the require renewal period.
- Any other document required by the Ministry of Labor.

Second: After studying the license application and review the assessments and violations detected on the office, the Ministry of Labor may take one of the following decisions:

- Approval of the license renewal request. The office will be provided with a document of the new period signed by the Minister or by his representative and stamped by the Ministry seal.

- Rejection of the request of license renewal provide the decision is the reason. In this case, the Ministry shall notify the relevant authorities thereof. The office shall cease to practice its activity when the license expires. The office shall liquidate its all liabilities towards its employees, employers and clients dealing with it. The office owner shall be subject to the Ministry's authority and responsible for the violations that may occur or actions resulting in rights to third parties. The Ministry of Labor shall keep the bank guarantee for two years from the date of expiry of the license.

Article (27)

The office owner may request cancelation of the license. This shall be done before ninety days from the proposed date for license cancelation according to the following procedures:

First: the office owner shall submit to the Ministry a request of license cancelation along with the following:

- Undertaking from the office owner to fulfill all the obligations arising from the license to be canceled. The undertaking shall include his declaration that in case of delay of fulfilling the obligations the Ministry of Labor shall deduct the corresponding value of these obligations from the bank guarantee to cover it without objection made by him.
- A statement of dealing with the liabilities and rights resulting under the cancelation.
- A statement of the contracts concluded by the office in mediate in recruitment and visas it obtains and the employees have not been recruited.

- A statement of the workers brought by the office for the provision of labor services and the impact of this cancelation on their rights and how their status could be remedied.
- A statement of the number of its employees and determination of how far the cancelation affect its financial liabilities towards them.

Second: the office shall stop practicing its activity on the date it determined for cancelation. The office shall liquidate its liabilities towards its employees, employers and the client dealing with it. The Ministry of Labor shall notify relevant authorities of the cancelation resolution. The office owner shall remain subject to the Ministry authority and liable for the violations that occur or actions resulting in rights to third parties. The Ministry shall maintain the bank guarantee for two years from the date of license cancelation.

Article (28)

The recruitment office may make agreement with any authority to receive and housing the employees until delivered to employers in accordance with the procedures established by the Ministry of Labor by coordinating with relevant authorities. The Ministry shall oblige the office to receive and accommodate the employees.

Article (29)

Exercise of mediation activity in the recruitment of employees would be by concluding one of the following contracts by the licensee with the employer, as the case may be:

- A contract called "Contract of mediation in the recruitment of employees".
- A contract called "Contract of mediation in the recruitment of house laborers"

As per the Form designed by the Ministry of Labor in which the parties' obligations and rights, the required number of employees, their professions, qualifications, experience, wages, employee's probation period, required time for recruitment, delay penalties and any other requirement agreed by the parties shall be identified.

Article (30)

The licensee shall be responsible for the employee of whom he mediated in recruiting for a period not less than ninety days starting from the date of delivering him to the employer, in the following cases:

- An employee's refrain from work for reasons that do not belong to the employer.
- Absence from work.
- Non-compliance of employee with performing his tasks in accordance with the employment contract concluded with him.
- Lack of experience.
- Employee's disease that does not enable him to perform his work.
- Validity of the medical and security checks carried out on the employee was proven incorrect.

Article (31)

Limit of licensee's responsibility for the employee shall be pursuant to one of the following options:

- Return the cost of recruitment to the employer from which the equivalent of the period spent by the employee in the work shall be deducted according to the following equation:
- (The total cost of recruitment ÷ the period of employee's employment contract by months) x the remaining period of the employee's employment contract in months.
- Secure an alternative employee for the employer - after his written approval - from within the Kingdom of

> Saudi Arabia, of the same nationality so that the employer bears the value of the monthly wage specified in the employment contract of the employee. The licensee shall bear the difference between this value and the actual cost of the alternative employee for the remaining period of the recruited employee's employment contract.

The licensee shall bear the costs of the employee's return to his country in the two previous cases unless the Ministry issues controls and procedures that organize utilization of recruited employee with another employer.

Article (32)

If the employees, whose recruitment is mediated by the licensee, increase the percentage of absenteeism and refusal to work, the Ministry may stop the service of concluding contracts of mediation and any other service for a period not exceeding six months in the first time during 24 successive months. In case of repletion the period of stopping shall double so that the employees calculated within the percentage in the first time shall not enter one again when repeated.

Article (33)

A licensee shall exercise provision of labor services in accordance with the following procedures:

- Apply to the Ministry for visas to bring in labor to provide labor services.
- Selection of male and female workers, taking into account the availability of professional, scientific or practical expertise compatible with the professions they have been recruited for.
- Conclude employment contract with the employee stating that:

a. Licensee's right to provide employee's services to his clients in any region in the Kingdom of Saudi Arabia without employee's objection.

b. Licensee's right to deduct fines and deductions from employee's salary in accordance with the Labor Law and regulations.

c. Employee's compliance with the regulations and rules organizing the work with licensee's clients, concerning determination of methods, times of work, periods of vacations and other provisions provided for in the Labor Law and regulations.

d. Employee's compliance with not to perform any work, which is not required by his profession with the licensee's clients whether directly or indirectly.

Under this contract, a direct contractual relationship is established between the licensee and the employee so that the licensee is responsible for paying all the employee's rights arising from such relationship.

Licensee shall, as the case may be, conclude with the client one of the following two contracts:

a. A contract called "Labor Services Provision Contract"

b. A contract called "House Labor Services Provision Contract"

As per the Form designed by the Ministry of Labor. The contract shall include as follows:

a. Number of employees, employees' positions, qualifications and experience of work, which they have been required for.

b. Client's right to request licensee to replace the employees whose services are provided with other employees having the same qualifications and necessary experience to perform the work to which they have been requested.

c. Contract period to provide the services.

d. The remuneration received by the licensee for the provision of labor services.

Article (34)

The Licensee, in any case, may not employ employees of a particular category or profession for the employment of another category or profession without the approval of the Ministry.

Article (35)

Employees who provide services to a licensee's client of legal persons are included in the employment on which Saudization rates are calculated unless the Ministry of Labor sets certain conditions for calculating such employment in the Saudization ratio.

Article (36)

The licensee shall comply with the Saudization requirements at its customers issued by the Ministry of Labor from time to time and shall refrain from offering his employees to the customer whenever the employees offered to him will violate the Saudization rate that should be complied with.

Before the arrival of the applicant to the Kingdom of Saudi Arabia, the licensee must verify the following procedures:

- Train the employee on the required work, advise him of his obligations, rights and everything related to the nature of customs, traditions, living conditions and regulations in force in the Kingdom of Saudi Arabia.
- Conduct a comprehensive medical examination of the employee to ensure that he is healthy according to the established standards and does not suffer from any chronic or contagious illness and he is free from physical disabilities and other diseases that would prevent him from working or harming the employer or his dependents.
- Security check on an employee shall be conducted by the competent official authorities in the employee's country to ensure he is free from any criminal precedents.

Article (38)

A licensee shall comply with the following:

- Provisions of these controls, the provisions of the Labor Law, its Executive Regulations, the Cooperative Health Insurance Law and other related regulations.

- Registration of all employees at the General Organization for Social Insurance.
- Standard contract forms developed and approved by the Ministry of Labor.
- Saudization rate according to percentages determined by the Ministry of Labor.
- Practice the activity in an independent place without exercising any other activity in this place for the duration of the license.

Article (39)

A license shall refrain from and shall not:

- Conduct any of the practices that constitute traffic in persons or otherwise assist third parties, in accordance with the Anti-Traffic in Persons Law and International Agreements ratified by the Kingdom of Saudi Arabia.
- Conduct any of the practices that constitute an encroachment on employees or assist third parties in doing so.
- Mediation in recruiting children and juveniles to work including the circumstances in which the licensee knows that the age of the child mentioned in the documents submitted to him to prove his eligibility to work is contrary to the fact of his age.
- Dealing in mediation to bring workers from unauthorized parties to practice any of the activities stipulated in these controls or dealing with entities with which dealing is stopped or prohibited, whether inside or outside the Kingdom of Saudi Arabia.
- Dealing with mediation agencies to hire employees abroad that practice any of the acts that constitute, contribute or facilitate traffic in persons, juveniles or child labor, in accordance with the standards set forth in

the regulations in the kingdom of Saudi Arabia and the applicable international legislation. In addition, the entities that practice any of the acts criminalized in accordance with the national laws.

- Dealing with any employer that practices any of the acts that constitute, contribute or facilitate traffic in persons, abuse of workers or child labor.

Article (40)

Licensee shall take into account the appropriateness of the amounts he collects in return for mediation in the recruitment, provision of labor services or the transfer of services in accordance with the activities licensed to him and the costs incurred therein. The Ministry of Labor, where appropriate, may determine the value of such amounts.

Article (41)

Licensee may not obtain any amounts from employee for mediation in the recruitment of the employee or for provision of labor services.

Article (42)

The Ministry of Labor is competent to apply the provisions of these controls, supervise and monitor such implementation. The Ministry of Labor shall issue necessary resolutions to improve and organize the recruitment market and licensee's performance.

Article (43)

The Minister may, at the time of the licensee's activity, increase the value of the bank guarantee by a percentage not exceeding (50%) of the value of the security in force whenever the need arises.

Article (44)

The Ministry of Labor May stop the services provided to the licensee by the Ministry and relevant authorities or withdraw any amounts from the bank guarantee to pay his liabilities or both of them. The Ministry of Labor may do the forgoing after giving the licensee a grace period of fifteen days from the date on which he was notified to pay such liabilities if any of the following conditions are true:

- Licensee's failure or inability to pay the entitlement of his employees, or pay the expenses of their return home and the resulting fines or penalties.
- Licensee's failure or inability to comply with his contractual obligations with the employer or its clients and refuses to pay back the amounts he received from the clients or pay the indemnity provided for in the contract.
- In implementation of a decision or a final judicial judgment issued against the licensee.
- The penalties imposed by the Ministry on the Licensee in accordance with the Labor Law.
- Any other amount that the Ministry considers to be paid from the bank guarantee is the result of the application of the provisions of these regulations.
- Licensee's commission of any statutory violation.

Article (45)

In case of withdrawal from the bank guarantee, the licensee shall complete the bank guarantee to the extent of what has been withdrawn from it within one month from the date of notification of withdrawal. Otherwise, the Ministry may suspend the services provided to the licensee and the services provided by the relevant authorities.

Article (46)

If the number of complaints against the Licensee exceeds the percentage determined by the Ministry or exceeds 50% of the value of the bank guarantee provided by the licensee, the Ministry of Labor may suspend the services provided to him and the services provided by the relevant authorities and refrain from renewing the license at the end of its term.

Article (47)

Licensee may dispose of the license by transfer the ownership to third parties provided that the assignee should have the same conditions prescribed by the licensee in accordance with the provisions of these controls with the same procedures followed to grant initial approval and grant the license provided for in these controls. If the Ministry approves the transfer of ownership, the assignee shall be given a new license for the remaining period of the original license signed by the Minister of Labor or his authorized representative and stamped with the Ministry's stamp.

Article (48)

Licensee, directly or indirectly, shall not license third party to engage in the activity or grant the third parties the right to use the license by any means, even if it is free of charge.

Article (49)

Labor inspectors shall be responsible for controlling the violations of these controls. All premises of the licensee and the places designated for housing the employees shall be subject to the provisions of the labor inspection procedures contained in the Labor Law.

Article (50)

The Labor Office shall study complaints concerning the exercise of the activities stipulated in these regulations and shall, for that purpose, take any of the following measures:

- Amicable settlement between the parties and offer of reconciliation.
- To inform the parties to resort to the competent judicial authority in accordance with the specific procedural dates of each authority in case of failure to reach an amicable settlement so that the jurisdiction shall be according to the following:
- a. With respect to the claims to which the licensee and employer or the client are parities, the competent court shall have jurisdiction.
- b. With respect to the claims to which the licensee and his employees are parties therein, labor dispute

settlement commissions or the labor courts shall be competent in the event they commence their work.

- Refer the violations of the provisions of these controls to the labor inspectors to control them and take the applicable procedures to impose the penalties stipulated in the two schedules of violations and corresponding penalties issued by the Minister of Labor Decree No. (4786) of 28/12/1436 e and the amendments thereto.
- Recommending the suspension of the services of the Licensee or withdrawing from the bank guarantee in accordance with Article 44 of these Controls.

Article (51)

The competent department of the ministry shall constitute one or more committees consisting of three members, including a legal advisor. The Committee's terms of reference shall be to decide on all or some of the following applications:

- Initial approvals to obtain the license.
- Grant a license.
- Renewal of license.
- Modify the license from an activity to another activity provided for in these controls.
- Cancellation of license.
- Transfer of license ownership.
- Stop the services provided by the Ministry and the relevant authorities to the Licensee.
- Withdrawal from the bank guarantee provided by the licensee
- Any other functions assigned to the Committee by the Ministry of Labor.

The Minister of Labor or his representative shall approve its resolutions.

Article (52)

These controls override all decisions and provisions that conflict with them. Currently existing companies and offices licensed to exercise any of the activities set forth in these controls at the time of issue shall adjust their status in accordance with the provisions of these controls within six months from the date of implementation. A decision of the Minister may extend this grace period for another period.

CHAPTER 10

ANNEX NO. 7 MODEL EMPLOYMENT CONTRACT

NOTE: *employment contracts have moved on-line, onto the Qiwa platform. Here is an example of such a Qiwa-generated contract.*

[MODEL]EMPLOYMENT CONTRACT

Contract ID: [Generated by the Qiwa platform] This contract was created electronically under the supervision of the Ministry of Human Resources and Social Development, Kingdom of Saudi Arabia on 02-08-1445 (12-02-2024), between:

FIRST PARTY:

Company/Corporation:
National Unified Number: [•]
Establishment Number: [•]
Commercial Registration: [•]
Address: [•]
Work Location: Tabuk
Email Address: [•]
Represented by: [•] as [•] hereinafter referred to as (First Party),

. . .

SECOND PARTY:

Name:
Profession: Lawyer
Employee Number: [•]
Nationality: [•]
Date of Birth: [•]
Identity Number: [•] or passport number
ID Type: National ID/passport
ID Expiry Date: [•]
Gender: [•]
Religion: Muslim, [Xtian for Christian]
Marital Status: [•]
Education: [•]
Speciality: Law
IBAN: [•] for receiving salary payments
Bank Name: Al Rajhi Bank
Email Address: [•]
Mobile Number: +966 [•] Saudi mobile number
hereinafter referred to as the (Second Party),

The two parties have agreed that the second party will work for the first party under its management and supervision with the job of Lawyer and carry out the work assigned to him/her in proportion to his/her practical, scientific and technical capabilities in accordance with the needs of the work and in a manner that does not conflict with the controls stipulated in Articles (58, 59, 60) of the Saudi Labor Law.

Term

The term of this contract starts from [•], noted that the date of commencement (joining date) of the second party's work is [•].

The second party is subject to a trial period of 90 days starting from the date of commencing work, during which Eid al-Fitr and Eid al-Adha holidays and sick leave are not included in the calculation. Both parties have the right to terminate the contract during this period, unless the contract specifies the right of one party to terminate.

Working Days and Hours Normal working days are set as 5 days per week and working hours are set as 8 daily hours. The first party is obliged to pay the second party an additional wage for the overtime hours equal to the hourly wage plus 50

The obligations of the first party The first party pays the second party a basic fee of [•] Saudi Riyals, which is due at the end of each month

The second party deserves for each year a paid annual leave of 21 days, and the first party determines its dates during the year of entitlement according to work conditions, provided that the leave wage is paid in advance when it is due, and the first party has to postpone the leave after the end of the year of entitlement for a period not exceeding 90 days, and with the consent of the party Second, in writing, to postpone it to the end of the year following the year of entitlement, according to the requirements of work conditions.

Medical:

The first party is obligated to provide medical care to the second party with health insurance in accordance with the provisions of the Cooperative Health Insurance Policy.

The first party is obligated to pay the contributions of the General Organization for Social Insurance according to its regulations.

The obligations of the second party:

- To perform the work entrusted to him in accordance with the principles of the profession and according to the instructions of the first party if there is nothing in these instructions that contradicts the contract, order or public morals and there is nothing in their implementation that puts him at risk.

- To take adequate care of the tools and tasks assigned to him and the raw materials owned by the first party placed at his disposal or in his custody and to return to the first party the non-expendable materials.
- To provide assistance and support without requiring additional pay in cases of dangers threatening the safety of the workplace or the persons employed in it.
- To undergo any medical examinations required by the first party before or during joining the work to verify that he/she is free from occupational or communicable diseases.

The second party is committed to good manners and work ethics while at work, and at all times abides by the rules, customs, norms and ethics in force at the Kingdom of Saudi Arabia, as well as the rules, regulations and instructions in force at the first party and bears all the financial penalties resulting from his violation of these regulations.

The first party hereby approves deductions of the prescribed percentage from the monthly wage for participation in the General Organization for Social Insurance.

Expiration or Termination of The Contract Either party is obligated upon termination of the contract to notify the other party in writing before the termination for a period of not less than 30 days

The first party has the right to terminate the contract of the second party without award, notice or compensation according to the cases mentioned in Article (80) of the Labor Law, provided that the second party is given the opportunity to express reasons for his opposition to the termination.

The second party has the right to leave work and terminate the contract without notifying the first party while retaining his right to obtain all his dues according to the cases mentioned in Article (81) of the Labor Law.

End of Service Reward Upon termination of the contractual relationship by the first party, or with the agreement of the two parties, or with the end of the contract period, or as a result of force majeure, the second party is entitled to a reward of fifteen days' wages for each of the first five years and a months wage for each year of the following. The employee is entitled to a reward for the parts of the year in proportion to what she/he spent in work, and the remuneration is calculated on the basis of the last wage.

If the termination of the employment relationship due to the resignation of the second party, the employee is entitled to one-third of the reward in case of a service period no less than two consecutive years and not more than five years, and two-thirds of the reward if the service period exceeds five consecutive years and has not reached ten years, and a full reward if the service period exceeds ten years.

Applicable Law and Jurisdiction: This contract is subject to the labor regulations and its executive regulations and the decisions issued in its implementation in all cases where no provision is made in this contract. This contract replaces all previous verbal or written agreements and contracts if any.

In the event that a dispute arises between the two parties regarding this contract, the Jurisdiction shall be convened for the labor cases qualified authority in the Kingdom of Saudi Arabia.

Notices: Warnings and notifications between the two parties are made in writing through the electronic communication channels in the Qiwa platform for each of the parties.The address and email address registered in Qiwa platform will be considered legally applicable, and both parties are obligated to update them on Qiwa platform in the event of any change.

This model contract was exported electronically and is accessible to both parties via the Qiwa platform.

This contract is approved by the Ministry of Human Resources and Social Development.

CHAPTER 11

CIRCULAR REGARDING THE CONTROLS OF THE CONTRACTUAL RELATIONSHIP OF DOMESTIC WORKERS

FIRST: The controls for providing domestic labor services shall be approved according to the formula attached to this decision.

Second: Recruitment offices and companies licensed to provide labor services to domestic workers must document the contracts for the activity of providing labor services for domestic workers between them and their individual clients, in accordance with the[se] controls starting from 01/01/2020.

Article 1: Scope

This Circular applies to all domestic workers employed in private households throughout the Kingdom.

Article 2: Contractual Agreement

- A written contract must be concluded between the employer and the domestic worker prior to commencement of employment.

- The contract shall be in Arabic and include a copy provided to the worker.
- The contract shall specify at least the following:
  - Nature and duration of work
  - Working hours and rest periods
  - Monthly wage and method of payment
  - Rights and duties of both parties
  - Procedures for termination and notice period

Article 3: Working Hours and Rest

Domestic workers shall have daily working hours not exceeding 10 hours, with appropriate rest breaks, and shall be entitled to at least one day off per week.

Article 4: Wages and Payment

Employers shall pay wages promptly on the agreed date without unauthorized deductions. Wages must comply with the minimum standards set forth by the Ministry.

Article 5: Accommodation and Food

Employers must provide adequate accommodation, food, and medical care to domestic workers during the employment period.

Article 6: Leave Entitlements

Domestic workers shall be entitled to annual paid leave of at least 21 days, in addition to official public holidays.

Article 7: Termination of Contract

- Either party may terminate the contract by providing written notice in accordance with the agreed notice period.
- Termination without notice is permitted only for justifiable reasons, such as breach of contract or misconduct.

Article 8: Dispute Resolution

Any disputes arising from the contractual relationship shall be settled amicably between the parties or, if necessary, by referral to the competent labor authorities.

Article 9: Prohibited Practices

Employers shall not:

- Confiscate passports or identity documents of domestic workers.
- Impose penalties or fines beyond those stipulated in the contract or by law.
- Engage in any form of physical, verbal, or psychological abuse.

Article 10: Monitoring and Enforcement

The Ministry shall oversee compliance with this Circular through periodic inspections and investigations of complaints. Violations may result in penalties according to the Labor Law and other applicable regulations.

Final Provisions

This Circular shall be effective as of the date of issuance and shall be disseminated to all relevant parties.

Chapter Six: Supervision and Monitoring

Supervision (Article 51)

The Ministry shall undertake the following supervisory and enforcement responsibilities:

i. Conduct periodic and unannounced inspections.
ii. Verify compliance with licensing terms.
iii. Investigate complaints from any party.
iv. Impose administrative penalties.
v. Refer criminal violations to competent authorities.
vi. Publish names of violators.
vii. Maintain a central database.

Final Provisions

Amendment Authority

The Ministry may amend or repeal provisions of these Regulations.

Repeal of Conflicting Provisions

These Regulations supersede all prior rules inconsistent with their provisions.

Effective Date

These Regulations shall enter into force on the date of publication.

CHAPTER 12

THE GUIDANCE GUIDE TO THE RIGHTS AND OBLIGATIONS OF DOMESTIC WORKERS IN THE KINGDOM OF SAUDI ARABIA

[CITE THIS DOCUMENT AS: *The Guidance Guide to the Rights and Obligations of Domestic Workers in the Kingdom of Saudi Arabia*, Ministry of Human Resources and Social Development, issued on: 3 Shaban 1446 H (2 February 2025)

1. Introduction The domestic workers regulations and those in their position includes the consent based on knowledge and knowledge, and ensures that the domestic employer and the domestic worker are aware of the conditions of work, the nature of work, the place, and the wage, and during the daily and weekly daytime as follows Which has been activated by the regulation, and it is required that this be done by a worker and his departure from his home country. The Ministry of Human Resources Unit Domestic 14 The arrangement does not currently affect the scope of employment, and the Kingdom of Saudi Arabia has organized the Department of Domestic Workers between companies, offices and partners who work according to what it wants internationally .

Terms

Domestic Workers Every natural person - male or female - who performs domestic work or the like directly or indirectly for the domestic employer and any member of the staff under his supervision who performs domestic work or someone who takes his place. **Approved Platform**: An electronic platform used to detect the operations of those licensed such as "Musaned" and "Ajir Recruitment,"[and] any [other] platform chosen by the Ministry. **Sending offices**: Every office, company, or recruitment agency outside KSA that has obtained a license in it s country to employ simple support workers, and is approved on the electronic platform to provide services and employ various support workers, matching the specifications approved by the Ministry.

3. 3. What are the professions available for domestic use The professions available for domestic workers include the following:

i. Domestic worker
ii. Private driver
iii. Education
iv. Home nurse
v. Home cook
vi. Home planning
vii. Home travel
viii. Home life
ix. Home manager
x. Home guard
xi. Personal assistant
xii. Home farmer
xiii. Physical therapy specialist
xiv. Home coffee maker
xv. It is included by any other person within the household tasks

4. 4. Digital services for domestic workers Microsoft provides services dedicated to domestic use. These services include the approved list. 1. The platform provides comprehensive and integrated services related to recruiting workers 2. Electronic documentation between local recruitment offices and offices The sender, and electronic contracting between recruitment offices and workers, 3. The Kingdom also provided a service for domestic workers and marketing labor disputes electronically, you can find more digital services on the website of the Ministry of Human Resources and Humanitarian Affairs. 4. Amicable service for labor disputes (https://www.hrsd.gov.sa/ministry-services/services/269970) 5. Licensed human resources and recruitment companies and domestic labor recruitment offices It is necessary to prepare domestic workers on the list of human resources companies for workers and labor recruitment offices approved by the Ministry periodically.(https://www.musaned.com.sa/recruitment-offices).

6.Rights of domestic workers

According to the provisions of the domestic regulations and those like them, and the domestic worker:

- Not to be charged for his recruitment fees, profession change fees, service transfer fees, residence fees, work permit fees and renewal fees, and any resulting fines caused by the domestic employer
- Not to take any decision or change after him from the career path.
- The wage as originally stated in the unified contract signed by the employer and the worker.
- Not to expose him to reasons that cause him complete harm.
- One day a week, according to what the two parties need in the contract.

- The continuous cost shall not be less than eight hours.
- A one-month leave with full pay and you wish to take a two-year leave.
- He shall not be employed under the service more than once with the employer himself, unless he draws attention to the fact that the domestic worker works in a job different from his first job
- The value of the travel ticket to his original country at the employer's expense every time every six years in accordance with electronic transactions and regulatory laws for domestic workers
- Obtaining a final exit visa to leave the Kingdom upon the expiration of the contract period Money for some otherwise.
- End of service bonus Monthly wage, if you have been in the service of the employer for four consecutive years.
- Sick leave of 30 days per year comprehensively decided the necessity of proving the need for leave
- Repair of special documentary documents such as passports, ID, etc.

Obligations of the Domestic Worker

The domestic worker is obligated to the following:

- Perform the work himself according to and outside the supervision of the employer and members of the people, and in accordance with what is specified in the employment contract, and to exercise the necessary care in performing it.
- Preserving the employer's property, work tools, and everything in his custody or at his disposal, taking necessary care of them, and taking all necessary measures to preserve and ensure their safety.

- Not to assault verbally or commit any act of violence against members of society or members of society.
- To preserve the families of the employer and family members and people who are in the house that they see during work or because of it and not disclose it to others.
- Not to refuse work or serve papers without an acceptable excuse.
- Not to work for his own account or have rights or work in a profession other than the blogger
- Not to harm the dignity of the employer and family members and not to interfere in what concerns them.
- To respect the Islamic religion and adhere to the regulations in force in the Kingdom and the customs and traditions of Saudi society and public morals and not to engage in any activity that harms the family.

7. Obligations of the Domestic Employer

- The employer must conclude an employment contract with the worker in accordance with the form and mechanisms approved by the Ministry.
- The employer is committed to the obligations stated in the contract, in addition to:
  - Providing the requirements for performing the agreed upon work.
  - Providing a suitable place to live and providing suitable food, or a financial alternative to them.
  - Enabling the worker to communicate with his family.
  - Issuing and renewing residency and paying the fees due.
  - Completing the requirements for licenses or permits necessary to practice the profession and renewing it

and paying all related fees, and any fees or costs imposed by the Government.
  - The employer pays the full wage to the domestic worker as agreed upon in the employment contract.
  - To allow the domestic worker to enjoy continuous daily rest for a period of not less than eight hours per day.
  - Health care for the domestic worker in accordance with the regulations and instructions approved in the Kingdom.
  - Not to assault the domestic worker physically or verbally or commit any act that involves violence against the domestic worker.
  - Not to assign the domestic worker to work other than the agreed upon work.
  - Not to hire the domestic worker's service or allow him to work for his own account.
  - Not to assign the domestic worker to any dangerous work that threatens his health or physical safety or affects his human dignity.
  - Complete the procedures for shipping the body upon the death of the domestic worker.

8. Obligations of the Licensee

Human resources and recruitment companies and domestic labor recruitment offices must commit to the following:

- Inform the worker of the type and nature of the work and the amount of wages.
- Attach evidence of his fitness, health, psychological and professional condition.
- Conduct the necessary medical examinations for the

worker within a period not exceeding (30) days at most prior to his entry into the Kingdom.

- Educating and familiarizing the worker with the customs and traditions of Saudi society and public morals.
- Receiving and housing domestic workers whom he mediates in bringing in until they are handed over to the employers and providing them with food.
- Providing suitable housing and food for the domestic workers whom he mediates in bringing in in the event of absence or refusal to work for the employer
- Treating the worker well and not exposing him to violence.
- Educating the worker about the competent authorities to consider his complaint regarding any violation of his rights and freedoms.
- Not to receive sums from the domestic worker in exchange for bringing him in
- Concluding a contract between the recruitment company/office and the domestic employer through the mechanisms approved by the Ministry, so that the contract generally includes the terms and specifications specified by the employer in the domestic worker whom the office is tasked with bringing in.
- The licensee must provide an alternative domestic worker or return the costs of bringing him in to the employer in accordance with the contract concluded between them. If the licensee violates the stipulated terms and specifications, the employer has the right to refuse to employ the domestic worker and return him during the trial period.
- Recruitment companies and offices are prohibited from submitting an advertisement that includes a false offer, statement or claim or is formulated with phrases that may directly or indirectly mislead the client.

- Recruitment companies and offices are prohibited from submitting an advertisement that includes terms or phrases that may affect the dignity of domestic workers and do not respect the regulations related to human rights.

9.Settlement of Disputes and Complaints

In the event of any dispute between the domestic worker or the domestic employer, either of them has the option to file a complaint with the Ministry. The Ministry is responsible for settling the case between the two parties amicably within five working days, starting from the date of submitting the complaint to the Ministry. If an amicable settlement is not possible, the dispute shall be referred to the competent court.

10. Penalties for Domestic Workers

According to Article (Thirty) of the *Domestic Workers and Those in Their Care* regulations, a domestic worker who violates the provisions of the Regulations shall be punished as follows:

- 1. A fine not exceeding two thousand riyals, or by permanently preventing him from working in the Kingdom, or both.
- 2. Fines shall be multiplied by the number of violations proven against the domestic worker.
- 3. The violating domestic worker shall bear the costs of his return to his home country.

11. Penalties for the Domestic Employer

According to Article (Twenty-Nine) of the *Domestic Workers and Those in Their Care Regulations*, a domestic employer who violates the provisions of the Regulations shall be punished as follows:

- 1. A fine not exceeding twenty thousand riyals or preventing him from recruiting for a period not exceeding three years, or both.
- 2. Preventing the violator from recruiting permanently
- 3. The penalty imposed on the violator may be doubled in the event of a repeat violation
- 4. Fines shall be multiplied by the number of persons against whom the violation occurred.

12. List of violations of the regulations of the Kingdom of Saudi Arabia and the penalties resulting from them.

Penalties for Violations Related to Residency and Labor Laws

1. Penalty for an expatriate who works for his own account ("loose labor"):

- **First offense:** Fine of 10,000 riyals and deportation.
- **Second offense:** Fine of 25,000 riyals, imprisonment for one month, and deportation.
- **Third offense:** Fine of 50,000 riyals, imprisonment for six months, and deportation.

2. Penalty for a citizen or resident who transports, employs, shelters, or assists violators of residency or labor regulations (including helping them find jobs, housing, or transport):

- **First offense:** Fine of 15,000 riyals and deportation if the violator is an expatriate.

- **Second offense:** Fine of 30,000 riyals, imprisonment for three months, and deportation if the violator is an expatriate.
- **Third offense:** Fine of 100,000 riyals, imprisonment for six months, and deportation if the violator is an expatriate.

3. Penalty for a citizen or resident who enables his own workers to work for his own account, or to work for another party:

- **First offense:** Fine of 15,000 riyals, deprivation of recruitment for one year, and deportation if the violator is an expatriate.
- **Second offense:** Fine of 30,000 riyals, imprisonment for three months, deprivation of recruitment for two years, and deportation if the violator is an expatriate.
- **Third offense:** Fine of 100,000 riyals, imprisonment for six months, deprivation of recruitment for five years, and deportation if the violator is an expatriate.

13.Legal provisions regulating the recruitment and employment of Domestic Workers

The *Domestic Workers and Those in Their Care*regulations regulate work relations with domestic workers in the Kingdom, and determine the responsibilities of the parties to the relationship in a manner that guarantees their rights and obligations in a balanced manner. It also regulates the provision of a suitable work environment for them in accordance with the applicable international legislation and agreements in the Kingdom. Decisions related to the recruitment and employment of domestic workers:

- Rules for dealing with expatriates who violate the regulations (https://www.hrsd.gov.sa/knowledge-centre/decisions-and-regulations/regulation-and-procedures/813383)
- Rules for practicing the activity of recruitment and providing labor services (https://laws.boe.gov.sa/BoeLaws/Laws/LawDetails/a910b5ff-6770-4978-99f5-a9a700f2c140/1)
- Controls for improving the contractual relationship of domestic workers and those in their care https://www.hrsd.gov.sa/en/knowledge-centre/decisions-and-regulations/regulation-and-procedures/04042024

CHAPTER 13

DOMESTIC SERVANTS AND SIMILAR OCCUPATIONS REGULATIONS

COUNCIL OF MINISTERS RESOLUTION No. 310 dated 7/9/1434 H (7-July-2013). *Material in brackets is not part of the regulation.*

Article 1 {Definitions}

Unless the context requires otherwise, the following words are defined as follows::

Regulation: This Regulation.

Minister: The Minister of Labor.

Home: The place of residence of the family whether permanent or temporary.

Employer: A natural person who has contracted by himself, or through a licensed Recruitment Office directly or indirectly, for a domestic service worker to perform domestic service.

Family: The employer and the people who live with him in his house, and associated with them by a family relationship, or affinity, or who are under his responsibility for moral or regular reasons.

Domestic service: direct or indirect personal services performed for a fee by a domestic worker for the employer or any family member.

Domestic service worker: A natural person performing household services directly or indirectly for the employer, or for any of his family. During the performance of the service he is under the supervision and guidance of the employer or his representative. Domestic service workers include but are not limited to domestic workers, chauffeurs, gardeners and security guards. When used it in this Regulation, the term domestic service worker refers to both household and other domestic service workers.

Wage: The amount received by the domestic service worker at the end of the month for the work agreed upon in the contract.

Committee: The committee provided for in this Regulation, which adjudicates disputes arising under this Regulation.

Parties: the employer and the domestic service worker.

Article 2 {Primacy of Contract, No Secondments}

The employer should not assign the domestic service worker a task which is not contained the contract, or to work for others.

Article 3 {Written Contract}

- The working relationship between domestic worker and employer is based on a written contract, the Arabic version of which will prevail.
- The contract shall be produced in triplicate, with one copy going to each party and the third copy shall be deposited at the National Recruitment Office.

Article 4 {Contract Contents}

The contract should include — in addition to the other terms and conditions agreed upon by the two parties, and not inconsistent with the provisions of these Regulations— the following core elements:

- The type of work to be performed by the domestic service worker.
- The amount of the wage to be paid by the employer to the domestic service worker.
- The rights and obligations of the parties.
- The duration of the probationary period.
- The duration of the contract and provisions for extension.

Article 5 {Probationary Period}

- The parties cannot agree to a probationary period in excess of 90 days. During this period the employer has to check the quality of the domestic service worker's performance, attention to safe practices and personal conduct.
- The employer may terminate the contract without cause during the probationary period.
- Domestic service workers may not be placed on successive probationary periods by the same employer unless the domestic service worker is assigned a new position.

Article 6 {Duties of Domestic Worker}

The Domestic Service Worker is required to:

- Perform the work agreed upon, to a customary standard of care.
- Follow the orders of the employer and members of his family, related to the agreed work.
- Safeguard the property of the employer, and the members of his family.

- Refrain from harming family members, including children and the elderly.
- Keep the secrets of the employer, family members, and people in the house, whether these are learned on the job or because of it, and not disclose these secrets to others.
- Not to refuse to work or leave the service of the employer without a legitimate reason.
- Not work for himself.
- Not adversely affect the dignity of the employer and family members, or to interfere with the family.
- Respect the Islamic faith, and the regulations which are in force in the Kingdom; the customs and traditions of Saudi society, and not engage in any activity detrimental to the family.

Article 7 {Duties of Employer}

The employer:

- Must not assign the domestic worker tasks not covered by the contract, except in cases of necessity, where the additional duties are fundamentally different from the original work.
- Must not assign any work which threatens the health, safety, or which affects the human dignity of the domestic service worker.
- Must pay the agreed wage at the end of every Hijri month to domestic service workers, unless the parties agree otherwise in writing.
- Must pay the wage and the domestic service worker's dues in cash or by check, and documented by a receipt, unless the domestic service worker prefers payment into his specific bank account.

- Must provide suitable lodgings for the domestic service worker.
- Permit the domestic service worker a period of rest of at least nine hours each day.
- Must not rent the services of the domestic service worker to third parties or allow him to work for his own account.

Article 8 {Rest Periods}

The domestic service worker shall have one day each week to rest, according to what is agreed upon by the parties in the contract.

Article 9 {Wage Deductions}

The employer may make no deductions from the wage of the domestic service worker except in the following cases but deductions may not exceed half of the wage:

- The cost of property the domestic service worker had destroyed or neglected.
- In respect of any loan made by the employer.
- Garnishment of wages in implementation of a judicial ruling, or an administrative decision issued against the domestic service worker unless the judicial ruling or administrative decision states that garnishment may exceed half of the wage.

Article 10 {Paid Leave Entitlement}

Domestic service workers are entitled to paid leave of one month after two years of service upon contract renewal for a similar period.

Article 11 {Sick Leave}

Domestic service workers are entitled to paid sick leave of no more than thirty days each year when proven by a medical certificate.

Article 12 {Health Care}

Health care must be provided to the domestic service worker in accordance with rules and regulations in force in the Kingdom.

Article 13 {Leaving Employment (Abscondment)}

When a worker abandons his place of employment, the employer has to inform the police station nearest to his home, and the police station must do the following:

- Notify the Immigration Department that the worker has absconded, in order to take necessary action.
- Notify the Labour Office; to insure that there is no pending lawsuit between the parties. If there is a suit, the Labor Office must so inform the Immigration Department by.
- Provide the employer with a copy of the police report.

Article 14 {Death of Contracting Parties}

The Contract ends upon the death of the employer or the domestic service worker. If the employer's family wishes to continue the service of the domestic service worker, they must enter the name of the new employer at the Labor Office.

Article 15 {Repatriation Costs}

The employer must bear the costs of repatriation of the domestic service worker if the contract term expires, if the employer terminates the contract for an illegal reason or if the domestic service worker terminates the contract for a legitimate reason.

Article 16 {End of Service Benefit}

A domestic service worker is entitled of an end of service benefit in the amount of one month's wages after completing four consecutive years in the service of the employer.

Article 17 {Employer Fines and Penalties}

Without prejudice to the imposition of a more severe penalty, the employer who violates the provisions of these Regulations may be punished as follows:

- A finc not exceeding twn thousand riyals, or prevention of recruitment for one year, or both.
- A fine of not less than two thousand riyals, and not more than five thousand, or prevented from recruiting for two years, or both, for a repeat violation.
- Prevention of recruitment for a period of not less than three years,in the case of a third violation.

Article 18 {Worker Fines and Penalties}

Without prejudice to the penalties contained in other regulations, the domestic worker who violates the provisions of these Regulations may be punished as follows:

- A fine not exceeding two thousand riyals, or a prohibition on working in the Kingdom permanently or both.
- Fines shall be multiplied by the number of offenses committed by the domestic services worker.
- A domestic service worker violator must bear the costs of repatriation. If he does not have sufficient funds to pay any fines imposed, he will be deported at the expense of the state less any proceeds realized from the imposition of any fine imposed in conformity with this Article 18 of these Regulations.

Article 19 {Use of Fines}

Fines provided for in this Regulation shall be deposited into a bank account to contribute to the cost of shelter and deportation for domestic and migrant workers in accordance with the directives adopted by the Minister.

Article 20 {Complaints}

Notwithstanding any other provision of law, the Labor Offices shall receive complaints and file claims that arise between the domestic service worker and the employer, and maintain records relating to such claims.

Article 21 {Domestic Workers Disputes Committee}

- The composition of the Committee will be in accordance with a decision of the Minister— in accordance with the jurisdiction of each office. The Committee will consist of a chairman and two members, one of whom shall be a legal adviser of the Ministry of Labor, to consider, study and adjudicate both financial claims arising between domestic workers and employers, and non-criminal violations of these regulations and to impose sanctions provided for in this Regulation

- The Committee shall be guided by the actions contained in the system of legal proceedings.
- The Committee will summon the defendant. The Committee must consider the dispute in the presence of the parties or their agent. A summoned party will be considered as present, even he was absent and did not appear.
- The Committee will try to settle the dispute amicably between the parties within five working days of filing a matter before the Committee. If unable to reach a settlement, the Committee shall consider the matter and may take action at the first session, or in a second session to be held within ten working days. The Committee will issue its decision. Minutes must be prepared and then signed by the Chairman of the Committee and its members.
- The Committee shall issue its decision on the dispute submitted unanimously or by majority vote, within a period not exceeding ten days from the date of the second session.
- The Minister shall issue a directive illustrating the working procedures of the Committee, and the duration of the term of committee members, procedures for re-appointment, procedures for the maintenance of records and compensation for Committee employees.
- Within ten days of receipt of an adverse decision, a party may appeal a decision of the Committee to the Labor Court. After ten days the Committee's decision may be enforced.

Article 22 {Implementing Regulations}

The Minister shall issue directives necessary for the implementation of these regulations from the date of their entry into force.

CHAPTER 14

CONTROLS TO IMPROVE THE CONTRACTUAL RELATIONSHIP OF DOMESTIC WORKERS AND THEIR EQUIVALENTS

(*NOTE: "CONTROLS" in this chapter means "rules" or "requirements."*)

Article 1: Definitions:

The following words and phrases, wherever mentioned in these controls, are meant by the meanings shown beside each of them unless otherwise required by the context: **The Ministry**: Ministry of Human Resources and Social Development. **The Competent Sector**: The executive general supervision of domestic workers in the Ministry of Human Resources and Social Development. **Domestic Employer**: Any person of a normal nature who has recruited the domestic worker themself, or through a licensed recruitment office or contracted them, directly or indirectly, to perform a domestic service. **Domestic Worker**: Any person of a normal nature performing a direct or indirect domestic service to the employer, or any of their family members, being under the supervision and instruction of the employer or those in their place, such as a female/male domestic worker, private driver, gardener, or a housekeeper and their equivalents. The phrase 'domestic service worker' means the domestic worker and their equivalent when used in this regulation. **The Company**: A company licensed to practice the activities governed by the provisions of "the rules of practicing the recruitment activity and providing labor services" **Both Parties**: Employer (person, institution), domestic worker. **Committee**: The committee provided for in the regulation of domestic workers and their equivalents.

Article 2:

First: Objective: These controls aim to develop workers' transportation and absence mechanisms to enhance the contractual relationship, based on: Paragraph (2) in article 7 of the Labor Law issued in the Royal Decree no. M/51 on 23/8/1426 AH, and its amendments which stated that 1- "[T]he following shall be exempted from the implementation of the provisions of this Law:

- A. The employer's family members, namely the spouse, ascendants and descendants who constitute the only workers of the facility.
- B. Players of clubs and leagues, and their coaches.
- C. Domestic workers and their equivalents.
- D. Private agriculture workers, herders and their equivalents.
- E. Sea workers who work on ships with less than 500 tons of cargo.
- F. Non-Saudi workers who came to perform a specific task for a period that does not exceed two months."

2-"[Where] [t]he Minister issues one or more regulations in coordination with the concerned authorities, for the groups mentioned in paragraphs (A), (C), (D), (E) and (F) from paragraph (1) of this article; that includes the other private rights, obligations and provisions relevant to each group."

- Cabinet Decision No. 12366/M B on 12/11/1426 AH, on the delegation of the Ministry of Labor and Social Development to take any action it deems appropriate for transferring the service in accordance with the changing labor market requirements.
- The Regulation for Domestic Workers and their Equivalents No. 310 adopted by the Council of Ministers on 7/9/1434 AH, and its amendments.
- Ministerial Decision No. (212875) dated 29/11/1443, to approve the transfer of a domestic worker's services to another employer without the approval of the current one.
- The (first) item of Ministerial Decision No. (212875) on 29/11/1443, which stipulated that "by implementing the provisions of the fifth article of the domestic workers' and their equivalents regulation, the Ministry applies procedures allowing the domestic worker to finally quit at the end of the contractual relationship."

Second: Applicability: These controls apply to the following groups:

- - The domestic employer
- - The domestic worker
- - Human resources and recruitment companies
- - Recruitment offices

Article 3:Absence from Work

A domestic employer shall file an absence report to the absent domestic worker, the controls and conditions below are required to be observed:

A. Controls for the domestic employer:

- - If the absent domestic worker's residency is valid, having the border number is enough if the report was during their probation period.
- - The domestic worker is not on the job.
- - The absent worker has a verified contract on the "Musaned" platform.
- - [There is] No claim against the employer by the Domestic Workers' Disputes Committees.

[Then]: The employer is allowed to withdraw the absence report within (15) days from submitting it, after which the report is considered final and cannot be withdrawn.

The employer is not allowed to withdraw the report if submitted within the first (90) days since the worker entered the Kingdom of Saudi Arabia.

The domestic worker's information is dropped from the current employer after (60) days from submitting the absence report, and is not included within their workers' information.

B. Controls for the domestic worker:

- No request for service transfer registered on "Musaned" platform.
- - No final exit visa issued to the worker.
- - The domestic worker coming to work in the Kingdom of Saudi Arabia with a new domestic contract within (60)

days after the absence report, is allowed to request a final exit visa starting from the date of submitting the absence report, with the worker's status as absent from work in the related ministry and authority systems.

[Then]:

The domestic worker is allowed to transfer their services to a new employer, or request a final exit visa starting from the date of submitting the absence report after two years from his first entry to the Kingdom of Saudi Arabia, within (60) days after submitting the report, with the worker's status as absent from work in the related ministry and authority systems.

In case the worker failed to submit a request to transfer services or a final exit visa, they are considered violating the residency system.

Article 4: [Employee Transfer]:

The Ministry is allowed to do the following while processing the domestic worker's services transfer to a new employer:

- - Extending the grace period in case there was a refused request being processed one day or more before expiration, as the new employer is not eligible to the recruitment requirements.
- - Searching for a new employer, whether natural or legal, according to the status in paragraph (A), after the worker approves that the legal employer be represented in the form of a human resources company or as a licensed recruitment of it by the Ministry.

Article 5: [Transfer of Services]

First: The necessary conditions when transferring the domestic worker's services [to a new employer are as follows]:

Controls for the new domestic employer:

- - The employer's eligibility based on the controls of granting individual visas for recruiting domestic workers and their equivalents.
- - Verifying work contracts for all domestic workers on the "Musaned" platform.
- - Compliance with the requirement to transfer the domestic worker's wages via the payment channels associated with the Wage Protection Initiative on "Musaned" platform.
- - No claim against the employer at the Domestic Workers' Disputes Committees.

Controls for the new company employer:

No penalties or violations imposed on the company by the Ministry.

Controls for the domestic worker:

- 1) The domestic worker's residency is valid.
- 2) The domestic worker has a verified work contract on "Musaned" platform.
- 3) The domestic worker ended the contractual relationship with the current employer.

- 4) No claim against the domestic worker at the Domestic Workers' Disputes Committees.

Second: The transfer of domestic workers' services requires the new domestic employer to do the following:

i. Pay the planned services transportation fees.
ii. Bear the specified recruitment and operational costs on the electronic platform approved by the Ministry.

- Pay the planned services transportation fees.
- Bear the specified recruitment and operational costs on the electronic platform approved by the Ministry.

Third: The Ministry may transfer the domestic worker services to another employer without the approval of the current one in the following cases:

- Where the employer has been not paying the worker's wages for three consecutive [periods] or sporadically without reason.
- Not picking the domestic worker up from the intermediary recruitment office or shelter homes within (15) days from notifying the employer of her arrival by the office.
- The employer not obtaining a residence permit for the domestic worker, or not renewing it 30 days after obtaining or renewal expiration.
- The employer renting the worker's services to others.

- Assigning the worker to dangerous tasks that threaten their health and body's safety.
- Proving the ill-treatment towards the domestic worker by the employer or any of their family members.

- Where the worker filed a claim against the employer and the employer caused the prolonging of its consideration, unless the worker also caused or contributed to such delay.
- The employer or their representative failed to appear before the Domestic Workers' Disputes Committees for two sessions despite having been notified.
- Based on a recommendation from the concerned authority during the claim review, in order to avoid any potential harm to the domestic worker.
- If the employer is away for travel or imprisonment or any other cause, which resulted in not paying wages owed the domestic worker.
- Where the domestic worker's services have been transferred to another employer without their knowledge.
- Terminating the contract by the employer during the probation period.

Article 6: Applicability to New-Contract Workers

These controls do not apply to the domestic workers coming to work in the Kingdom of Saudi Arabia with a new domestic contract, unless the contractual relationship with the current employer ended on their first entry to the Kingdom of Saudi Arabia.

Article 7: Current Employer's Right to Compensation

The Ministry may make the necessary regulations for the cases in which the current employer deserves financial compensation, and how to calculate it through the electronic platform approved by the Ministry.

CHAPTER 15

RULES GOVERNING ILLEGAL FOREIGN WORKERS

(AS DISTRIBUTED by the Ministry of the Interior to Foreign Embassies in Riyadh via Diplomatic Note dated November 4, 2013) Material in brackets is not part of the regulation.

Article 1 {Pursuit of Employees and their Employers}

The Ministry of Interior, represented by its law enforcement agencies, shall undertake the following:

Pursue, apprehend, penalize and deport foreign workers who work for their own account (illegal labor) or abscond from work as well as overstayers (including holders of Hajj, Umrah, visit (of all types), tourism, medical treatment or transit visas) and infiltrators arrested outside the border area. Pursue anyone who employs offenders referred to in Article 1 of these Rules, allows his workers to work for their own account (illegal labor), provides cover, harbors or transports the same or aids them by any means, as well as recruiters who do not report the overstay of their recruits.

Article 2 {Costs of Deportation}

An offending foreign worker shall be deported at the expense of the employer, unless the worker absconds from work and this is reported in due time. In such case, the deportation cost shall be borne by the person employing him. An offending worker who works for his own account shall be deported at his own expense, but if he is unable to afford the travel ticket, he shall be deported at the expense of the State. Necessary and sufficient funds shall be allocated for such purpose.

An offending foreigner entering the Kingdom under Hajj or Umrah visa, visit visa of all types or other types of visa shall be deported at the expense of the person employing him. If he works for his own account, he shall be deported at his own expense; otherwise, he shall be deported at the expense of the company, establishment or person sponsoring his visit or at the expense of the carrier or the person providing him with cover.

Article 3 {Duty to Report Overstaying Pilgrims}

Hajj and Umrah companies and establishments shall notify the competent authority of any visitor who overstays his Hajj or Umrah visa.

Article 4 {Duty to Report Overstaying Visitors}

The person sponsoring a visitor shall immediately notify the competent authority of his guest's overstay. Otherwise, said sponsor shall be deemed to be committing an instance of cover-up.

Article 5 {Duty to Renew Residence Permits}

All companies, private establishments and individuals shall ensure that their workers obtain and renew iqama (residence) and work permits in due time, and shall not employ workers of third parties, nor allow their workers to work for third parties without following established statutory rules or work for their own account, and shall, within five days, notify the competent authorities of workers absconding from work.

Article 6 {Foreigners working for Government Agencies}

All government agencies shall ensure that all foreigners working for them or in fields falling within their jurisdiction have valid iqama and work permits or are employed under officially approved contracts.

Article 7 {Duties of Employers}

Any person found to be employing offending foreign workers, allowing his workers to work for their own account or for third parties or employing workers of third parties without following established statutory rules shall be deprived of the right to obtain work or visit visas for a period not exceeding five years.

Article 8 {Re-entry after Deportation}

Any deported foreigner shall be prohibited from entering the Kingdom in accordance with periods and procedures specified in regulations to be issued pursuant to a decision by the Minister of Interior.

Article 9 {Incarceration pending Deportation}

Offending foreigners referred to in these Rules shall be accommodated in centers created for this purpose pending deportation.

Article 10 {Penalties}

The Ministry of Interior shall apply to offenders referred to in Articles 1, 3 and 4 of these Rules penalties stipulated in Articles 4 and 5 of the Statute on Treatment of Persons Entering the Kingdom under Hajj, Umrah, Visit, Work or Other Visas issued pursuant to Royal Decree No. M/42 on 18/10/1404 H.

Article 11 {Review of Penalties}

Committees formed in the General Directorate of Passports and its branches shall review offenses referred to in these Rules and decisions thereof shall be subject to the approval of the Minister of Interior or his designee. The power to review such offenses may, pursuant to a decision by the Minister of Interior, be transferred to committees formed for this purpose at the Ministry of Interior.

Article 12 {Right to Appeal Committee Decisions}

Any person against whom an administrative decision is issued by the committees referred to in Article 11 of these Rules shall have the right to appeal said decision to the Minister of Interior within a period not exceeding thirty working days from the date of notification or knowledge of said decision.

Article 13 {Implementing Regulations}

The Minister of Interior shall issue the executive decisions required for the application of these Rules.

Article 14 {Publication, Effective Date}

These Rules shall be published in the Official Gazette and shall enter into force as of the date of publication.

CHAPTER 16

RULES FOR PRACTICING THE RECRUITMENT ACTIVITY

(DATED 1 Muharram 1443 AH (corresponding to 9 August 2021 G)

1. Definitions

- **Recruitment Activity**: The act of practicing mediation or recruitment services to supply workers to third parties for a fee.
- **Private Recruitment Office**: An establishment licensed to engage in recruitment activity under these rules.

2. Licensing Requirements

- Must be a Saudi national or wholly Saudi-owned company.
- Must meet financial solvency and operational capacity standards as defined by the Ministry.
- Must not have committed labor violations in the past three years.

- Submit an application through the Ministry's electronic platform.

3. Obligations of Licensed Entities

- Comply with all labor and recruitment laws and executive regulations.
- Maintain transparency in contract terms, including wages, working hours, and duties.
- Ensure that workers are not charged fees for recruitment services.
- Submit quarterly reports on operations to the Ministry.

4. Prohibited Practices

- Charging workers directly for recruitment services.
- Practicing without a valid license.
- Misrepresentation of job offers or working conditions.
- Retaining worker passports or personal documents.

5. Penalties and Enforcement

- Fines ranging from SAR 10,000 to SAR 50,000 depending on the violation.
- Suspension or revocation of license.
- Blacklisting and public disclosure of non-compliant entities.

6. Transitional Provisions

- Existing recruitment offices must comply with new

licensing and operational requirements within 12 months from the effective date.

CHAPTER 17

FINANCIAL RIGHTS AND BENEFITS REGULATIONS

Introduction

THESE REGULATIONS ESTABLISH the financial rights and benefits entitled to employees working within the Kingdom of Saudi Arabia, in accordance with the Labor Law and relevant ministerial decisions.

Article 1: Scope

These Regulations apply to all employees subject to the Saudi Labor Law, unless otherwise stipulated.

Article 2: Wages

- Employees shall be paid wages agreed upon in their employment contracts.
- Wages shall be paid at least once a month on a fixed date.
- Unauthorized deductions from wages are prohibited except as permitted by law.

Article 3: End-of-Service Benefits

Employees are entitled to an end-of-service gratuity calculated as follows:

- Half a month's wage for each of the first five years of service.
- One month's wage for each subsequent year of service.

Article 4: Annual Leave Pay

Employees shall receive full wages during their annual leave as prescribed by the Labor Law.

Article 5: Sick Leave Pay

Employees are entitled to sick leave with pay as specified under the Labor Law and health regulations.

Article 6: Maternity Leave Pay

Female employees shall be entitled to maternity leave with full or partial pay according to Labor Law provisions.

Article 7: Social Insurance Contributions

Employers shall make all required social insurance contributions on behalf of their employees as mandated by the General Organization for Social Insurance (GOSI).

Article 8: Work Injury Compensation

Employees injured during work shall receive compensation

according to the provisions of the Work Injury Insurance Regulations.

Article 9: Overtime Pay

Employees working beyond normal working hours shall be compensated with overtime pay as prescribed by the Labor Law.

Article 10: Salary Increases and Bonuses

Salary increases and bonuses shall be governed by company policies and applicable regulations and shall not contravene the Labor Law.

Article 11: Payment Methods

Payments shall be made through authorized banking channels to ensure transparency and traceability.

Article 12: Dispute Resolution

Disputes related to financial rights and benefits shall be resolved in accordance with the Labor Law dispute resolution procedures.

Final Provisions

These Regulations shall come into force on the date of publication and shall be enforced by the Ministry of Human Resources and Social Development.

CHAPTER 18
EMPLOYER COMPLIANCE GUIDE

Introduction

THIS GUIDE PROVIDES a comprehensive overview of employer obligations and best practices to ensure compliance with the Saudi Labor Law and related regulations. It is intended to assist employers in maintaining lawful and ethical employment practices.

Licensing and Registration

- Ensure all recruitment agencies and labor service providers engaged are properly licensed by the Ministry.
- Register your company and workforce with the relevant government platforms, such as the *Nitaqat* system.

Employment Contracts

- Use written contracts in Arabic that clearly define the terms of employment, including job title, duties, salary, benefits, and duration.

- Provide employees with a signed copy of their contract before starting work.

Wages and Benefits

- Pay salaries on time via approved banking channels.
- Ensure wages meet or exceed the minimum wage and comply with agreed terms.
- Provide end-of-service benefits, annual leave pay, sick leave pay, and other financial entitlements as required by law.

Working Hours and Leave

- Comply with statutory working hours, rest periods, and overtime pay rules.
- Grant annual leave, public holidays, sick leave, maternity leave, and other leaves as stipulated.

Saudization and Workforce Nationalization

- Adhere to Saudization quotas and policies to increase employment of Saudi nationals.
- Submit periodic reports on workforce nationalization progress.

Health and Safety

- Maintain safe and healthy workplace conditions.
- Provide employees with required safety training and equipment.

Worker Rights and Protection

- Respect workers' rights to non-discrimination and fair treatment.
- Avoid retention of passports or identity documents.
- Establish mechanisms for worker complaints and dispute resolution.

Recordkeeping and Reporting

- Maintain accurate employment records for all workers for at least five years.
- Submit required reports and notifications to the Ministry and other authorities timely.

Inspections and Enforcement

- Cooperate with Ministry inspections and investigations.
- Promptly address any violations or corrective actions mandated by authorities.

Conclusion

Compliance with Saudi labor laws and regulations protects both employers and employees, ensuring a productive and fair work environment. Employers should stay informed of legal updates and seek professional advice as needed.

- **Initiatives Supporting Private Sector Establishments and Entrepreneurs**
- **Employer Rights**
- **Control Procedures**

CHAPTER 19

IMPLEMENTING REGULATIONS OF THE RULES FOR PRACTICING THE RECRUITMENT ACTIVITY AND PROVIDING LABOR SERVICES

Chapter One: General Provisions

Scope and Purpose

THESE REGULATIONS AIM to define the procedures, conditions, and obligations related to practicing recruitment and labor services activities.

Applicability

These Regulations apply to all private sector entities licensed to practice recruitment or labor mediation within the Kingdom.

Definitions

Terms used in these Regulations shall have the meanings ascribed to them in the Labor Law and its Implementing Regulations.

Chapter Two: Licensing Procedures

Licensing Requirement

Practicing recruitment or labor services requires a license from the Ministry of Human Resources and Social Development.

Conditions for Licensing

Applicants must:

- Be a Saudi national (if a natural person), or a registered Saudi company.
- Submit a Commercial Registration (CR), financial statements, and office lease.
- Not have a criminal record involving moral turpitude.

License Validity

Licenses shall be valid for three years and renewable upon fulfillment of regulatory requirements.

Chapter Three: Operational Controls

Obligations of Licensed Entities

Licensed entities shall:

- Maintain records of recruitment contracts and workers.
- Submit periodic reports to the Ministry.
- Cooperate with inspections.

Notification of Changes

Any changes in the business's structure, ownership, or location must be reported to the Ministry within 30 days.

Office Standards

The entity must comply with health and safety standards for offices.

Chapter Four: Prohibited Practices

Prohibitions

Licensed entities are prohibited from:

- Charging workers for recruitment services.
- Advertising jobs without approval.
- Retaining workers' passports.
- Subcontracting without authorization.

Chapter Two: Licensing Procedures

Article 11: Trade Name Restrictions

The licensee may not operate under a trade name that suggests unauthorized activities.

Article 12: Non-transferability

The license is non-transferable without the Ministry's approval.

Article 13: Legal Status Changes

A new license must be obtained in the event of legal status change (e.g., merger or division).

Article 14: License Renewal

Renewal applications must be submitted 60 days before expiry.

Article 15: License Suspension

Licenses may be suspended for violations of the Labor Law or these Regulations.

Article 16: License Reinstatement

A suspended license may be reinstated upon rectification and Ministry approval.

Article 17: License Cancellation

License cancellation may occur for repeated or serious violations.

Article 18: Office Maintenance

Licensed entities must maintain a physical office in compliance with Ministry requirements.

Article 19: Office Facilities

The office must be equipped to provide client and worker services, including:

- Interview rooms

- Secure storage for documents
- Waiting areas

Article 20: Staff Training

All staff must be trained and knowledgeable about labor law and ethical recruitment.

Article 21: General Manager

The licensee shall employ a general manager with relevant experience and qualifications.

Article 22: Internal Complaints System

The entity must have an internal complaints and compliance system.

Article 23: Saudization Compliance

The licensee must comply with Saudization requirements.

Article 24: Scope of Activity

Licensees must refrain from practicing any activity beyond their licensed scope.

Article 25: Periodic Reporting

Licensees must submit quarterly reports and statistics to the Ministry.

Article 26: Notification of Changes

Any change in ownership, management, or location must be reported within 30 days.

Article 27: Record Keeping

Licensees must maintain comprehensive records for a period of five years.

Article 28: Confidentiality

The entity must ensure confidentiality of worker and client data.

Article 29: Display of License

The license must be publicly displayed in the office.

Article 30: Staff Identification

Staff must carry ID cards showing their position and authority.

Article 31: Contract Templates

The Ministry may prescribe templates for contracts and agreements.

Article 32: Pricing Compliance

All services provided must be consistent with the approved pricing structure.

Article 33: Customer Satisfaction

Customer satisfaction surveys must be conducted periodically.

Article 34: Use of Digital Platforms

Licensees must use the Ministry's digital platforms for transactions and communications.

Article 35: License Inactivity

A license may be revoked for inactivity exceeding 180 days without justification.

Article 36: Compliance with Directives

Licensees must comply with Ministry circulars and directives.

Article 37: Subcontracting

Subcontracting is prohibited unless authorized by the Ministry.

Article 38: Prohibited Activities

A licensed recruitment or labor services company shall be prohibited from:

i. Employing a worker in a job inconsistent with the agreed qualifications or job title.
ii. Charging the worker directly or indirectly for recruitment costs.
iii. Collecting any financial compensation from the worker for recruitment or mediation services.

iv. Transferring a worker to another employer without written approval from the Ministry and the consent of the worker.
v. Advertising for recruitment without obtaining prior approval from the Ministry.
vi. Violating the terms and conditions stated in the license or the recruitment contract.
vii. Engaging in any form of human trafficking or exploitation.
viii. Retaining the passports or identification documents of workers, except as legally permitted.

Violations of this article may lead to license suspension,

CHAPTER 20

LIST OF VIOLATIONS OF THE REGULATIONS OF THE KINGDOM OF SAUDI ARABIA AND THE PENALTIES RESULTING FROM THEM.

Penalties for Violations Related to Residency and Labor Laws

1. Penalty for an expatriate who works for his own account ("loose labor"):

- **First offense:** Fine of 10,000 riyals and deportation.
- **Second offense:** Fine of 25,000 riyals, imprisonment for one month, and deportation.
- **Third offense:** Fine of 50,000 riyals, imprisonment for six months, and deportation.

2. Penalty for a citizen or resident who transports, employs, shelters, or assists violators of residency or labor regulations (including helping them find jobs, housing, or transport):

- **First offense:** Fine of 15,000 riyals and deportation if the violator is an expatriate.

- **Second offense:** Fine of 30,000 riyals, imprisonment for three months, and deportation if the violator is an expatriate.
- **Third offense:** Fine of 100,000 riyals, imprisonment for six months, and deportation if the violator is an expatriate.

3. Penalty for a citizen or resident who enables his own workers to work for his own account, or to work for another party:

- **First offense:** Fine of 15,000 riyals, deprivation of recruitment for one year, and deportation if the violator is an expatriate.
- **Second offense:** Fine of 30,000 riyals, imprisonment for three months, deprivation of recruitment for two years, and deportation if the violator is an expatriate.
- **Third offense:** Fine of 100,000 riyals, imprisonment for six months, deprivation of recruitment for five years, and deportation if the violator is an expatriate.

CHAPTER 21
LEGAL PROVISIONS REGULATING THE RECRUITMENT AND EMPLOYMENT OF DOMESTIC WORKERS

THE *DOMESTIC WORKERS and Those in Their Care* regulations regulate work relations with domestic workers in the Kingdom, and determine the responsibilities of the parties to the relationship in a manner that guarantees their rights and obligations in a balanced manner. It also regulates the provision of a suitable work environment for them in accordance with the applicable international legislation and agreements in the Kingdom. Decisions related to the recruitment and employment of domestic workers:

- Rules for dealing with expatriates who violate the regulations (https://www.hrsd.gov.sa/knowledge-centre/decisions-and-regulations/regulation-and-procedures/813383)
- Rules for practicing the activity of recruitment and providing labor services (https://laws.boe.gov.sa/BoeLaws/Laws/LawDetails/a910b5ff-6770-4978-99f5-a9a700f2c140/1)
- Controls for improving the contractual relationship of domestic workers and those in their care https://www.

hrsd.gov.sa/en/knowledge-centre/decisions-and-regula tions/regulation-and-procedures/04042024

CHAPTER 22
IMPLEMENTING REGULATIONS OF THE RULES FOR PRACTICING THE RECRUITMENT ACTIVITY AND PROVIDING LABOR SERVICES MINISTERIAL RESOLUTION NO. (1982) DATED 28/06/1436 AH (AS AMENDED BY MINISTERIAL DECISION NO. (70273) DATED 11/04/1440 AH)

CHAPTER One: General Provisions

Article 1: These Regulations aim to define the procedures, conditions, and obligations related to practicing recruitment and labor services activities.

Article 2: The Regulations apply to all private sector entities licensed to practice recruitment or labor mediation within the Kingdom.

Article 3: Terms used in these Regulations shall have the meanings ascribed to them in the Labor Law and its Implementing Regulations.

—

Chapter Two: Licensing Procedures

Article 4: Practicing recruitment or labor services requires a license from the Ministry of Human Resources and Social Development.

Article 5: The license applicant must: 1. Be a Saudi national (if a natural person), or a registered Saudi company. 2. Submit a

Commercial Registration (CR), financial statements, and office lease.
3. Not have a criminal record involving moral turpitude.

Article 6: Licenses shall be valid for three years and renewable upon fulfillment of regulatory requirements.

Article 7: The Ministry shall determine the types of licenses and service categories.

Article 8: The applicant must satisfy technical and administrative competency standards.

Article 9: Applications shall be submitted through the Ministry's electronic platform.

Article 10: The Ministry shall respond to complete applications within 30 working days.

Article 11: The licensee may not operate under a trade name that suggests unauthorized activities.

Article 12: The license is non-transferable without the Ministry's approval.

Article 13: A new license must be obtained in the event of legal status change (e.g., merger or division).

Article 14: Renewal applications must be submitted 60 days before expiry.

Article 15: Licenses may be suspended for violations of the Labor Law or these Regulations.

Article 16: A suspended license may be reinstated upon rectification and Ministry approval.

Article 17: License cancellation may occur for repeated or serious violations.

—

Chapter Three: Operational Controls

Article 18: Licensed entities must maintain a physical office in compliance with Ministry requirements.

Article 19: The office must be equipped to provide client and worker services, including: 1. Interview rooms 2. Secure storage for documents 3. Waiting areas

Article 20: All staff must be trained and knowledgeable about labor law and ethical recruitment.

Article 21: The licensee shall employ a general manager with relevant experience and qualifications.

Article 22: The entity must have an internal complaints and compliance system.

Article 23: The licensee must comply with Saudization requirements.

Article 24: Licensees must refrain from practicing any activity beyond their licensed scope.

Article 25: Licensees must submit quarterly reports and statistics to the Ministry.

Article 26: Any change in ownership, management, or location must be reported within 30 days.

Article 27: Licensees must maintain comprehensive records for a period of five years.

Article 28: The entity must ensure confidentiality of worker and client data.

Article 29: The license must be publicly displayed in the office.

Article 30: Staff must carry ID cards showing their position and authority.

Article 31: The Ministry may prescribe templates for contracts and agreements.

Article 32: All services provided must be consistent with the approved pricing structure.

Article 33: Customer satisfaction surveys must be conducted periodically.

Article 34: Licensees must use the Ministry's digital platforms for transactions and communications.

Article 35: A license may be revoked for inactivity exceeding 180 days without justification.

Article 36: Licensees must comply with Ministry circulars and directives.

Article 37: Subcontracting is prohibited unless authorized by the Ministry.

—

Chapter Four: Prohibited Practices

Article 38: A licensed recruitment or labor services company shall be prohibited from: 1. Employing a worker in a job inconsistent with the agreed qualifications or job title. 2. Charging the worker directly or indirectly for recruitment costs. 3. Collecting any financial compensation from the worker for recruitment or mediation services. 4. Transferring a worker to another employer without written approval from the Ministry and the consent of the worker. 5. Advertising for recruitment without obtaining prior approval from the Ministry. 6. Violating the terms and conditions stated in the license or the recruitment contract. 7. Engaging in any form of human trafficking or exploitation. 8. Retaining the passports or identification documents of workers, except as legally permitted.

Violations of this article may lead to license suspension, cancellation, or financial penalties in accordance with the Labor Law and relevant Ministerial Decisions.

—

Chapter Five: Inspection and Penalties

Article 39: The Ministry may conduct announced or unannounced inspections.

Article 40: Inspections aim to verify compliance with these Regulations and related laws.

Article 41: Inspectors may request access to premises, records, and staff.

Article 42: Obstruction of inspections is a violation subject to penalties.

Article 43: Violations are recorded in an official inspection report.

Article 44: The Ministry may impose: 1. Warning notices 2. Administrative fines 3. Temporary suspension 4. Permanent revocation of the license

Article 45: Penalties shall consider the severity, recurrence, and harm of the violation.

Article 46: Licensees may appeal administrative decisions through designated channels.

Article 47: Criminal violations shall be referred to competent authorities.

Article 48: Penalties may include publication of violator names.

Article 49: Penalties do not preclude civil or criminal liability under other laws.

Article 50: The Ministry may issue further enforcement procedures.

—

Chapter Six: Ministry Oversight

Article 51: The Ministry shall undertake the following supervisory and enforcement responsibilities: 1. Conduct periodic and unannounced inspections of recruitment offices and labor service providers. 2. Verify compliance with licensing terms, contractual obligations, and legal standards. 3. Receive and investigate complaints from workers, employers, or the public. 4. Impose administrative penalties including fines, license suspension, or revocation as stipulated in the implementing regulations. 5. Refer cases involving criminal violations to the competent authorities. 6. Publish the names of violators and the nature of their violations in accordance with applicable regulations. 7. Maintain a central database of licensed recruitment agencies and labor service providers, accessible to the public.

Article 52: The Ministry shall provide guidance and support to promote compliance.

Article 53: The Ministry shall develop performance indicators and monitoring tools.

—

Chapter Seven: Final Provisions

Article 54: These Regulations may be amended by the Ministry in coordination with relevant authorities.

Article 55: Any provision conflicting with these Regulations is hereby repealed.

Article 56: These Regulations shall be published and enter into force upon publication.

Note: This English version is an unofficial translation for reference only. The original Arabic text published by the Ministry of Human Resources and Social Development shall prevail in legal interpretation.

CHAPTER 23
RECRUITMENT ACTIVITY IMPLEMENTING REGULATION

ISSUED BY: Ministry of Human Resources and Social Development
Effective Date: 1 Muharram 1443 AH (corresponding to 9 August 2021 AD)

—

Article 1: Scope of Application

This Regulation applies to all natural or legal persons engaged in recruitment or labor mediation services within the Kingdom of Saudi Arabia.

Article 2: Licensing Procedures

- Applications must be submitted electronically via the Ministry's designated platform.
- The applicant shall attach:
    - Commercial Registration (CR) certificate
    - Proof of financial solvency
    - Certified lease contract for office premises

    - Police clearance certificate for owners and managers
- The Ministry shall decide on complete applications within 30 days.

Article 3: License Validity and Renewal

- Licenses shall be valid for a period of 3 years.
- Renewal applications must be submitted no less than 60 days prior to expiration.
- Failure to renew on time may result in automatic suspension.

Article 4: Operational Standards

- Licensed entities must maintain a physical office with signage clearly indicating their licensed status.
- Offices must be equipped to handle client and worker needs, including private interview space.
- Staff must have appropriate training and knowledge of labor laws.

Article 5: Recruitment Contracts

- All recruitment arrangements must be governed by a written contract.
- Contracts shall include:
    - Job description and location
    - Duration and terms of employment
    - Compensation and benefits
    - Grievance mechanisms

Article 6: Worker Protection

- Workers may not be charged any recruitment-related fees.
- Workers shall be provided copies of their contracts and informed of their rights.
- Recruitment offices shall not retain workers' passports or identification documents.

Article 7: Complaints and Dispute Resolution

- Complaints may be submitted to the Ministry by any party.
- The Ministry shall investigate and respond within 45 days.
- Mediation services may be offered by the Ministry prior to formal adjudication.

Article 8: Monitoring and Inspection

- The Ministry may conduct unannounced visits to verify compliance.
- Inspection results will be documented in a formal report.
- Violations may result in warnings, fines, or license suspension.

Article 9: Penalties

- Violations of this Regulation may lead to:
  - Fines up to SAR 100,000
  - Suspension or cancellation of license
  - Publication of violator names

Article 10: Final Provisions

- The Ministry reserves the right to amend these regulations.
- Any matter not explicitly covered shall revert to the provisions of the Labor Law.

CHAPTER 24

DIPLOMATIC SERVICE EMPLOYMENT REGULATIONS

TABLE OF CONTENTS

Chapter 1: Definitions

Article (1): The following terms and phrases, whenever used herein, shall have the meanings assigned thereto:

• **Regulations**: Regulations of Diplomatic Jobs

• **Minister**: Minister of Foreign Affairs

• **Ministry**: Ministry of Foreign Affairs

• **General Court**: The ministry's offices, branches, and offices in the kingdom.

• **Functions of the Corps**: Functions of the Diplomatic

Corps (Attaché-Third Secretary-second secretary-First Secretary-adviser-Minister Plenipotentiary-Ambassador).

• **Host Nation**: The country where the headquarters of the mission is located.

• **Mission**: The embassy, or the permanent mission to international or regional organizations inside and outside the country, or the consulate, or the offices affiliated with the ministry abroad.

• **Head of Mission**: A person who is selected to work in this capacity

• **Deputy Head of Mission**: A person who is selected to work in this capacity

• **Member of the Mission**: Anyone who works within the mission, including the head of the mission and their deputy.

• **Technical Attaché Office**: The technical office is affiliated with a government agency within the mission.

• **Attaché**: An employee of the government agency was selected to oversee the technical attaché office.

• **Council of the Corps**: Council of the Diplomatic Corps

• **Member of the Corps**: An employee of the ministry who holds one of the jobs of the Corps.

• **Difficult cities to live**: Cities with a lower quality of life compared to Riyadh, measured based on political and economic conditions, health infrastructure, and entertainment, availability of consumer goods, housing and education services, climate conditions, and social environment.

• **High-[cost of] living cities**: Cities with high living costs. The index of high living costs is measured based on the difference in lost purchasing power from living in those cities compared to living in Riyadh.

• **Family of a Diplomatic Staff Member**: Husband, wife, male children under the age of eighteen, and unmarried females.

• **Diplomatic Representation**: Sending a member of the Corps to work within the mission.

• **Basic Salary**: The monthly amount received by a diplomatic staff member according to the salary scale outlined in the salary, allowances, and benefits tables.

• **Housing Allowance**: The monthly amount that a member of the Corps receives to secure suitable housing for him inside the kingdom.

• **Transposition Allowance**: The monthly amount received by a member of the Corps for the purpose of moving to and from the place of work within the kingdom.

• **Transportation Allowance**: The monthly amount received by a member of the Corps for the purpose of moving to and from the place of work within the Host Nation.

• **Advantages of Moving**: Benefits that are granted to a member of the Corps when moving to another state

• **Diplomatic Representation Allowance**: The fixed monthly amount received by the member of the Corps assigned to represent the kingdom in the mission.

• **Additional Representation Allowance**: The monthly amount received by the head of the mission for representing the kingdom in another country in addition to the receiving state.

• **Living Difficulty Allowance**: The monthly amount that a member of the Corps receives is based on the index of the difficulty of living in the receiving city.

• **Accommodation Allowance**: The monthly amount received by a member of the Corps in order to secure housing within the city where the headquarters of the mission is located outside the kingdom.

Chapter 2: Scope of Validity

Article (2): The provisions of the regulations apply to those holding positions within the diplomatic corps and do not apply to others except to the extent specified. In matters not specifically addressed in the regulations, the Civil Service System and its executive regulations, along with relevant laws, decisions, and orders, shall apply to those holding diplomatic jobs.

Article (3): The disciplinary rules and sanctions contained in the job discipline regulations and its executive regulations shall apply to the corps member.

Article (4): The relevant regulations of the host nation apply to the contractor at the mission who is not a Saudi citizen.

Chapter 3: Council of the Diplomatic Corps

Article (5): The Council of the Diplomatic Corps shall be formed in the Cabinet of the ministry, by a resolution of the minister, and it shall be chaired by him, and the resolution shall determine the Council of the Diplomatic Corps members. The minister may reconstitute the council whenever necessary.

Article (6): In addition to the terms of reference contained in the regulations, the Council of the Diplomatic Corps shall do the following:

- a. Nominate heads of missions after coordination with human resources in the ministry.
- b. Format committees that help him to perform his duties.
- c. Coordinate meetings with heads of missions.
- d. Propose and review the rules governing its work, and propose what is necessary to develop them in accordance with the relevant orders, laws, regulations, and resolutions. It shall be approved by the minister.
- e. Any other task within his competence is assigned to him by the minister.

Article (7): The Council of the Diplomatic Corps shall have a secretary from the corps members whose job is not less than (adviser), and he is assigned for a period of (three years maximum, and may be extended for a similar period. His assignment and termination of his assignment shall be by a decision of the minister.

Article (8): The secretary of the Council of the Diplomatic Corps shall prepare its agenda follow up the implementation of its decisions and recommendations, and carry out any other task in his field of competence assigned by the chairman of the Council of the Diplomatic Corps.

Chapter 4: Appointment and Transfer

Article (9):

• a. Whoever is chosen by royal order as an ambassador from non-holders of corps jobs is appointed to the job of (Ambassador).

• b. Whoever is selected by a royal order to work in one of the missions from non-holders of corps jobs is appointed in accordance with the manual of scientific and practical qualifications, which is approved by agreement between the Ministry and the Ministry of Human Resources and Social Development.

Article (10): Subject to the requirements of other regulations, the appointment of a candidate to the jobs of the Corps is subject to the following conditions:

• a. Candidate shall be of Saudi origin.

• b. Candidate shall have a good biography and ethics.

• c. His health fitness shall be proved by a report issued by the competent medical committee.

• d. Candidate shall have a bachelor's degree or equivalent, equivalent to a certificate from the competent authority if it is from a university outside the Kingdom, and possess the required qualifications for the job.

• e. Candidate shall not have been convicted of a Shariah-prescribed punishment, *qisas* (Retribution), a prison sentence exceeding one year, or any of the following crimes: bribery, forgery, embezzlement, drug or alcohol trafficking, promotion, or trade. If previously convicted, at least one year shall have passed since the completion of the sentence or exemption from it.

• f. Candidate shall not be dismissed from the state service for disciplinary reasons, or he was dismissed and at least one year has passed since the date of dismissal.

• g. Candidate shall not be married to a non-Saudi national.

• h. Candidate shall have proficiency in Arabic and English. The minister may make an exception to the English language proficiency requirement if the candidate is fluent in at least one other living language in addition to Arabic.

• i. Candidate shall undertake in writing to work at the general court or any mission to which a decision is issued to transfer him.

Article (11):

• a. Subject to the provisions of Article (9), the appointment shall be based on a job (Attaché), and no consideration shall be given to the candidate's scientific qualifications, practical experience, training, or preparatory programs that exceed the conditions of appointment set out in the regulations.

• b. The appointment to the job of (Adviser(or below shall be by a decision of the minister, and the appointment to the job of (Ambassador) or (Minister Delegate) shall be by a decision of the Council of Ministers based on the nomination of the minister.

Article (12):

• a. The member of the Corps shall take the following oath before the minister after the issuance of the decision to appoint him: (*I swear by Almighty God to be faithful to my religion and then my king and my homeland, not to divulge a secret of the state, to preserve its interests and regulations at home and abroad, and to perform my work with honesty, faithfulness, and sincerity*).

• b. The person appointed as an ambassador to a country or permanent delegate to regional or international organizations for the first time before the king or his deputy, takes the following oath: (*I swear by Almighty God to be faithful to my religion and then my king and my homeland, not to divulge a secret of the state, to preserve its interests and regulations at home and abroad, and to perform my work with honesty, faithfulness, and sincerity*).

• c. The appointed consul general upon his first appointment shall take the following oath before the minister: (*I swear by Almighty God to be faithful to my religion and then my king and my homeland, not to divulge a secret of the state, to preserve its interests and regulations at home and abroad, and to perform my work with honesty, faithfulness, and sincerity*).

Article (13): An appointed to the position of (Attaché) shall be considered to be on probation for one year from the date of joining the job. This period shall be extended for an additional year if they do not achieve the required performance level during the first year of the probation period. If the appointee is absent from work for any lawful or other reason without resulting in the termination of his service, the probation period will be extended by the duration of the absence. If the appointee is found unsuitable during the probation period, the Minister shall issue a decision to terminate his employment.

Article (14):

• a. The appointee to the position of (Attaché) shall undergo a basic training program determined by the ministry. They may also be seconded during the probation period to work in regional or international organizations in accordance with the regulatory procedures followed in this regard.

• b. It is not allowed during the entire probation period to transfer or assign the appointee to a job (Attaché) to work a job from a category other than the job to which he was appointed.

Article (15): An employee who occupies a position not covered by the provisions of the regulations may be transferred to one of the Corps' jobs after the approval of the minister, provided that the conditions for filling the Corps' jobs are met. This transfer shall be after reclassifying the employee and determining the appropriate job for him according to the scientific and practical qualifications manual, which is approved by agreement between the Ministry and the Ministry of Human Resources and Social Development.

Article (16): By a decision of the minister, the Recruitment and Transfer Committee for the jobs of the Corps shall formed of five members, including the first official of human resources in the ministry, it shall be as follows:

• a. Determine the requirements for the appointment.

• b. Identify sources of attracting competencies.

• c. Interview procedures and supervision of tests required for recruitment or transfer.

• d. Determine the basic salary of the appointee ranging from the minimum to the average of the basic salary range for the position to which he was appointed, in accordance with controls established by the Committee.

Article (17): Selection of the head of mission in embassies or regional or international organizations shall be from those holding the position of (Advisor) or higher, in accordance with relevant regulations and based on the minister's recommendation. The selection of other heads of missions shall be by decision of the minister, provided that the position of the selected person is not lower than (Advisor).

Chapter 5: Duties and Obligations

Article (18): The member of the mission shall:

• a. Appear in an appropriate manner, adhere to the general and personal conduct befitting Saudi society's values and ethics, as well as the provisions of Islamic Sharia, and perform the duties imposed by their position and representative capacity with utmost honesty and dedication.

• b. Perform the tasks and duties assigned to him at his workplace to serve the interests of the kingdom.

• c. Comply with the provisions of the Code of Professional Conduct and ethics of the public office, the system of awarding decorations and gifts and the issued regulations and rules related to that.

• d. Take care of the affairs of Saudi citizens, provide assistance to them, and defend them within the competence of the mission, whether they are natural or legal persons.

• e. Not engage in any professional or commercial activity in the receiving state for the purpose of achieving any personal gain.

• f. Not marry non-holders of Saudi citizenship.

• g. Not make any statements and not express political opinions to the local or foreign media or within social media except with the approval of the ministry or with the authorization of the head of the mission and within the limits of the tasks assigned to him, and in accordance with the general policy of the state.

• h. Not issue newspapers, magazines, or bulletins or participate in them except with the approval of the ministry or with the authorization of the head of the mission and within the limits of the tasks assigned to him, and in accordance with the general policy of the state.

• i. Comply with the rules and regulations issued regarding the use of social media.

• j. Not belong to organizations, bodies, or political parties, and not work for them and participate in propaganda and promotion in any way.

• k. Not benefit from diplomatic or Consular Privileges except for the purposes granted for them.

• l. Not interfere in the internal affairs of the receiving state, respect for its regulations, laws, prevailing customs, and traditions.

• m. Oblige all members of his family and accompanying employment to the rules of conduct contained in the regulations.

• n. Stay in the city where the headquarters of the mission is located and in accordance with the requirements of the host nation.

• o. Compliant with the relevant provisions and obligations contained in the Vienna Convention on Diplomatic Relations of 1961 G and the Vienna Convention on Consular Relations of 1963 G.

• p. Complete the delivery and receipt procedures when transferring him in accordance with the instructions for this and the Disclaimer Form, and settle all financial and other obligations before departure.

Chapter 6: Performance Management and Promotion

Article (19): The evaluation of the performance of the corps member shall be annually according to the performance indicators, merits, and models adopted by the ministry in coordination with the Ministry of Human Resources and Social Development.

Article (20): Promotion shall be a means of advancement and career development for a corps member and shall be associated with performance evaluation. It is not, under any circumstances, considered a right for the diplomatic corps member.

Article (21): A member of the Corps may be promoted under the following conditions:

- a. Vacancy of the position to be promoted to.
- b. The promotion shall be to the position that directly follows his current position.
- c. Completion of training hours for special training programs specified by the ministry for the positions of (Attaché - Third Secretary Second Secretary - First Secretary).
- d. Passing the assessment of (behavioral or technical) diplomatic merits, as approved by the ministry for promotion to positions (Adviser - Minister Plenipotentiary - Ambassador).
- e. Proficiency in at least one living language, other than Arabic, for promotion to the positions of (Adviser - Minister Plenipotentiary-Ambassador).

Article (22): The regular periods required for promotion shall be as follows:

- a. At least three years for promotion from a position (Attaché) to a position (Third Secretary).
- b. At least two years for promotion from a position (Attaché) to a position of (Third Secretary) in the event that the member of the Corps holds a master's degree, doctorate, or equivalent before being appointed to a position (Attaché), taking into account that this qualification shall be obtained from abroad equivalent from the competent authority in the kingdom.
- c. At least three years for promotion from the position of (Third Secretary) to (Second Secretary).
- d. At least three years for promotion from the position of (Second Secretary) to (First Secretary), provided that he has worked for at least three years in one of the missions abroad.
- e. At least five years for promotion from a position (First Secretary) to a position (Adviser), and it may be reduced to four years in case of obtaining (four) minimum performance evaluations (Exceeding Expectations) or equivalent.
- f. At least four years for promotion from a position (Adviser) to

the position of (Minister Plenipotentiary), and it may be reduced to three years in case of obtaining (three) performance evaluations with a minimum (Exceeding Expectations) or equivalent.

• g. Six years for promotion from the position of (Minister Plenipotentiary) to the position of (Ambassador), and it may be reduced to five years in case of obtaining (five) minimum performance evaluations (Exceeding Expectations) or equivalent.

Article (23): Subject to the provisions of articles (31) and (22) of the Regulation, the minister may nominate whoever he deems appropriate for promotion to the job of (Minister Plenipotentiary - Ambassador). He may, in the cases he deems appropriate, exclude the corps member from achieving the specified level required in the performance evaluation.

Article (24): The following periods are not counted for promotion purposes:

• a. The duration of the extraordinary leave.

• b. The loan period is for non-regional or international organizations or offices affiliated with the ministry.

• c. The duration of the scholarship, sending for study or study leave if the purpose of any of them has not been achieved.

• d. The duration of the absence of official Leave is not counted.

• e. The duration of the suspension from work duties if a member of the Corps has been sentenced to a penalty.

Article (25): A member of the Corps may not be considered for promotion in the following cases:

• a. If he is on a scholarship, sent to study, or attached to a training course for more than (six) months at home or abroad.

• b. If he is on study or exceptional leave.

• c. If he is suspended from work duties or referred to trial in matters related to public office or matters prejudicial to honor, honesty, or good conduct and morals.

• d. If he receives a performance evaluation below the required level, according to the following:

– 1. A performance evaluation that is less than (Meets Expectations) or its equivalent in the last (three) years is considered during promotions to the positions of (Third Secretary - Second Secretary - First Secretary)

– 2. A performance evaluation that is less than (Meets Expectations) or equivalent in the last (two years), upon promotion to the position of (Third Secretary) in accordance with Paragraph (B) of Article (22) of the regulations.

– 3. A performance evaluation that is less than (Meets Expectations) or equivalent in the last four years, when I was promoted to the two positions (Adviser - Minister Plenipotentiary).

– 4. A performance evaluation that is less than (Meets Expectations) or equivalent in the last (six) years, when promoted to the position of (Ambassador).

Article (26):

• a. The criteria for promotion to the positions of (Third Secretary - Second Secretary - First Secretary) are as follows:

– 1. The level of performance evaluation.

– 2. Training and Development hours.

– 3. Any additional item determined by the promotions committee of the ministry.

• b. The elements of trade-off for promotion to the positions of (Adviser - Minister Plenipotentiary - Ambassador), according to the following:

– 1. The level of performance evaluation.

– 2. Evaluate diplomatic skills (behavioral or technical).

Article (27): A member of the Corps holding the position of (First Secretary) or (Advisor) may be promoted exceptionally to the position that directly follows his current position, with the following conditions:

• a. Candidate shall have obtained a job performance evaluation result in the last year that is not less than (Ideal) or equivalent.

• b. The age of the candidate shall not exceed (fifty-five) years.

• c. Candidate shall have spent a minimum of five years in the Corps jobs.

• d. Candidate shall have held the position he holds for at least a year.

• e. The exceptional promotion of a member of the Corps shall be only once and for only one job during his career in the Corps jobs.

• f. The number of people promoted in the fiscal year shall not exceed a percentage (1

• g. Do not combine more than one promotion during one year.

Article (28): The promotions committee shall be formed by a resolution of the minister from five members, including the chief human resources officer at the ministry, and the committee shall consider the promotions of the corps members and supervise the promotions procedures, in particular as follows:

• a. Ensure the availability of general conditions for promotions.

• b. Apply the criteria and elements of trade-off and their weights approved by the minister.

• c. Determine when to make a trade-off for promotion.

• d. Prepare minutes for the promotion of corps members nominated for promotion.

• e. Submit the minutes of promotions to the minister, including the nomination for promotion in preparation for approval.

• f. Propose and review the criteria and elements of the trade-off and their weights, and determine the weighted element in case of equality, and approved by a resolution of the minister.

Article (29): The ministry's human resources shall prepare lists of corps members who meet the conditions for promotion to vacant positions, the choice of which is by promotion.

Article (30): The promotion resolution shall be issued by the entity that has the authority to appoint and the promotion shall be effective from the date of issuance of the resolution, and shall not be retroactive.

Article (31): After promotion, a member of the Corps shall be granted a minimum salary of the promoted position, or an increase of (10) percent of the basic salary of the position before promotion, whichever is higher, and not exceeding the upper limit of the promoted position.

Chapter 7: Salaries, Allowances, and Benefits

Article (32): A member of the Corps shall be paid a basic salary according to the values indicated by the salary scale contained in the salaries, allowances, and benefits scales.

Article (33): A corps member shall be paid a housing allowance of (25%) of the basic salary up to a maximum (120.000) SAR per year, and it is not permissible to combine the provision of housing in-kind inside the kingdom with the disbursement of [a] housing allowance.

Article (34): Health care shall be provided to a member of the Corps, his spouse, parents, unmarried daughters, and sons up to the age of 25 years, provided that they are not covered by other health care.

Article (35): A member of the Corps assigned outside the kingdom shall be paid a secondment allowance according to the values indicated in the salary, allowances, and benefits scales for corps members.

Article (36): A member of the Corps transferred to one of the missions or to the General Staff shall be paid a secondment allowance for travel days in accordance with the numbers indicated in the salary, allowances, and benefits scales for corps members.

Article (37):

- a. Both the head of the mission and his deputy abroad are provided with permanent housing, and the Council of the Corps determines its standards and controls.
- b. In the event that there is no permanent accommodation for the head of the mission upon arrival at the mission headquarters or he is not ready, he shall be provided with temporary accommodation in a hotel for a period not exceeding (90) a day.
- c. In the event that the deputy head of the mission does not have permanent housing or is not ready, he shall be paid a residence

allowance until permanent housing is secured for him, provided that this is within a period not exceeding (180) a day.

Article (38): Upon arrival at the headquarters of the receiving mission, the corps member shall be provided with accommodation in a residence for (twenty-one) days.

Article (39): A delegating member of the Corps shall be paid a residence allowance in accordance with the figures indicated in the salary, allowances, and benefits scales for corps members, and in cases determined by the Council of the Corps, the housing may be provided in kind under the regulations governing that.

Article (40): A member of the Corps in the host nation may not combine housing in kind with a residence allowance.

Article (41): The housing allowance shall continue to be paid to the corps member when he is sent to work at the mission.

Article (42): A member of the Corps shall be paid a transportation allowance when he is sent to work at the mission in accordance with the values indicated in the salary, allowances, and benefits scales for Corps members, and it may not be combined with the transportation allowance.

Article (43): A delegating member of the Corps shall be paid a representation allowance, including the costs incurred when purchasing appropriate clothing for the requirements of the diplomatic job, according to the values indicated in the salary, allowances, and benefits scales for members of the Corps.

Article (44): The head of mission accredited to an additional country or countries shall be paid an additional representation allowance in the proportion of (25%) of the representation allowance in the country in which he is mainly accredited.

Article (45): A delegating member of the Corps to one of the high-living cities shall be paid a high-living allowance according to the values indicated in the salary, allowances, and benefits scales for Corps members, and the calculation of the allowance is based on the following elements and calculation equation:

- a. Delegating City.

• b. Annual Basic Salary.

• c. The number of his family members.

• d. The value of the spendable income in the country as a percentage of the annual basic salary (65%) for married, and (60%) for single.

• e. The index of high-living cities. Cost of living index – 100/100 × Spendable income = Living height allowance

Article (46): A delegating member of the Corps to a difficult-to-live city is paid a high-living allowance in accordance with the values, standards and weights indicated in the salary, allowances, and benefits scales for corps members.

Article (47): The value of the high-living allowance is calculated as a percentage of the basic salary, not exceeding (40%) depending on the indicator of the difficulty of living in the receiving city to which the corps member is sent, and according to the values indicated in the salary, allowances, and benefits scales for corps members.

Article (48): The Ministry shall take care of the education fees of the corps member's children abroad according to the values of the tuition fees indicated in the salary, allowances, and benefits scales for corps members, and shall disburse them to schools immediately after verifying their enrollment.

Article (49): The Ministry shall bear the tuition fees for the children of a member of the Corps from the age of six to the age of eighteen in the Kingdom and a maximum of (20,000) Saudi riyals per year for each son and no more than three sons.

Article (50): The children of diplomatic corps members, who have been ordered to return to the Kingdom due to political, security, natural, or health-related disasters in the countries where they reside, are included. Given their circumstances and educational paths, they are enrolled in foreign or private schools within the Kingdom, with their education fees covered. Payment of these fees shall be stopped as soon as directives are issued to allow diplomats and foreign workers to bring their children back abroad, without affecting their educational paths. The Ministry of Education shall facilitate the enrollment of those who wish to continue their studies in government schools.

Article (51): The annual allowance shall be paid to the corps member in accordance with the value indicated in the salary, allowances, and benefits scales for corps members.

Article (52):

• a. A Standing Committee shall be formed under the chairmanship of the Ministry and the membership of the Ministries of Finance, Human Resources, and Social Development. It shall make unanimous decisions and be responsible for updating and approving the allowances and benefits scales for members of the diplomatic corps. The Committee shall hold its meetings during the last quarter of each fiscal year, and its decisions shall come into effect from the first month of the following fiscal year.

• b. Except for what is mentioned in paragraph (a), the committee may convene before the last quarter of the fiscal year in cases of wars or conflicts in cities where missions are located or upon the opening of diplomatic missions in new cities. This is for the purpose of reviewing and determining allowances and benefits and their amounts. In this case, its decisions shall come into effect from the date specified in the decision.

Article (53): The secretariat of the committee shall be at the Ministry and shall be responsible for providing data on allowances and benefits and their amount from one of the International Houses of Expertise.

Article (54): A member of the diplomatic corps shall be entitled to transfer benefits upon being delegated to work in the mission or upon the end of their delegation, in accordance with what was stated in the salary, allowances, and benefits scales for members of the diplomatic corps.

Article (55): In cases where a member of the Corps is called up or withdrawn for a temporary period based on the requirements of public interest and exceptional emergencies witnessed by the host nation from security or political unrest, infectious epidemics, natural disasters, or in the event of the closure of the mission, the member of the Corps shall be treated in terms of financial benefits as follows:

• a. Taking into account the provisions of Article (50), the payment of all allowances related to the delegation shall be suspended from the date of departure from the host nation until the member's return to their workplace, except for the accommodation allowance. In this case, the continued payment of the accommodation allowance is conditional upon providing evidence of their housing commitments in the host nation.

• b. The transportation allowance shall be paid until his return and commencement at the mission headquarters. A Committee shall be formed in the Ministry to consider assessing the value of the damages resulting from this recall, and its recommendations in this regard shall be submitted to the Minister.

Article (56): Flight tickets for the member of the diplomatic corps, his family, and those dependents who are legally residing with him are provided one way when the member of the diplomatic corps is delegated to one of the missions or transferred to the General Court.

Article (57): Flight tickets for the member of the diplomatic corps, his family, and those dependents who are legally residing with him are provided round trip in the following cases:

• a. If the member of the diplomatic corps has spent a minimum of eleven months at his place of work.

• b. In the event of the death of his wife, spouse, one of his parents, children, brothers, or sisters.

Article (58): Flight ticket for the member of the diplomatic corps shall be provided round trip in the following cases:

• a. If the member of the diplomatic corps is seconded at home or abroad for a period not exceeding (90) a day.

• b. If the member of the diplomatic corps is called to testify before one of the courts or bodies located outside his place of work.

• c. If the member of the diplomatic corps is summoned to appear before a medical commission, an investigative body or a court for work-related matters.

Article (59): It is permissible to compensate in cash for the value of the plane ticket, according to the regulations agreed between the Ministry and the Ministry of Finance.

Article (60): Flight tickets for the member of the diplomatic corps, his family, and those dependents who are legally residing with him in the following cases:

- a. Incumbent (Head of Mission) or (Ambassador): First Class (or Business Class if First Class is unavailable).
- b. Incumbent (Minister) or (Advisor): Business Class.
- c. Incumbent (First Secretary), (Second Secretary), (Third Secretary) or (Attaché): Hospitality Class.

Article (61): The flight class may be upgraded to business class for holders of positions (Attaché) to (First Secretary) in any of the following cases:

- a. If the duration of delegating is not less than (twelve) months.
- b. If he is part of an official delegation.
- c. If he is accompanying the Minister.
- d. If the duration of the trip is more than six hours with stops, if any.

Article (62): In the event that a member of the Corps is prevented from accompanying his family, or a decision has been issued to return it to the kingdom for any circumstance, the member of the corps shall be provided with a boarding ticket to the kingdom by plane twice a year, provided that the period of these circumstances is not less than (six months) and the work is related to the extent of the continuation of those circumstances.

Article (63): Round-trip airline tickets shall be provided for the family of the diplomatic corps member and those legally dependent on him when the duration of the secondment or recall exceeds ninety days.

Article (64): Round-trip airline tickets shall be provided for the children of the member of the mission (with one accompany) to the

Kingdom or to the nearest city with a Saudi school for the purpose of taking final exams.

Article (65): Round-trip airline tickets shall be provided for the wife of the head of mission when accompanying him on his official duties in the receiving country.

Article (66): In the event of the death of a member of the Corps or one of his family members or his legal dependents accompanying him, the Ministry shall bear the costs of processing the body and burial in the country accredited to the mission, according to the desire of his relatives, or transfer the body to the kingdom.

Chapter 8: Termination of Service

Article (67): Taking into account the reasons for termination of service provided by the regulations, the service of a member of the Corps shall be terminated for one of the following reasons:

- a. Resignation.
- b. Approval of the request for referral to retirement before completing the statutory retirement age.
- c. Dismissal for disciplinary reasons.
- d. Dismissal by order of the Prime Minister or by a decision of the Council of Ministers, if the public interest so requires.
- e. Death.

Article (68): The Ministry may terminate the service of a member of the Corps for one of the following reasons:

- a. If the member of the Corps has been absent from work without valid justification for a total of fifteen consecutive days or thirty scattered days during the previous year the decision is issued.
- b. If the member of the Corps did not implement the transfer decision without valid justification within 30 days from the specified for commencing the transferred work.

Article (69): The Minister may extend the service of a member of the Corps who holds a position (Ambassador or Minister Plenipotentiary) once or more until his completion at the age of sixty-five. The Minister may extend the service of a person holding the position of Ambassador after reaching the age of sixty-five to not exceed the age of seventy, in accordance with the following conditions:

• a. An order has been issued to be accredited as an Ambassador of the Custodian of the Two Holy Mosques or the Kingdom in any of the international organizations.

• b. That his services are needed for his practical adequacy, and there is no alternative to him.

• c. Be medically fit.

• d. The extension of his service shall be annually.

Article (70): If a member of the Corps dies, is injured, goes missing or is captured, due to terrorist acts, war or targeting with the intention of offending the kingdom, as well as any member of his family if he is accompanied by him while working abroad, he shall be treated in accordance with the relevant regulations and decisions issued by the competent authority.

CHAPTER 25

GUIDELINES FOR CLASSIFICATION OF WORK PERMITS BY SKILL CATEGORIES

INTRODUCTION

BASED on the Ministry's commitment to regulating the labor market and enhancing human competencies, and with reference to Ministerial Resolution No. (4602) dated (10/1/1447AH) concerning the classification of work permits by skill categories, this document aims to raise awareness among labor market stakeholders (establishments/non-Saudi workers) regarding the segmentation of work permits based on skill categories, in alignment with the objectives of Saudi Vision 2030. The Ministry seeks to establish a new mechanism and develop a regulatory framework for the recruitment of non-Saudi workers into the labor market by classifying work permits according to skill categories. These categories have been identified based on the Saudi Standard Classification of Occupations (primary occupational groups and job codes) and specific classification criteria, including:

- Educational qualifications,
- Professional experience,
- Professional skills,
- Wages, and
- Age.

This initiative aims to foster an attractive labor market and empower human competencies within a professional and sustainable work environment.

The ministerial decree aims to achieve several strategic objectives, including:

• 1. Enhancing the performance of workers and transferring expertise to the Saudi labor market by attracting high skills workers.

• 2. Building an environment that supports innovation and invests in the future through the recruitment of talented individuals.

• 3. Strengthening compliance with the Saudi Standard Classification of Occupations* and ensuring that non-Saudi workers possess the skills required to meet the demands of the Saudi labor market, in accordance with Cabinet Resolution No. (195) dated 04/04/1443H.

• 4. Implementing best practices for attracting high-level talents and skills.

• 5. Developing mechanisms for verification and understanding the distribution rates of skill categories among non-Saudi workers in the Kingdom, enabling entities to manage them more effectively.

The provisions outlined in this guide will be implemented in two key phases. The first phase will commence on Wednesday, July 5, 2025, and the second phase on Tuesday, August 3, 2025, as detailed under the implementation stages later in this document.

DEFINITIONS

The Ministry: The Ministry of Human Resources and Social Development **The Entity**: Every entity managed by a natural or legal person that employs one or more workers for any type of remuneration. **The Non-Saudi Skilled Worker**: Any non-Saudi natural person who works for an employer and under their management or supervision in return for remuneration, even if not under their direct oversight. **Skill Categories** A classification of work permits according to the following categories:

• 1. High-Skilled

- 2. Skilled
- 3. Basic

WORK PERMIT CLASSIFICATION CRITERIA

Base criteria through which work permits are classified for the specified Skill Categories, are as follows:

- 1. Managers
- 2. Specialists
- 3. Technicians and Associate Professionals
- 4. Clerical Support Workers
- 5. Service and Sales Workers
- 6. Skilled Agricultural, Forestry, and Fishery Workers
- 7. Craft and Related Trades Workers
- 8. Plant and Machine Operators and Assemblers
- 9. Elementary Occupations

PROFESSIONAL ACCREDITATION

A program aimed at verifying the qualifications and skills of workers and their alignment with the requirements of the Saudi labor market. **Professional Accreditation** is based on two main components:

- **Qualification Verification** Focuses on verifying the validity of the qualifications and experience of the **Non-Saudi Skilled Worker** in line with the professional requirements of the labor market. (*Qualification Verification applies to the main occupational groups 1 to 3*).
- **Skills Verification** Ensures that the **Non-Saudi Skilled Worker** possesses the necessary skills by performing a practical and theoretical test in their field of specialization. (*Skills Verification applies to the main occupational groups 4 to 8 and to some of the occupations in the group 9 according to the Saudi Standard Classification of Occupations, approved under Cabinet Resolution No.* (660) *dated* 24/10/1441*H*).

MECHANISM FOR CLASSIFYING WORK PERMITS

Work permits will be classified according to skill levels (High-Skilled, Skilled, and Basic) as explained below:

Criteria for Classifying Work Permits

- **Educational Qualifications**: Determining the suitability of the educational level to the requirements of the profession.
- **Professional Experience**: Verifying the required years of professional experience according to the specific requirements for each skill level.
- **Professional Skills**: Meeting the requirements of the Professional Accreditation Program, based on the nature of the profession.
- **Remuneration**: The wage thresholds set by the Ministry for each skill level, depending on the economic activity.
- **Age**: The age group specified for each profession according to its nature and requirements.

METHODOLOGY USED FOR CLASSIFICATION

: The above mentioned criteria for classifying work permits will be adopted to build a balanced methodology for classifying work permits for non-Saudi workers into three categories, as follows: 1. High-Skilled Level Work permits for the High-Skilled Level will be classified according to the following criteria:

- a. The profession must fall within one of the main occupational groups (1 to 3) as per the Saudi Standard Classification of Occupations.
- b. The worker's total wage must not be less than the minimum threshold for the High-Skilled Level, as determined by the Ministry for the economic activity.
- c. The worker must meet the requirements of the Professional Accreditation Program defined by the Ministry for the main occupational groups (1 to 3).

• d. The worker must pass the points-based system set by the Ministry for this level, which is based on three main criteria: educational qualifications, professional experience, and wage.

2. Skilled Level Work permits for the Skilled Level will be classified according to the following conditions:

• a. The profession must fall within one of the main occupational groups (4 to 8), as per the Saudi Standard Classification of Occupations.

• b. The worker's total wage must not be less than the minimum threshold for this level, as determined by the Ministry.

• c. The worker must meet the requirements of the Professional Accreditation Program defined by the Ministry for the main occupational groups (4 to 8).

• d. The profession may fall within one of the main occupational groups (1 to 3) if the worker does not meet the minimum wage threshold set for the High-Skilled Level.

2. Basic Level Work permits for the Basic Level will be classified according to the following conditions:

• a. The profession must fall within the main occupational group (9), as per the Saudi Standard Classification of Occupations.

• b. If applicable for the profession, the worker must meet the requirements of the Professional Accreditation Program defined by the Ministry for the main occupational group (9).

• c. The age of the non-Saudi worker must not exceed 60 years.

• d. The profession may fall within one of the main occupational groups (1 to 8) if the worker does not meet the minimum wage threshold set for the Skilled Level.

IMPLEMENTATION STAGES

The Ministry has ensured a smooth and gradual implementation of this methodology, which will be launched in two main phases:

Phase 1: Classification of work permits for workers currently employed in the Kingdom

(Effective from July 5, 2025) This phase targets non-Saudi workers who are currently employed in the Kingdom. The skill level of these workers will be assessed based on their professions and wages.

PHASE 2: CLASSIFICATION OF WORK PERMITS FOR INCOMING WORKERS TO THE KINGDOM

(Effective from August 3, 2025) This phase involves classifying the work permits of workers entering the Kingdom for the first time, in accordance with the work permit classification mechanism outlined in Section 3.

The classification process for both phases will be automated, with the skill level of work permits appearing directly through the establishment's account on the Ministry's systems (Qiwa Platform). Workers whose skill level is not accurately classified can submit a request to correct their skill level. If they meet the specified criteria for the desired skill level, their classification will be updated accordingly.

FREQUENTLY ASKED QUESTIONS (FAQS)

What are the different skill levels introduced? What changes will occur in the labor market after implementing the classification of work permits by skill levels?

Ans. After implementing this mechanism, every non-Saudi worker, whether currently employed in the labor market or newly arriving in the Kingdom, will have their work permit classified according to skill levels. The classification will be displayed through the establishment's account on the Ministry's systems (Qiwa Platform).

The skill levels will be classified as follows:

- • High-skilled

- • Skilled
- • Basic

How does the points-based system work for applicants seeking high-skilled work permits, and what criteria are considered?

Ans. The points-based system evaluates applicants based on three main criteria: academic qualifications, professional experience, and wages. A specific number of points are allocated to each criterion based on the applicant's performance. If the total points earned by the applicant exceed a certain threshold set by the Ministry, they will qualify for a high-skilled work permit. This system is characterized by flexibility, allowing applicants to compensate for not meeting some criteria with stronger performance in others. For example, if an applicant has extensive experience but does not meet the education/experience requirements, they can still qualify for a high-skilled work permit based on their performance in the remaining criteria.

Will the new classification criteria apply to the current expatriate workforce in the Kingdom?

Ans. The classification will apply to all expatriate workers currently employed in the Kingdom. The classification can be corrected by verifying and ensuring that job titles are accurately reflected in the documented work contract on the Qiwa platform.

Will work permit holders be allowed to change their skill level?

Ans. Yes, work permit holders will have the flexibility to change their skill level, provided they meet the specified criteria for the desired skill level they wish to transition to.

CHAPTER 26
DEFINITION OF WAGE

THIS CHAPTER IS *a legal analysis classifying types of payments made to employees and whether these constitute part of the "wage" for the purposes of the End of Service Benefit.*

A. Part of the Wage

The Ministry now offers an online calculator to simplify the calculation of the End of Service Benefit. The calculator can be found at: https://www.hrsd.gov.sa/en/ministry-services/services/end-service-benefit-calculator.

1. Awards

Awards are treated as bonuses and are part of the wage.

2. Base Salary

The base salary is part of the wage. It includes any and all increases in the salary.

3. Bonuses

Contract completion bonuses or project completion bonuses are considered part of the wage, whether provided for in the employment contract or otherwise agreed upon. They are also includable in the wage if the employee is prevented by the employer, without a legal excuse, from the completing the contract or project. An employee forfeits his right to such a bonus if he reasons without a valid reason or if he is discharged for a valid reason. If such a bonus was paid in pro rata monthly installments simultaneously with the employee's salary, the installments actually received are considered part of the wage even if the contract is not completed. To the extent these pro rata bonus sums are already paid, they can never be recovered by the employer even if the employee resigns without justification or is discharged for a valid reason.

4. Commissions, Percentages and Tips

These are normally considered part of the wage. However, under Royal Decree No. M/2 of 7.2.1403A.H., the employer and employee may agree that all or some of the commission sums, as well as the percentages on the prices of sales and similar elements of wages paid to the employee shall not be used as a basis to compute the EOSB. Further, Article 2 defines commissions as being part of the "actual wage" and not "base wage." This would suggest that commissions are not to be used in the calculation, but such an interpretation would deprive an employee whose income was exclusively derived from commissions from his EOSB. This issue will undoubtedly be clarified by the courts in the future.

5. Cost of Living Allowance

Any paid Cost of Living Allowances constitute and are considered part of basic wages.

6. Extended Work Week Bonus

Some non-Saudi companies pay this bonus to their expatriate workmen transferred to Saudi Arabia form overseas. It represents compensation for the Saudi work period in excess of that of the workman's home country. The work week in Saudi Arabia, unless specified otherwise in the employment contract, is forty-eight hours long, not forty, except during the holy month of Ramadan. The bonus is part of the wage.

7. Family Allowances

Any extra sum paid to an employee in consideration of the employee's family obligations is considered part of the wage.

8. Food Allowance

Food allowances are part of the wage. If provided in kind, it is our view that food allowances are not part of the wage.

9. Tuition Fees

Any sum paid for the schooling of the employee's children is considered part of the wage, whether paid directly to the employee or directly to the school.

10. Foreign Service Premium

This differential is part of the wage.

11. Housing Allowance

A housing allowance paid in cash is part of the wage. A housing allowance paid in kind (i.e. making company housing available to the employee, or the company renting an apartment which is then made available to the employee) is part of the wage unless provided in a remote area.

12. Insurance Premiums

If the employer pays the employee's share of mandatory contributions to the Social Insurance Fund without deduction, these sums are considered part of the wage.

13. Pocket Money/Miscellaneous Expense Allowance

Where this is a sum given to the employee, or made available to him for minor expenses, such as coffee and the like, these sums are considered part of the wage.

14. Remote Area Premium

This differential is part of the wage.

15. Taxes

The amount of any income tax owed by the employee and paid by the employer whether inside or outside Saudi Arabia, and whether to the employee directly or to the tax collection authorities is considered part of the wage. Most countries base income tax on residency, but with respect to those few that base income taxation on citizenship, this provision would apply.

16. Transportation

Cash allowances are part of the wage, but transportation provided in kind is not part of the wage.

17. Uniform or Tool Allowance

These are part of the wage unless provided in kind.

B. Not Part of the Wage

1. Commuting Expenses

These are not part of the wage, whether paid in cash or kind.

2. End of Service Benefit

3. Excess Baggage Expenses

4. Extra Payments not Required by Law

Payments made by the employer on religious, historical, cultural or any other days of significance which are not provided for in the employment contract or otherwise agreed upon and are paid at the sole discretion of the employer are not part of the wage. However, if repeated with regularity, they may become acquired rights of the employee and as such, includable in the wage.

5. Household Goods Storage Expenses

6. Overtime Payments

Irregular overtime is not part of the wage. However, if overtime work is performed and compensated for during eight months of the year, overtime payments will be includable in the wage because the employee will have begun to rely on them. This "eight month" or 75% rule is not hard and fast and in each case will depend on the circumstances.

7. Repatriation Expense

The Employer has a responsibility to the Government to repatriate foreign workers. The costs incurred in meeting this obligation are not considered part of the wage.

8. Travel Expenses

Food, travel and hotel expenses while traveling on behalf of the employer are not part of the wage.

9. Vaccination Expenses

10. Visas and Passport Expenses

CHAPTER 27

NITAQAT (RANGES) TABLE

NITAQAT (RANGES) TABLE

Nitaqat (Ranges) Table

Activity	Blue	Green	Yellow	Red
Financial Institutions and Banks	90	50-89	20-49	0-19
Public Service Offices; Recruiters	90	30-89	10-29	0-9
Security Guards	86	76-85	51-75	0-50
Employment Agencies	86	76-85	51-75	0-50
Oil and Gas Extraction	80	30-79	10-29	0-9
Girls' private and public schools	80	50-79	40-49	0-39
Maritime Transport	70	25-69	10-24	0-9
Preschools and Post-Secondary Education	70	35-69	12-34	0-11
Community and Social Services	65	17-64	5-16	0-4
Personal Services (excluding domestic)	65	13-64	5-12	0-4
Electricity, Gas & Water	64	15-63	6-14	0-5
Gold & Jewelry Sales	60	20-59	10-19	0-9
Collection Offices and Real Estate Services	60	18-59	5-17	0-4
Insurance and Business Services	55	20-54	5-19	0-4
Mines and Quarries	45	20-44	6-19	0-5
Petrochemical, Coal and Rubber	45	25-44	8-24	0-7
Cement	40	25-39	6-24	0-5
Hotels and Tourism	40	18-39	5-17	0-4
Urban Passenger Transport (including taxis)	40	12-39	5-11	0-4
Storage	40	20-39	10-19	0-9
Consulting Services	40	12-39	6-11	0-5
Printing, Publishing & Media	40	20-39	10-19	0-9
Boys' Private and Public schools	40	20-39	15-19	0-14
Maintenance Workshops and Facilities	35	7-34	3-6	0-2
Wholesale & Retail Trade	34	17-33	5-16	0-4
Laboratories	31	16-30	11-15	0-10
Manufacturing	30	15-29	6-14	0-5
Pharmacies	30	13-29	6-12	0-5
Health Services	30	16-29	10-15	0-9
Foreign Schools	30	15-29	7-14	0-6
Building Materials and Construction	28	6-27	2-5	0-1
Construction Maintenance & Cleaning, Operation and Upkeep	28	6-27	3-5	0-2
Nutritional Services	28	7-27	2-6	0-1
Agriculture, Fishing, Grazing, Farmers, Fisherman, Herdsman	27	6-26	2-5	0-1
Agriculture and Livestock Production	27	8-26	4-7	0-3
Interurban Passenger and Cargo Transport	25	9-24	5-8	0-4
Urban Transport of Goods (trucking)	21	11-20	7-10	0-6

CHAPTER 28
ABOUT THE AUTHOR

MICHAEL O'KANE HAS PRACTICED in Saudi Arabia for two decades. He has been involved in several high-profile matters such as United States v. Noriega, BCCI and the ``British Bombers" case in Saudi Arabia. He is a former special legal advisor to the Kingdom of Saudi Arabia and in that capacity drafted a legal code for the Kingdom's Economic Cities project. His works include, *Doing Business in Saudi Arabia, Saudi Arabia Civil Transactions Law 2026, Saudi Arabia Labor Law and Practice 2025, Saudi Securities Law* and others. His creative works include *El pueblo* and *Miami Babilonia.* He has also translated José María Álvarez' *La esclava instruída* into English.

He can be reached at mok@mu7ami.com.

Made in the USA
Monee, IL
05 November 2026

67845299R00239